THINKING THROUGH ARCHAEOLOGICAL COMPLEXITY

Thinking Through Archaeological Complexity explores how archaeologists can engage with complex adaptive systems, examining dynamic interactions between humans and environments across space and through time. It offers a roadmap for integrating theory, method, and data through a complexity science lens.

This volume bridges archaeology and complexity science, offering a transdisciplinary framework for understanding long-term socio-ecological dynamics. It provides a substantive overview of how complex adaptive systems science is used in archaeology. Drawing from case studies in the Ancestral Pueblo Southwest, it demonstrates how tools like agent-based modeling, ecological and social network analysis, and settlement scaling reveal emergent patterns in the archaeological record. The book critically examines concepts such as resilience, adaptation, innovation, and transformation, offering alternatives to overly linear narratives. Emphasizing methodological transparency, it provides practical guidance for scholars interested in modeling, data integration, and working across disciplinary boundaries while grounding in theoretical pluralism. By situating archaeological knowledge within broader scientific conversations, the book encourages readers to reimagine the past not as static or collapsed, but as complex, entangled, and instructive for contemporary challenges.

This book is essential reading for students, researchers, and practitioners in archaeology as well as complexity science. It will also appeal to scholars in anthropology, environmental studies, geography, and network science interested in long-term human-environmental dynamics and the application of complex systems approaches in historical contexts.

Stefani A. Crabtree is Associate Professor in Social-Environmental Modeling in the Department of Environment and Society at the S.J. and Jessie E. Quinney College of Agriculture and Natural Resources at Utah State University. She is also an External Professor at the Santa Fe Institute.

THINKING THROUGH ARCHAEOLOGICAL COMPLEXITY

Stefani A. Crabtree

Designed cover image: Stefani A. Crabtree

First published 2025
by Routledge
4 Park Square, Milton Park, Abingdon, Oxon OX14 4RN

and by Routledge
605 Third Avenue, New York, NY 10158

Routledge is an imprint of the Taylor & Francis Group, an informa business

© 2025 Stefani Crabtree

The right of Stefani Crabtree to be identified as authors of this work has been asserted in accordance with sections 77 and 78 of the Copyright, Designs and Patents Act 1988.

All rights reserved. No part of this book may be reprinted or reproduced or utilised in any form or by any electronic, mechanical, or other means, now known or hereafter invented, including photocopying and recording, or in any information storage or retrieval system, without permission in writing from the publishers.

Trademark notice: Product or corporate names may be trademarks or registered trademarks, and are used only for identification and explanation without intent to infringe.

ISBN: 978-1-032-95511-7 (hbk)
ISBN: 978-1-629-58555-0 (pbk)
ISBN: 978-1-003-58525-1 (ebk)

DOI: 10.4324/9781003585251

Typeset in Times New Roman
by SPi Technologies India Pvt Ltd (Straive)

To my father, Tom, the best researcher I've ever known.

CONTENTS

List of Figures   *viii*
List of Tables   *xi*

1 Introduction   1

2 Scaling Theory and Archaeology   19

3 Agent-Based Modeling and Archaeology   34

4 Network Analysis and Archaeology   53

5 Settlement Scaling and Agent-Based Modeling   73

    Case Study: How to Make a Polity (in the Central Mesa Verde Region)   77

6 Network Analysis and Food Webs Case Study   112

    Case Study: Reconstructing Ancestral Pueblo Food Webs in the Southwestern United States   116

7 Conclusions   148

Glossary   *153*
Index   *157*

FIGURES

1.1 A large flock of Sandhill Cranes as well as Ross's geese and snow geese fly in Bosque del Apache National Wildlife Refuge   4
1.2 A woman in 1895 in Ohio poses to demonstrate her "Gay 90s" fashion. More importantly, her hat demonstrates the breeding plumage that was pilfered from birds throughout the Americas, leading to their rapid decline   12
2.1 Kleiber's law, discovered by Max Kleiber in the 1930s, demonstrates that animals' basal metabolic rates scale at a power of roughly 3/4   22
3.1 The "Segregation" model in the NetLogo library, an agent-based model version of Schelling's model of segregation (1969). In this model agents are one of two colors, light or dark, and they are either happy or unhappy based on the percent of neighbors who are the same color as them. Agents move until they are "happy." Schelling showed that with agents only wanting 2/3 of their neighbors the same color as themselves that there would be system-wide segregation   39
3.2 Simple decision tree of data types on the left and types of models on the right. There are, of course, many other types of models but this is a basic way of thinking through which type of model to pursue   42
4.1 A map of Konigsberg, Prussia and the islands that the city's citizens would try to reach by crossing the seven bridges, juxtaposed with a network that would be required to solve the problem. Here the circles are the littorals and the edges are the bridges   55

5.1	Location of the VEP I study area (shown by simulation boundary) within the VEPIIN area, which encompasses the most populous portion of the central Mesa Verde region	79
5.2	Expected social group sizes represented by kiva floor areas, calculated from kiva diameters assuming circular shape; PII, left column; PIII, right column. NSJ data are in the top row, MSJ data in the second row, and the CCP in the third row. Axes are standardized	87
5.3	Power-law analysis of the expected social group sizes represented by kivas of various sizes, by period and region. Power-law probability values from Table 5.1 are reported in the upper right-hand corner of each panel	90
5.4	Central tendencies for simulated human population through time for each of 36 parameter combinations (in color), with each of the 540 unique runs plotted in grey over blocky histograms representing the empirical population estimates for the simulation area (from Varien et al., 2007). Schwindt et al. (2016) created newer population estimates, but for a larger region, so the older population estimates are retained here	96
5.5	Panel 5.5a: Average territory sizes through time for the largest groups of which each simple group is a member, for Run 1 and replicates, and Run 35 and replicates. 5.5b: annual deaths from warfare. Grey lines indicate means for all runs with replicates; Run 1 and replicates and Run 35 and replicates are shown in black. 5.5c: average number of households through time for Run 1 and replicates, and Run 35 and replicates, shown over blocky histograms representing the empirical population estimate for the simulation area. 5.5c: average annual potential maize productivity for the simulation area	97
6.1	Central Mesa Verde area; box shows study area used for this research. Sites used for analyses in this chapter (Grass Mesa Pueblo, Albert Porter Pueblo, and Sand Canyon Pueblo) represented by circles	119
6.2	Graph of overall food web. Trophic level on y-axis. Red nodes indicate primary producers, orange primary consumers, yellow-orange omnivores, true-yellow true carnivores. Humans pointed at by arrow. The common poorwill, an insectivore, is represented by the node in upper right-hand corner	127
6.3	Vulnerability measures of species to predation: maize is the most vulnerable plant in our study area	129

x Figures

6.4 Primary prey of humans, leporids (cottontail and jackrabbit), deer and turkey taken from composite web. Red nodes are nodes that are connected to humans through predation. Size of node and thickness of edges approximates importance of species to consumer, with narrow edges being not important, and wide edges being very important. Maize makes up between 70 and 85 percent of diet. Deer, leporids and turkey each became important in human diet through Pueblo occupation. Primary prey of humans, leporids (cottontail and jackrabbit), deer and turkey taken from composite web. Red nodes are nodes that are connected to humans through predation. Size of node and thickness of edges approximates importance of species to humans. Maize makes up between 70 and 85 percent of diet. Deer, leporids and turkey each became important in human diet through Pueblo occupation 130
6.5 Ideal Clustering Coefficients. In (a) all species prey on each other, showing a complete connectance (or 1). In (b) only one predator preys on all other species, which do not prey on each other, showing a clustering coefficient close to 0 131
6.6 Clustering coefficient for the overall food web. Humans are mapped at point 51 on the x-axis, showing that humans are connected, but are well below the median species in this food web 131
6.7 Connectivity measures. Here, humans are the 37th most connected species with a score of 1.987 132
6.8 Human specific food web for Grass Mesa Pueblo, Pueblo I period. Arrow identifies humans 133
6.9 Human specific food web, Albert Porter Pueblo, Pueblo II period. Arrow identifies humans 134
6.10 Human specific food web, Sand Canyon Pueblo, Pueblo III period. Arrow identifies humans 134

TABLES

2.1 Populations of megacities in 2016 in millions and projected population of megacities in 2030. Note that while Tokyo is projected to have a decline, all other cities are projected to increase   26

5.1 Summary of conformity of kiva-size distributions to power-law expectations. "Power-law probabilities" between 0.1 and 1 indicate inability to reject the hypothesis that the data could have been generated by a power law. "Compare distributions" values of 0.6 to 1 indicate a power law; values from 0 to 0.4 indicate a log-normal distribution; intermediate values are ambiguous. Positive values for the "Test statistic" indicate power-law distributions; negative values indicate log-normal distributions   91

5.2 Summary of degree of conformity of VE PII N settlement-size distributions to power-law expectations. "Power-law probabilities" between 0.1 and 1 indicate inability to reject the hypothesis that the data could have been generated by a power law. "Compare distributions" values of 0.6 to 1 indicate a power law; values from 0 to 0.4 indicate a log-normal distribution; intermediate values are ambiguous. Positive values for the "Test statistic" indicates power-law distributions; negative values indicate log-normal distributions   92

5.3 Parameters varied in the runs of the simulation reported here. This created 36 unique runs, each replicated 15 times; replicates are reported in Supplemental Table 4. Max simple group size is the number of households beyond which the group will fission. S is the percentage of fighters the smaller

	group will accept as casualties; e.g., a fight between a group with 100 warriors and a group with 200, and an s value of 0.02, will result in up to 2 fighters dieing. β is the tax on the net return to the public goods game, while μ is the tax on beta	95
5.4	Summary of conformity of simulation territory-size distributions to power-law expectations, evaluated in the last year of each of the empirically derived periods. "Power-law probabilities" between 0.1 and 1 indicate inability to reject the hypothesis that the data could have been generated by a power law. "Compare distributions" values of 0.6 to 1 indicate a power-law; values from 0 to 0.4 indicate a log-normal distribution; intermediate values are ambiguous. Positive values for the "Test statistic" indicate power laws; negative values indicate log-normal distributions	99
5.5	Summary of analysis results for empirical and simulated distributions	100
6.1	Periods and sites examined here	120
6.2	Scores for human trophic level, generality, vulnerability, connectivity, and clustering coefficient by food web	127
6.3	Vulnerability and generality scores of primary prey for humans. White-tailed jackrabbit and snowshoe hare were not originally coded in the dataset but were positively identified in an archaeological assemblage. Consequently, their vulnerability score only reflects being eaten by a few top species (humans, bobcat, cougars) and thus should not be taken as a true vulnerability score for these leporids	128
6.4	Generality scores for both empirical data and the reduced food web, where only the most important species to Pueblo diet were included. These include corn, beans, squash, deer (before being hunted out), rabbit/hare, and turkey (after being introduced as a food source)	135

1
INTRODUCTION

Ascending the Grapevine over the Tahachapi Mountains and looking down on the sprawling Los Angeles metropolitan area, it is almost impossible to imagine a small town adjacent to acres of orchards. With a population of 5,728 in 1870, even Galesburg, IL (population 10,158) was more populous. How and why did these two towns develop the way they have? To answer this, we can access census records and historical documents to understand the historical trajectory of L.A. versus Galesburg. We know that the discovery of oil in California led to an increase in population, as did the nascent film industry. As the film industry grew in the region (largely attributed to a trifecta of cheap land, year-round good weather promoting year-round production, and being a long distance from the mercurial Thomas Edison), the city's growth continued apace, and with growth came more opportunities, including a large manufacturing economy (Cherny et al., 2024). Galesburg, on the other hand, grew to a standard small-town-America size, and has more-or-less flirted with 30,000 citizens for the better part of a century. It did not experience an oil boom, nor a motion picture industry influx, yet thanks to being home to a good Liberal Arts college, it has stayed a respectable size. Los Angeles, though, is in the millions to multi-millions, depending upon where along the concrete you draw the line.

What is clear from these two cities is that there are compounding effects that influence population growth. If we want to understand those latent effects, we can calibrate census records with local and global events. This can help us understand the history of these two regions (or really any modern city) and potentially help us to predict the growth of other cities worldwide.

But when there is no historical record, or the records are incomplete, how can you detect the reasons for a city's growth? If we were able to travel back to

DOI: 10.4324/9781003585251-1

the mid AD 800s to the locality of Chaco Canyon, NM, would we predict that some small settlements would over the course of the next 300 years grow to one of the largest and most complex communities on the continent (Plog, 2015)? What were the reasons that Chaco Canyon grew to the importance that it had in the mid 1100s? Why did it happen *there* and not in other areas of the Four Corners region?

How would the fortunes of Southern California have changed had a cheap way of creating moving pictures been innovated in, say, France along the Riviera, or Australia in the boroughs surrounding Sydney? What if the small Knox College had turned into a[n] (even greater) powerhouse of intellectualism, spawning captains of industry and future presidents[1]? Would we today be talking about Illinois as 1/5 of the world's economy instead of California? How can we know anything about the contingencies of history without historical records to set us straight?

A Complex Adaptive Systems Science Approach

This is why this book is called "thinking through archaeological complexity." There are countless challenges in trying to understand the processes that led to an outcome. In archaeology that challenge is magnified, for we are often confronted with the end points—the outcome—and want to know exactly the processes that led to what we find in the archaeological record. This book aims to demonstrate a way to think through these challenges while deploying the lens of complex adaptive systems science. This is what I mean by complexity—complexity science, or the study of complex adaptive systems.

Archaeologists have a unique set of challenges in their work as well as incredible opportunities for understanding humanity. The main challenge lies in what is preserved. Look around you, and think about the walls of your home or office, the pen sitting to your right, the coffee mug to your left, or perhaps even the book you have open; each of these may preserve 1000 years into the future for a future archaeologist to find. But the ideas that you have as you read, or the relationships you form with your friends and colleagues, would likely vanish unless these are written down. Because of this we must infer relationships and ideas from the material traces that are left behind. This is true for past peoples and past societies as well. This, then, is one of the largest challenges in archaeology—being able to get from the material record (lithics, pottery, bones, houses) to the relationships that formed among the people of the past.

Opportunities also lie in the archaeological record. Uniquely in the study of the past, we can see the beginning, middle, and end of a society's trajectory. The plethora of data that comes from *in situ* contexts can help us to understand past lifeways, past interactions with abiotic environments and with ecosystems, and can help us understand such diverse questions as the origins of inequality (Kohler and Smith, 2019) or the origins of the modern city (Ortman et al., 2014).

Yet, to get from the material remains that we find and catalogue to mechanistic explanations of societal change requires analysis, often of the invisible possible interactions among entities, to be able to make inferences about what formed the past. This is why this book focuses on complex adaptive systems science as a way to understand the past. Complex adaptive systems (CAS) science, or complexity science for shorthand, is a field that has been increasing in practitioners since its founding in the mid-to-late 20th century (Romanowska, 2023). At the most fundamental, complex adaptive systems science provides a way to study how the actions and interactions of individual components can lead to larger, overarching structures.

We can see how complex adaptive system science aids archaeology in the definition of complex adaptive systems. Melanie Mitchell, a computer scientist, defined a complex system as "a system in which large networks of components with no central control and simple rules of operation give rise to complex collective behavior, sophisticated information processing, and adaptation via learning or evolution" (Mitchell, 2009, p. 13). Murray Gell-Mann, one of the original founders of the Santa Fe Institute (which itself was formed as a place to study complex adaptive systems) defined it as

> a complex adaptive system acquires information about its environment and its own interaction with that environment, identifying regularities in that information, condensing those regularities into a kind of 'schema' or model, and acting in the real world on the basis of that schema.
>
> *(Gell-Mann, 1995, p. 117)*

Further, complex adaptive systems are present when "things relate but don't add up, if events occur but not within the processes of linear time, and if phenomena share a space but cannot be mapped in terms of a single set of three-dimensional coordinates" (Mol and Law, 2002, p. 1). When these statements are true, the system being studied is likely a complex system, and approaches from complex systems, such as network analysis or agent-based modeling, may help in its examination.

The theoretical underpinnings of complexity science as applied to archaeology can be stated in a few precepts:

1. individuals matter, so we need to study the actions and interactions of individuals;
2. system-wide behaviors cannot simply be understood via the summing of individual parts, but when individuals interact together they create larger systems;
3. system behaviors typically include nonlinearities, so an increase in one factor does not lead to a proportional increase in the output;
4. change and adaptation are typical of complex systems, yet maladaptive behaviors may survive and even proliferate under certain circumstances.

4 Thinking Through Archaeological Complexity

In a classic example of how complex systems function, Reynolds (1987) showed that when individual birds create complex murmurations they follow just three simple rules: (1) retaining alignment with the flock; (2) steering toward the average of the neighbors' headings; and, (3) maintaining adequate space between oneself and one's neighbors. When individual birds follow these rules, the flock becomes a complex, moving system, able to respond to exogenous effects (such as the presence of obstacles or being attacked by a predator, which likely have their own rules) in ways that wouldn't be predicted by looking at the individual strategies alone. Complexity science in this way can help researchers understand nuances that may otherwise be obscured by larger group processes or provide candidate mechanisms for the emergence of group structure at larger scales (Figure 1.1).

Complex adaptive systems theory thus provides a way to see not just individual behaviors (the choices of individual birds), or system behaviors (the movement of the flock), but how individuals influence one another and how individual behaviors impact system-wide behaviors. Complex adaptive systems theory tells us that we must pay attention to how individuals connect to one another via networks, and to understand the properties of the networks we must examine how information or goods flow among individuals. Small changes in how individuals interact can have dramatic effects on the system, but we cannot understand the system merely via the summation of its parts.

FIGURE 1.1 A large flock of sandhill cranes as well as Ross's geese and snow geese fly in Bosque del Apache National Wildlife Refuge. Photo by Tom Crabtree.

We know, however, that humans are infinitely more complex than birds. We shall take an archaeological example to see how individual actions can lead to larger complex structures. Take, for example, the exchange of a pot across 200 km of the American Southwest. We know that this happened, as we see, for example, Salado Polychrome in areas far from where it was manufactured (VanPool and Savage, 2009). But the sherd we find represents not only a whole pot but also interactions among individuals. We may expect that one or more individuals traded that pot across the landscape; thus, we can potentially see the interaction of two or more individuals linked together though the movement of a pot. Moreover, we may be able to understand that transaction via a complex systems approach, since trade was likely not limited to one ceramic vessel. Here, if we looked at the suite of traded pots we may be able to connect them via a social network, suggesting that people at the source of the ceramic material traded with those at the source of the finished pot, creating a link between these two communities (Peeples, 2018). Thus, complex adaptive systems, and network science specifically in this example, enable us to see the individual ceramic maker (and ceramic receiver) as well as the overarching trade network that links many actors together in a complex interconnected sphere.

The theoretical platform of complexity science—that individual decisions matter, that these decisions will have cascading effects on the system, and that individuals and groups will change and adapt—can provide a novel approach for examining the archaeological record. We can examine the individual, the family, the group, and the overarching structure, all by applying a simple suite of rules.

On "Complex"

One challenge with words in English is that we have a general understanding of what a word likely means but it can mean different things to different people. Here the word "complex" can be a culprit for assumed meaning. When I use the term complex I do not denote "complicated" but mean that something is part of a complex adaptive system.

In archaeology the notion of complex societies muddies the terminology for using complex adaptive systems science to understand archaeology. Kohler demarcates the difference well:

> Many archaeologists immediately connect the term complexity with the cultural-evolutionary literature of the 1950s and 1960s, and the large literature in archaeology dealing with how "more complex" societies (meaning societies exhibiting inegalitarian social relations and political hierarchies) evolved from more egalitarian, smaller-scale societies. This is an interest of complexity theory—since it involves the emergence of new political actors,

levels of organization, and social relations—but the scope of complexity theory is much broader, and encompasses even the smallest-scale human societies (and, for that matter, societies of ants, and networks of neurons inside an ant's brain).

(Kohler, 2012)

In a recent book, Dries Daems tackles the challenge of complex societies using complex adaptive systems science to help understand the development of complex societies (Daems, 2021). In a more classic work, Tainter looks at how societies that get more and more complicated can experience a societal restructuring (which he calls "collapse") using complexity theory (Tainter, 1988). There are many other books and works that look at how complex societies can be understood from the lens of complexity theory. This book does not, however, look at complex societies in more depth than purely incidentally. While Chapter 5 examines the development of hierarchy from egalitarian antecedents (i.e., the growth of "complexity") the goal of the study is not to understand the development of complex societies, but rather to understand how particular processes unfold in particular areas and how complex adaptive systems methods and theory can help us to understand the invisible interactions of the past.

Yet there are many works that use complexity in the same ways that I mean in this volume. In the past decade and a half there have been several thorough summaries of complex systems within archaeology. Kohler (2012) covers the most thorough description of the beginnings of complexity theory and how it led to developments within archaeology, while an older volume (Bentley and Maschner, 2003) provides a complimentary approach. Other recent chapters and books have offered similar treatments and updates (Daems, 2021; Davis, 2024; Romanowska, 2023; Romanowska et al., 2021). Finally, the Santa Fe Institute recently published a four-volume set called *The Foundational Papers in Complexity Science*, which spans about 80 years and reprints papers that guided complex adaptive systems science, including papers in archaeology, anthropology, and ecology (Krakauer, 2024). The book that you are reading herein offers my viewpoint on complex adaptive systems and archaeology: how it can help us to understand the intractable aspects of the past and how it can help us link the archaeological past to the present and the future.

Thus, in this book (as with the aforementioned books) the term complex will always mean something relating to complex adaptive systems and complexity, unless I specify otherwise within the context of the sentence how I will be using that word.

On Models

Archaeologists love to create models. Oftentimes, though, these models are not formalized; they are instead verbal. Many times, these models are unintentional.

In the years I spent doing cultural resource management archaeology throughout the Mountain West I heard archaeologists create countless models:

> Example 1: "We should check along that draw because in every other draw we have found lithic scatters."
> Example 2: "Pay extra attention as you come up to that rise; that seems to be a prime place for eagle traps."
> Example 3: "This slope is 45 degrees. There's no way there's a site along here, so let's get this part of the survey done quickly."

What the crew chief did in each of these occasions was create mental maps between data they had accumulated from their expertise of years of completing archaeology in the region to the data they saw on the ground. From this they built inference, which then helped us with informal predictive models of where to locate archaeological sites.

For the first example we were completing a survey on a recently drained reservoir as part of dam compliance. There was a naturally occurring lake in the region that had been dammed to create a large reservoir, and since the 1950s commercial boaters had enjoyed the area for recreation. With the lake drained so the dam could be repaired, we were hired to do on-the-ground survey. Early on we noted that there were larger quantities of lithic debitage where drainages led to the natural lakebed. Thousands of flakes, dozens of formalized tools, and even a few pot sherds congregated in these areas. Once the crew chiefs noticed this pattern, we spent a little more time surveying when we noticed a drainage coming to the lakebed.

In the second scenario, a survey in the plains of the Dakotas drew on both primary sources from the journals of Lewis and Clark and notes from an Army Corps survey in the 1950s. Observers had noted eagle traps on high areas in the 1950s that seemed to correspond to descriptions written in primary sources. When I came to resurvey the area in the early 2000s, eagle traps were bound to look like small divots in the ground because of aeolian processes. The crew chief knew, based on the primary sources, that some bluffs and high spots would have been prime locations for eagle traps. They told us to pay attention, so when we came across features that looked relatively natural, we knew these could be eagle traps, so we spent extra time analyzing them.

In the third scenario I was working with a crew in Colorado in a very mountainous region, surveying for natural gas deposits along the Western Slope. The priors for the crew chief were that sites had seldom been found along high-degree slopes in arid Colorado. We still needed to survey the area, but according to the mental models we didn't need to comb it as closely as we would other regions.

Were each of these justified? It's possible they weren't. In some draws we didn't find sites, on some slopes over 45 degrees we found sites. Detecting eagle traps was incredibly difficult (and I apologize to future archaeologists reading

8 Thinking Through Archaeological Complexity

my site forms recording them). But each of these cases serve as an opportunity to illustrate what a model is.

A model is a formalized set of expectations or beliefs about a system. It is itself a microcosm of a real system. It serves to simplify reality. A model distills reality down to a few variables. A model reduces the noise of the world to a few precepts: lithics are frequently found near drainages, eagle traps are found on rises, sites are seldom found on steep slopes. There are always exceptions to the rules, but our models tell us when to *pay attention in closer detail*. Importantly, they help us to refine our understanding of the real world, and when things do not conform to model expectations, they can help us understand that something quite interesting is going on.

As Clarke (1972, p. 2) states, "models are pieces of machinery that relate observations to theoretical ideas." Even models built on simple rules can help eliminate poor hypotheses, clarifying the understanding of a system. Even when a model is wrong (as "all models are wrong, but some are useful" (Box and Draper, 1983, p. 424)) we can glean a better understanding of the system by slowly building the model up from simplicity and studying simplified processes of complex systems. Yet, as Kohler and van der Leeuw tell us "models are not true or false in the manner of hypotheses, though to be useful, they must be clear and internally consistent" (Kohler and van der Leeuw, 2007, p. 3). In the preceding scenarios, the crew chiefs did not tell the crew to *not* survey on slopes because the model wasn't true or false—they told us to spend a little less time there because sites were unlikely, though still possible. The model was clear and consistent but would be updated with new information when it was found ("sites seldomly are found on slopes over 45 degrees, but they sometimes are").

All anthropologists and archaeologists build models, yet the models aren't always formalized. Indeed, some may say they seldom are, and they remain verbal models. Formalizing models—writing them down in a mathematical way—however, helps to demonstrate the power of the hypotheses a scientist puts forth. The formalization process also helps us to become better scientists. Formalizing a model is a courageous act: it takes our simple observations and challenges others to prove them wrong. Building models, in my opinion, requires the scientist to put down ego and invite criticism.

What if our models are wrong? What if the sites are found not along drainages, but on the high points? What if we discover site after site along precipitous slopes in Colorado? What then? Then we learn more about prehistory. Then we have to change our models. We alter our hypotheses to find better ways to understand the past.

To quote Salmon:

> Archaeology, even more than biology, studies extremely complex systems whose boundaries are not well defined. Modeling always ignores some, often fundamental, aspects of a system in order to focus on others. No one

model should or does model every feature of a system. Whether a model is good or bad depends partly on our purposes in constructing the model. Unless the components of a system and their systemic relationships are well understood it is difficult to decide which features may be ignored in constructing useful models. ...Much more must be known about crucial components of biological systems and their important relationships before they can be modeled successfully. And biologists, not systems theorists, are the ones who are equipped to do this sort of work. I believe that archaeology is in a position similar to that of biology in this respect.

(Salmon, 1978, p. 179)

On Maps as Models

One useful way to think about models is to think about how we build different types of maps. Maps are, after all, a model of how we experience the landscape put onto two dimensions.

Maps by early explorers in the Age of Exploration were representations of the state of knowledge of the places they were visiting. Often these were at least slightly incorrect topographically, with mountain ranges interpolated where there were none, or coastlines that didn't quite match. As more information was gleaned, the models—the maps—were updated. Sometimes the maps contained elements that on further inspection were absolutely wrong—sea monsters, dragons, mermaids—which as society advanced had to be removed from the models or only added with ironic whimsy. Sometimes maps would have to be updated as geography changed—the eruption of Mount St. Helens, for example, required dramatic updates to topographic maps. These examples show the way that models can evolve to reflect the data that is collected, to give a better representation of reality.

Maps are part of our daily lives, but often we don't question the inclusion or removal of certain aspects within them. A highway map may show where major roads intersect and where gas stations can be reliably found, but will likely not show other pieces of information. Topographical maps will show the changes in elevation in bands from lowest to highest points, but a topographical map would not necessarily show where to find a gas station. A tourist map may in fact not have a perfect scale of distances, instead trying to show relative locations of key sites to help tourists plan their visit to the city. Each of these are models of the real world, but each mapmaker makes decisions on how to simplify the world and what to focus on. This does not make the models incorrect; it merely helps the user to filter out unnecessary information in the service of focusing on specific aspects of the real world. Sometimes the user may *want* information found on another map. This does not make the first map (model) incorrect, just insufficient, so more models (maps) are needed.

A crossover between literature and complex adaptive systems science lies in the discussion of the utility of maps. A famous absurd story, told by many narrators, is the idea of a one-to-one scale map. The original, from Lewis Carroll (Carroll, 2017, chap. XI), I post below.

> "What a useful thing a pocket-map is!" I remarked.
> "That's another thing we've learned from your Nation," said Mein Herr, "map-making. But we've carried it much further than you. What do you consider the largest map that would be really useful?"
> "About six inches to the mile."
> "Only six inches!" exclaimed Mein Herr. "We very soon got to six yards to the mile. Then we tried a hundred yards to the mile. And then came the grandest idea of all! We actually made a map of the country, on the scale of a mile to the mile!"
> "Have you used it much?" I enquired.
> "It has never been spread out, yet," said Mein Herr: "the farmers objected: they said it would cover the whole country, and shut out the sunlight! So we now use the country itself, as its own map, and I assure you it does nearly as well."

In Lewis Carroll's original version, Mein Herr describes a map that is the size of a country itself, so grand that farmers protest that if it were unfolded it would block out the sun. Instead of people being able to use the map, they now use the country itself as a map. While the country may, indeed, be a perfect representation of itself, it certainly wouldn't provide a representation of a map for those who needed one.

Borges, the Spanish story teller, takes this idea further in his story "Del rigor en la ciencia" or "on exactitude in Science." In his short story (which he facetiously credits as being a translation of a story told in 1658), a principality wants to create the most exact maps possible, where only the precise representation of every minute detail can faithfully recreate the kingdom. As such, the art of mapmaking becomes the one-to-one representation on cartography. "[S]ucceeding Generations... came to judge a map of such Magnitude cumbersome... In the western Deserts, tattered Fragments of the Map are still to be found, Sheltering an occasional Beast or beggar..." (Borges, 1972).

Finally, this theme is explored by Umberto Eco in his story "On the Impossibility of Drawing a Map of the Empire on a Scale of 1 to 1" from his book *How to Travel with a Salmon & Other Essays*. Eco examines what would be required to make a 1-to-1 scale map, taking the absurd story initially written by Lewis Carroll a step further. He finds that because the map would actually obscure the underlying ground, its shadow would kill the ecosystem below, requiring *constant* updating of the map to showcase the changing earth (Eco, 1995, pp. 95–106).

These stories are meant to explore the absurd and demonstrate how ridiculous a one-to-one representation would be. There is little likelihood that an endeavor of a faithful replication of a region in one-to-one scale would even be followed. We can collectively laugh at the lack of wisdom of these individuals. Maps, we know, are made to help wayward travelers to understand the topography they are traveling in and focus on key aspects of that landscape. Maps may contain multiple layers, both topography and features of interest, but the more layers that are included the more difficult they may be to parse.

If we can understand that we need to simplify in order to maximize our understanding of a physical place, why, then, do so many scientists include so much exogenous information when they build models? How can there be such a large mismatch between the practice of understanding the world and the realities of building models? If we now understand that maps are models, and we would never faithfully reproduce everything we see in the world into our map, instead simplifying for the key features that are needed, why do so many well-intentioned scientists have a tendency to add so much to our models?

On Parsimony

Parsimony is the concept that we will add only what is necessary to understand the key tenets of something. In models we aim for parsimony—we don't want to make a one-to-one map. Instead, we simplify, but it isn't too simple. We have as much as is necessary to truly understand our system, and not any more than that.

To understand parsimony let's start with an example. Let's imagine that you have been hired by the Arkansas National Wildlife Refuge to model the reintroduction of whooping cranes, which almost became extinct at the beginning of the 20th century. You decide you need to build a model to understand the threats that might be facing whooping cranes today.

Whooping cranes are the tallest bird species in North America, and like many large species, they have a slow reproductive rate. They only lay two eggs per clutch and don't lay again until the young are out of the nest. Wild whooping cranes migrate 2500 miles from breeding grounds in Canada to wintering grounds along the Gulf Coast. They feed predominantly on crabs and berries in their wintering grounds (Cornell Lab of Ornithology, 2025).

You compile a team of experts to talk about what you should put in a model to help study the reintroduction of whooping cranes. You ask the group what items should go into your model. One person suggests that habitat loss should be included in the model—how does the shrinkage of habitat impact the birds? Another person suggests including the warming of the Gulf waters—will that impact the food supply? Another suggests climate change in general. Still another wants to make sure you understand the life cycle of the birds—how old they are when they mate, how often they reproduce, and so on.

Then, someone in the back says "We need to model ladies' hats!"

It turns out that one of the pressures on whooping cranes in the early 1900s was that their plumes were collected to adorn women's hats. The birds would be killed just to harvest the feathers, and this led to the rapid decline of their numbers (Learn, 2020). And while this may be factually true—that ladies' hats were a culprit in the loss of whooping cranes—including ladies' hats in a model of the challenges of reintroducing whooping cranes today would be ridiculous at best. It would be extraneous information that does not deserve to be in a model of modern challenges. It would not be parsimonious.

To build a parsimonious model you must remove the items that seem extraneous. While you can probably find a justification for including many parameters in a model, you must always ask yourself—is this item necessary, or am I modeling ladies' hats? (See Figure 1.2.)

Complex systems scientist Ross Hammond describes a good way to think of parsimony as thinking about building a model like going on a backpacking trip. Everything you put in takes space and creates weight. You want to make sure it doesn't weigh too much. While a full mattress would be more comfortable, we bring small camping pads to lie on. To create parsimony, you don't

FIGURE 1.2 A woman in 1895 in Ohio poses to demonstrate her "Gay 90s" fashion. More importantly, her hat demonstrates the breeding plumage that was pilfered from birds throughout the Americas, leading to their rapid decline. Photo from Toledo Lucas County Public Library.

overload the model, and to have a good backpacking trip you don't overload your backpack (Hammond, 2024).

So, to create good scientific models we don't want to build maps that are one-to-one; we need to simplify to the things that are most critical to understand our system. We also want to build models that are parsimonious and avoid the "ladies' hats" conundrum.

Next, I outline a very brief history of model building in archaeology. I move from the early model builders to formalized models in GIS to modern model builders using agent-based modeling and network modeling (and sometimes the two together) to understand more about systems of interest.

Models in Archaeological Systems

> We will teach you to ask big questions! But not how to answer those questions…
>
> *(Holland-Lulewicz, 2024)*

Archaeology in recent decades has focused on asking big questions, but as the preceding quote suggests, perhaps not how to answer them. The methods used in archaeology sometimes lag behind being able to ask large, overarching questions. But that is why tools from complex adaptive systems science, such as I am presenting here, are critical. They can help answer so many of the larger questions that traditional approaches cannot. And one of the ways that complex systems helps to answer the big questions is by helping us to build parsimonious models.

Archaeology as anthropology of the past (Willey and Phillips, 1958, p. 2) has made great advances in understanding the lives of people in pre- and protohistory. While many early studies focused on material culture by necessity (e.g., Strong, 1935), social-evolutionary narratives (e.g., Steward, 1955; White, 1949), processual archaeology (e.g., Binford, 1965), and post-processual archaeology (e.g., Shanks and Tilley, 1991) each moved the discipline further toward an understanding of the uniqueness of human lives in the past. Each of these approaches have used models in some way, although some of the approaches don't use the term "models". According to Nakoinz, the term *model* began being applied in archaeology in the 1960s, largely due to processual archaeology desiring to apply the scientific method to the study of the past (Nakoinz, 2018, p. 107), and the term fell out of use during post-processual's critique.

Nakoinz reviews models in archaeology, so a deeper discussion of those can be found there. However, his delineation of archaeological models into six types are useful for understanding how models are used in archaeology: predictive models, representative models, conceptual models, latent models, quantitative models, and simulations (Nakoinz, 2018, p. 107). Here I briefly define each of these types.

Predictive models are perhaps the most commonly used in archaeology, as we use observed features from an archaeological site (e.g., distance to water, elevation, etc.) and then identify those places on a landscape that have those features. We can then go survey in those regions to see if archaeological sites exist in those regions (e.g., Clarke, 2014).

Representative models include 3D models of a site. Representative models are simplified representations of the real world that can help guide more discovery. Visiting many archaeological sites today, you can download a visual 3D interpretation to your phone so you can see what the site would have looked like in the past; Ambrussum, France has a particularly compelling 3D representative model.[2]

Conceptual models, in Nakoins' view, are those models that define relationships among entities. For example, mental models of the trade of goods can be conceptual models. This leads into the idea of latent models, where there is an underlying relationship between entities that may not be observed. For example, the models in the American Southwest that assign certain pot sherds to different chronologies could be a conceptual model (the relationship of sherds to each other in time) or a latent model (there is an underlying unobserved variable that ends up sorting the sherds).

Quantitative models use mathematical constructs to understand the connection between entities. These types of models are frequently used in archaeology through the deployment of statistical techniques. For example, regression and cluster analysis are examples of quantitative models that define patterns in archaeological data.

Finally, simulations are representatives of the real system that include a component of time or space. A simulation takes the models that may be identified in a predictive model, and then adds heterogeneity to the system and examines "what happens *if* x occurred over y time?"

In this book I focus on quantitative models and simulations for understanding the archaeological past. While each of the aforementioned modeling techniques is useful and illuminates key aspects about the past, in complex adaptive systems science specifically, quantitative models and simulations have proven useful for illuminating the hidden ways that entities can interact to create something larger than the sum of its parts.

Archaeology itself is the study of humans in the past and everything humans did, including things like economics, epidemiology, politics, and ecology. Because of this, archaeologists have to be well-versed in how tools and concepts from other established disciplines can apply to the system the archaeologist is studying in the past. Many of these disciplines use models to understand the spatial and social interaction of people and environments, so we adopt those tools to our own study.

Quantitative models illuminate the real relationships between entities. Often, these relationships may be inferred, but applying statistical procedures describes the actual relationships. In Chapter 5 I review settlement scaling in archaeology, which deploys quantitative modeling to examine the ways that sites relate to each other in terms of their size.

Simulations are particularly well suited for archaeology because they can offer a way to examine *what if* scenarios without experimenting on the real system. Simulations are frequently used in other disciplines, such as epidemiology and astrophysics, where it would be unethical to experiment on the system (in the case of a disease outbreak) or impossible to access the system (in the case of distant stars) (Romanowska, 2023, p. 274; Romanowska et al., 2021, p. 4). In archaeology, because we only see the end point of the past, we need to use simulations built on an understanding of the ways the past society worked to refine our understanding of how the past system behaved. In Chapters 3 and 5 I review agent-based modeling in archaeology, a type of simulation modeling that has been particularly useful for refining our understanding of the past.

I also review network models within this book, specifically social network models and ecological network models, which can be seen as a hybrid between a simulation and a quantitative model. Networks examine the direct relationship between two entities, yet you can also simulate the topology of a network to examine *what if* scenarios. In Chapters 4 and 6 I look to two different types of network models, food webs and social networks, and their applications in archaeology.

Romanowska (2023) describes the difference between different methods in complex adaptive systems as either describing a system's behavior or a system's structure. She ascribes agent-based modeling as describing a system's behavior, while network analysis describes a system's structure. In the papers that proceed I also present work on settlement scaling theory, which describes a system's structure as well. However, each example in this book is built on an agent-based model, so it describes not only the behavior that developed the system, but the structure that underlies it as well.

The Structure of this Book

This book is divided into two sections: reviewing the state of the field as of the printing of this book, and case studies.

Chapters 2, 3, and 4 present review chapters. In Chapter 2 I introduce scaling and its uses within archaeology. Settlement scaling has become a cornerstone of complex adaptive systems approaches, and we will see why. I also review other scaling literature, such as metabolic scaling, to situate the theoretical underpinnings for this work.

Chapter 3 introduces agent-based modeling (ABM) as a methodological tool for understanding past interactions. While I review many published agent-based models, I also cite other works that go into more depth on just the subject of agent-based modeling, allowing for a foundation on the theory behind why to use ABM in one's work.

Chapter 4 introduces network analysis as a tool for understanding interactions between individuals and groups of individuals. I cover both social network analysis and ecological network analysis, two approaches that have been adopted strongly into archaeological work. Network analysis is perhaps the most familiar approach from complex adaptive systems in archaeology, but I show why the theories from network science can help us make the invisible visible.

The next section introduces the case studies. Chapter 5 introduces the settlement scaling case study which also is built on an agent-based model, so it draws on the concepts from Chapters 2 and 3. Chapter 6 introduces the food webs case study, which is a network method, drawing from concepts in Chapter 4 and building on concepts introduced in Chapter 5. In Chapter 7 I bring all these ideas together, to show how approaches from complex adaptive systems science can help us better understand the archaeological record.

Finding the Invisible Through Complex Adaptive Systems Approaches

I began this chapter by suggesting that it is difficult to understand past human relationships through traditional archaeological methods. The fact that artifacts preserve, but relationships disappear creates great challenges for the study of ancient humanity. While some societies have the benefit of writing, even the written record is biased as it often favors elites. Thus, we must augment our understanding of the past with other tools.

Complex adaptive systems approaches provide tools that can help us examine relationships among individuals in the past. Through these methods we can directly observe how individuals make decisions (in the case of agent-based modeling) or link to other individuals (in the case of network analysis) and can examine the effects of these actions and interactions on the larger structure (in the case of settlement scaling). Complex adaptive systems approaches thus help advance archaeological research to study not just the tangible (artifacts) but the intangible and invisible (relationships).

These approaches also enable us to not only examine one scale, but multiple scales of interaction, breaking limitations placed on research in the past. Complex adaptive systems, by allowing us to bridge scales, can help us to understand how individuals, who by definition should be looking out for themselves, nevertheless can find sufficient common interests to group into stable collectives and how these collectives leave tangible marks on landscapes of the past.

Complexity theory helps to unravel the archaeological record. While we can look at modern flocks of birds and understand them from individual behaviors, so, too, can we look to the archaeological record, which by nature is in aggregate, and understand its derivation from individual choices. As Dietler (2010, p. 381) remarked about Bronze Age France, "cultural change is an unintended result of a combination of decisions and actions by individuals and households experimenting with change, rather than by cultures or societies." Unintentionally, Dietler evokes theory parallel to that of complexity science: it is the choices of individuals that drive societal change. Thus, it is my hope that through the research presented here I am able to forge a pathway to examine the people in prehistory, the social structures they created, and the effects these had on environments as a whole.

Notes

1 Ellen Browning Scripps, part of the Scripps newspaper family, graduated from Knox College in Galesburg Illinois. She founded my Alma Mater, Scripps College in Claremont CA, and has lent her name to any number of higher education endeavors. Thanks to Knox College for allowing women to attend university, and thus leading to my own education!
2 See https://www.ambrussum.fr/visiter/ambrussum-3d/.

Works Cited

Bentley, R.A., and Maschner, H.D.G., 2003. *Complex Systems and Archaeology*. The University of Utah Press, Salt Lake City.
Binford, L.R., 1965. Archaeological Systematics and the Study of Culture Process. *American Antiquity* 31, 203–210. https://doi.org/10.2307/2693985
Borges, L., 1972. *A Universal History of Infamy*, First English Ed. EP Dutton.
Box, G.E.P., and Draper, N.R., 1983. *Empirical Model-Building and Response Surfaces*. Wiley Series in Probability and Statistics.
Carroll, L., 2017. *Sylvie and Bruno Concluded*. CreateSpace Independent Publishing Platform.
Cherny, R.W., Lemke-Santangelo, G., Griswold, R., and Castillo, D., 2024. *Competing Visions: A History of California*. Self-published.
Clarke, D.L. (Ed.), 2014. *Models in Archaeology*. Routledge. https://doi.org/10.4324/9781315748474
Clarke, D.L., 1972. Models and Paradigms in Contemporary Archaeology. In *Models in Archaeology*, edited by D.L. Clarke, Meuthen and Co. Ltd, London.
Cornell Lab of Ornithology, 2025. Whooping Crane [WWW Document]. Cornell Lab of Ornithology All About Birds. Ithaca, NY.
Daems, D., 2021. *Social Complexity and Complex Systems in Archaeology*. Routledge.
Davis, D.S., 2024. Past, Present, and Future of Complex Systems Theory in Archaeology. *Journal of Archaeological Research* 32, 549–596. https://doi.org/10.1007/s10814-023-09193-z
Dietler, M., 2010. *Archaeologies of Colonialism: Consumption, Entanglement, and Violence in Ancient Mediterranean France*. The University of California Press, Berkeley, CA.
Eco, U., 1995. *How to Travel with a Salmon & Other Essays*. HarperVia.
Gell-Mann, M., 1995. *The Quark and the Jaguar: Adventures in the Simple and the Complex*. Henry Holt and Company LLC, New York.
Hammond, R., 2024. Personal Communication.
Holland-Lulewicz, J., 2024. Personal Communication.
Kohler, T.A., 2012. Complex Systems and Archaeology. In *Archaeological Theory Today*, edited by I. Hodder. Polity Press.

Kohler, T.A., and Smith, M.E. (Eds.), 2019. *Ten Thousand Years of Inequality the Archaeology of Wealth Differences*. University of Arizona Press, Tucson, AZ.

Kohler, T.A., and van der Leeuw, S. (Eds.), 2007. *The Model Based Archaeology of Socionatural Systems*. The School for Advanced Research Illustrated Press, Santa Fe, NM.

Krakauer, D.C. (Ed.) 2024. *Foundational Papers in Complexity Science*. SFI Press, Santa Fe, NM.

Learn, J.R., 2020. *Species Spotlight: Whooping Cranes*. National Wildlife Federation.

Mitchell, M., 2009. *Complexity: A Guided Tour*. Oxford University Press, Oxford.

Mol, A., and Law, J., 2002. Complexities: An Introduction. In *Complexities: Social Studies of Knowledge Practices (Science and Cultural Theory)*, edited by J. Law and A. Mol. Duke University Press, Durham, NC.

Nakoinz, O., 2018. Models and Modelling in Archaeology. *Historical Social Research* 31, 101–112. https://doi.org/10.12759/hsr.suppl.31.2018.101-112

Ortman, S.G., Cabaniss, A.H.F., Sturm, J.O., and Bettencourt, L.M.A., 2014. The Pre-History of Urban Scaling. *PLoS One* 9, e87902.

Peeples, M.A., 2018. *Connected Communities: networks, Identity, and Social Change in the Ancient Cibola World*. University of Arizona Press, Tucson, AZ.

Plog, S., 2015. Understanding Chaco: Past, Present and Future. In *Chaco Revisited: New Research on the Prehistory of Chaco Canyon, New Mexico*, edited by C. Heitman and S. Plog. University of Arizona Press, Tucson, AZ.

Reynolds, C., 1987. Flocks, Herds, and Schools: A Distributed Behavioral Model. In *SIGGRAPH '87: Proceedings of the 14th Annual Conference on Computer Graphics and Interactive Techniques*. Association for Computing Machinery, pp. 25–34.

Romanowska, I., 2023. Complexity Science and Networks in Archaeology. In *The Oxford Handbook of Archaeological Network Research*, edited by T. Brughmans, B.J. Mills, J. Munson, and M.A. Peeples. Oxford University Press, Oxford, pp. 265–279.

Romanowska, I., Wren, C.D., and Crabtree, S.A., 2021. *Agent-based Modeling for Archaeology: Simulating the Complexity of Societies*. SFI Press, Santa Fe, NM.

Salmon, M.H., 1978. What Can Systems Theory do for Archaeology? *American Antiquity* 43, 174–183. https://doi.org/10.2307/279242

Shanks, M., and Tilley, C., 1991. *Social Theory and Archaeology*. Polity Press, Cambridge.

Steward, J., 1955. *Theory of Culture Change: The Methodology of Multilinear Evolution*. The University of Illinois Press, Urbana, IL.

Strong, W.D., 1935. *An Introduction to Nebraska Archaeology*. The Smithsonian Institution, Washington, DC

Tainter, J., 1988. *The Collapse of Complex Societies*. Cambridge University Press, Cambridge.

VanPool, T.L., and Savage, C., 2009. War, Women, and Religion: The Spread of Salado Polychrome in the American Southwest. In *Innovation in Cultural Systems: Contributions from Evolutionary Anthropology*, edited by M.J. O'Brien and S.J. Shennah. The MIT Press.

White, L., 1949. *The Science of Culture: A Study of Man and Civilization*. Grove Press, New York.

Willey, G.R., and Phillips, P., 1958. *Method and Theory in American Archaeology*. University of Chicago Press, Chicago, IL.

2
SCALING THEORY AND ARCHAEOLOGY

When *Homo sapiens* spread out of Africa as early as 125,000 years ago, they began to rapidly modify environments as they encountered them (Bird et al., 2021). While the initial impacts of humans on ecosystems may have been small in scale, focused on the direct impact of a new species arriving in a novel environment, over time human impacts across the globe compounded and intensified (Crabtree et al., 2021). From these simple antecedents, complex structures and tens of thousands of distinct cultures grew. Yet despite differences among these varying societies across the 510 million square kilometers of land on earth, human action may in fact be subject to unifying organization principles.

Complex adaptive systems theory can enable an understanding of the myriad ways that humans have shaped the globe and can provide a method for examining such disparate subjects as human mobility (Romanowska et al., 2017), settlements and cities (Bettencourt, 2013), and ecosystems (Crabtree et al., 2021) worldwide. In this book I focus on scaling theory, network science, and agent-based modeling as three of the methods from complex adaptive systems science that guide archaeological investigation. In this chapter we will focus on how we can look to scaling patterns in both modern and archaeological sites. Often the choices made by individuals and societies have cascading effects over time, lending naturally to using complex adaptive system science to understand culture.

Scaling theory is one of the pillars of complex adaptive systems used within archaeology. Why? Recall that complex adaptive systems science seeks to understand not only the large, overarching structures in the object of study, but how the actions and interactions of internal components can lead to something greater than the sum of its parts. Scaling theory helps us understand why large entities—bodies, social networks, settlements—are made up of

DOI: 10.4324/9781003585251-2

surprisingly smaller constituents and how those constituents interact. To understand how scaling theory is used within archaeology, we will first understand what scaling theory is by beginning with its foundations—metabolic scaling theory.

Metabolic Scaling Theory: A Primer

Complex adaptive systems science is useful for understanding the hidden order that governs social and ecological systems. We can build up our understanding from examining the ways that ecosystems both govern and are constructed by human systems, to the ways that interactions among people help to shape social systems. As we will see, even industrialized nations seem to be subject to the organizing principles of smaller-scale societies (Lobo et al., 2019; Ortman et al., 2014).

To understand scaling theory and the organization of constituent parts, we will look first at the human body itself and then look to organization beyond the skin to our societies past and present.

Scaling theory itself developed from understanding why lifespan and body size seem to correlate, yet this use of scaling theory is not in alignment with much of what we find archaeologically. To understand scaling theory in an archaeological context by looking at the size of settlements, we will begin by looking at the well-known work of the scaling of organisms to see what scaling is and how it can be useful for understanding hidden order.

Within our bodies, our circulatory system is governed by a system of networks—our blood vessels—that enable the efficient spread of blood throughout our bodies. These networks are hierarchical networks, where the routes that things spread on—the blood vessels themselves—get smaller the farther they move from the central hub point—the heart (West, 2018). These types of hierarchical networks exhibit fractal-like properties, whereby they look self-similar in both miniscule and majuscule, and can be found not only in the human body (although the human circulatory system is not strictly fractal (West, 2018 p. 129)), but also in the ways that nutrients flow from the trunk of a tree to the tips of leaves. The self-similarity within these systems seems to follow a ¼ power scaling law. A scaling law "describe[s] the functional relationship between two physical quantities that scale with each other over a significant interval" (Nature Portfolio, 2021). The reason for this scaling is the efficiencies they bring upon the flow of blood within the human body (or the flow of nutrients from trunks to leaves). For blood to reach the extremities of our fingers and toes it needs to be pumped quite hard. By decreasing the size of capillaries this allows for the blood pumped from the heart and within the largest blood vessels to reach the farthest extremities. Constricting the blood vessels allows the decreasing quantities of blood to be appropriately accelerated to their final destination in the tips of your fingers or toes (West, 2018).

Think of this as when you are watering your garden. If you are watering something up close, you just allow the water to pour out of the hose and let the water puddle at the base of the rose bushes. If you want the water to reach a long distance, say to scare away a rabbit that has entered the far end of your garden, you *constrict the flow of water* by putting your thumb strategically over the end of the hose. What this does is enable the water to flow faster and farther. The smallest capillaries are essentially the same as your finger over the end of the hose.

Scaling laws also apply to the metabolic rates in aging versus body mass, where larger animals live longer than a simple 1:1 scaling would suggest. Described another way, an animal that has twice as many cells as another (say, a vole to a golden mantled ground squirrel, which is roughly double the vole's size), doubling the amount of energy is not required to power those cells. Instead, there is an *economy of scale* that governs the process of doubling in size, where metabolic rate only increases by approximately 75 percent, or a power of ¾. This process is known as Kleiber's Law after Max Kleiber, the scientist who defined this work in the early 1900s (Kleiber, 1947; West, 2018). In the following figure (Figure 2.1), we can see how many common animals, from humans to horses to rats and mice, all fit neatly on a scaling graph of metabolic rate versus body mass with a scaling exponent of ¾ when they are log-normally graphed (West, 2018).

A challenge in understanding the growth of organisms lies in the juxtaposition of scaling of body size to metabolic rate and the ways that blood vessels branch within a mammalian body, creating a constraint in allometric scaling laws. It turns out that capillaries, the smallest of blood vessels, are size invariant across mammals, being of the same size in voles and blue whales (West, 2018). Capillaries allow for the exchange of matter between tissue and blood cells, most critically oxygen. When an organism doubles in size it does not have a doubling in the size of capillaries. Instead, the size of these increase by approximately ¾; if the capillaries doubled when the size of an organism doubled this would result in sizes beyond which would be impractical according to allometric scaling laws. An organism larger than a blue whale that would be constrained to allometric scaling laws would suffer tissue death, killing the animal. According to this rule, metabolically, humans come from a scaling relationship somewhere between a sheep and a sow (Figure 2.1).

Yet our metabolic rate can also tell us much about the process of aging and death. Larger organisms, like blue whales, elephants, and even humans, tend to live longer. If again we used a 1:1 ratio for doubling, we would not predict the longevity that is experienced by these larger mammals' lifespans. Wear and tear on the body seems to predict the *terminus ad quem* of an organism's lifespan, with greater wear and tear proportionally on smaller organisms. This is due to the fact that with each doubling in the size of an organism, a decrease of roughly 25 percent in the quantity of heart beats per minute is reached. A shrew

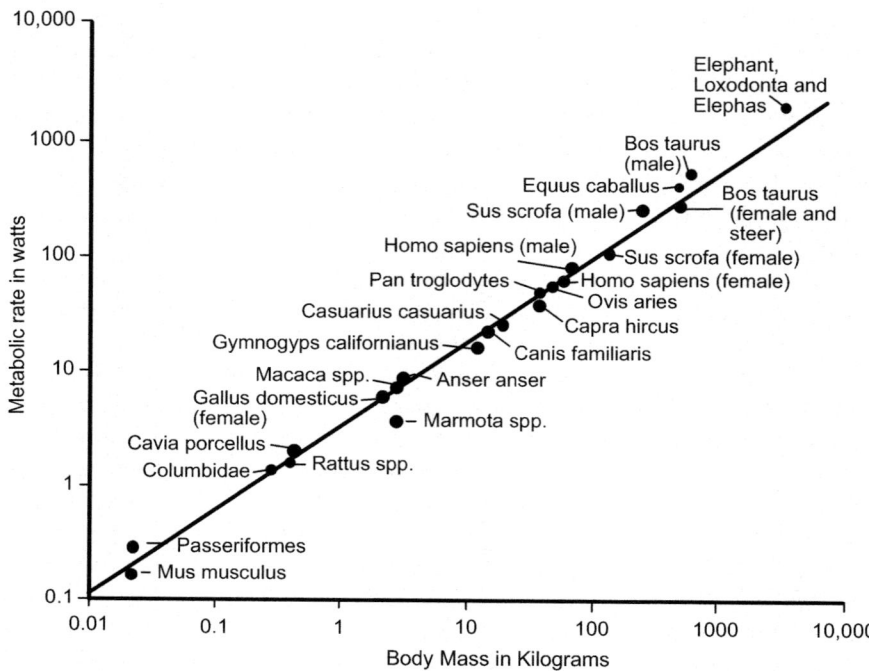

FIGURE 2.1 Kleiber's law, discovered by Max Kleiber in the 1930s, demonstrates that animals' basal metabolic rates scale at a power of roughly 3/4. Adapted from Kleiber, 1947.

experiences approximately 1000 beats per minute; a human roughly 70; a blue whale only 4–8 beats per minute. Metabolic processes cause significant stress on the body; this decrease in the number of beats means larger organisms generally enjoy longer lives. Lifespan scales as ¼ power of mass (West describes this as following the ¾ scaling exponent on "terminal units" with the number of cells scaling linearly, forcing lifespan to scale at ¼ power of mass) (West, 2018).

So, to recap, the human body is subject to scaling laws related to our body size and our metabolism. We grow to a certain size and live to certain lifespans because of the ¾ scaling exponent.

Scaling in Cognitive Function

I described metabolic scaling because of the ways that it is fundamental to complexity science for understanding the ways that certain properties relate to each other. In archaeology we may rarely care about metabolic scaling in the pure sense of that described earlier, but a fundamental understanding of scaling relationships is critical for understanding how scaling has been applied to human cognition and human societies.

Scaling impacts the ways that social relationships form among individuals and even within societies, which has perhaps more bearing on archaeological questions. One surprising output of scaling relationships is that physiological constraints limit the quantity of individuals we can maintain relationships with. In the early 1990s, anthropologist Robin Dunbar proposed that the size of the brain corresponded to the sizes of social groups among nonhuman primates, specifically finding that a limit of approximately 150 individuals would be reached among humans (Dunbar, 1992).

Since Dunbar first proposed this theoretical limit, appropriately now known as Dunbar's number, others have gone on to test this theory, such as work by Lewis et al. (2011) who discovered that the volume of the prefrontal cortex likely dictates the upper bound of the number of individuals we can recognize and befriend. This hardwired boundary limits the size of social network we can maintain (Dunbar et al., 2012). Unless brain size can increase, which anthropologists suggest is impossible due to the limits in the size of the birth canal (Dunsworth, 2016), the upper limit on our social network is around 150 individuals.

To move past this point, hypothetically, if babies were born premature and continued brain development outside the womb this social network size could expand, though this likely would require biohacking or a similar effect on a population scale to enable an expansion of Dunbar's number in a meaningful way.

Because of the universality of Dunbar's number an interesting side effect is that all *Homo sapiens* have likely had this constraint on the number of individuals they can recognize and befriend. This number should be invariant for the length of the *Homo sapiens* species, though presumably other hominins would experience different Dunbar numbers due to the size of their prefrontal cortexes. Further work by Aiello and Dunbar propose that language development in early humans allowed us to have long-distance social networks. Since our neocortex size is larger than that of Neanderthals, that likely gave humans an advantage over their larger-bodied cousins (Aiello and Dunbar, 1993). Yet even with these advantages, innovations would be required to move beyond this limit of around 150 individuals that is hard wired to the size of our neocortices.

Scaling and Settlements

If the number of individuals we can have direct contact with is hard-wired, then ways to move beyond those constraints include innovations such as *scaling our relationships*. Often, anthropologists look at modern nonindustrialized small-scale societies to see the development of social structures, since these societies provide a useful analogue for pre-industrialized societies. Among cross-cultural studies, researchers have found that groups typically form with a nested hierarchical structure, with family units of approximately 5, and language groups of 1500 individuals forming the upper bound, with a scaling ratio of approximately 3 for each level (5, 15, 50, 150, 500, and 1500) (Dunbar et al., 2012). Within these levels include foraging groups of 30–50, larger residential units of about 150, and sodalities or other groups of relatedness of about 500 people (Zhou et al., 2005).

A common feature exists between small-scale hunter-gatherer societies and village societies: the number of individuals we can have meaningful relationships with. While we recognize and maintain weak ties with a larger number of people, approximately 1500 with whom we can name and recognize by face at any given moment (Dunbar et al., 2012), the number of individuals we maintain strong ties with remains relatively consistent between mobile hunter-gatherers and modern industrialized cities due to the physical constraints upon our brains. Dunbar further tested this with social networks in the mid-1990s; in work by Hill and Dunbar they see that the average upper bound of Christmas card networks reaches 153.5 individuals, corresponding to the ~150 limit of a social group (Hill and Dunbar, 2003). More recently they find that even though social media enables us to maintain social ties with a larger number of individuals, studies suggest that we frequently interact among the same subset of 150 of our "friends." Even outsourcing a friendship network to a computer does not, it seems, enable us to move beyond a hardwired Dunbar's number (Dunbar, 2016).

Another way to maintain connection to the larger group beyond face-to-face contact can be codified in language, in stories, or rituals. In a study that makes use of ethnographic interviews of a living small-scale society, Fitzhugh finds that people living on the Kuril Islands maintain long-distance social ties specifically to help different groups survive disasters. Via oral tradition, distant groups pass down stories to subsequent generations; often, these groups will rarely have contact after the initial sharing of the story. The impact of these shared stories is critical, though, for the survival of the societies. The Kuril Islands are beset by natural disasters, including earthquakes and the follow-on impact of tsunamis. When a group is impacted by one of these events, they can then travel to another group hundreds of kilometers away. The telling of a shared story identifies them as part of a distant node in a social network. The long-held stories identify a connection in the social hierarchy (Fitzhugh et al., 2011).

This type of hierarchical communication, based on maintaining social ties without direct face-to-face contact, can be seen in other types of settlements and social organization. Cities are a prime example of ways to take advantage of scaling and the limits of our perception based on our neocortex. And these types of communications can show how scaling relationships organize much of the way that societies interact with each other.

A Modern and Ancient Source of Order

It turns out that the way modern cities are organized may be influenced by ancient systems. Cities, after all, are not a new invention, but have been in existence for millennia. Yet cities were not the norm in ancient times. Rather, most individuals lived in rural contexts, with cities being core locations that nonresidents would visit for business. There were those who lived within the cities, of course, but the predominant mode of living was not in them.

As before, to understand archaeological cities we will begin by looking at the modern example, then move to understand the archaeological cases.

What Makes the Modern City?

Recently, and for the first time in human history, populations shifted from being primarily agricultural to moving toward urban centers. In the year 2000, 70 percent of the population of *developed* countries lived in cities, with 40 percent of *developing* countries living in cities (Crane and Kinzig, 2005; UN, 2018). In 2016, there were 512 cities globally with a population of 1 million or more. Yet the United Nations projects that by 2030 there will be 662 cities with at least 1 million residents (UN, 2018).

A unified definition of a city is required before going further. Bettencourt (2013) suggests that human settlements are the physical manifestation of social networks, embedded across space. Geographers have long established cities as permanent settlements where people live in high densities (Kostof, 1991; Wirth, 1938) and where strangers are likely to come into contact with one another (Sennett, 1977). My undergraduate anthropology professor, Dan Segal, defined the city as "a settlement that cannot feed itself and has to import food from elsewhere" in his singular class "The World Since 1492." Combining these definitions together, cities are densely inhabited settlements where individuals can frequently interact with strangers, with the built environment representing the manifestation of social networks, and where the mode of production is usually outside its walls. With this definition, cities have been around for millennia, the first cities corresponding to the first permanent settlements during the Mesolithic such as at Çatalhöyük (Hodder, 2012). These settlements were founded before we were dependent on domesticates, suggesting that we wanted the benefits of aggregation before we realized the costs associated with sedentism, namely, abandoning our roots in hunting and gathering. Of course, today's cities are often denser, have higher proportions of strangers interacting, and often have the physical manifestation of social networks—roads and buildings—stretching for a longer extent due to efficiencies in modern transportation.

Movement requires cost. As noted by Lobo et al. (2019) "social interactions in space have, throughout history, involved travel, which carries monetary, energy and time costs." Moving to a dense urban environment can reduce those costs, especially when the costs of movement are incurred directly by humans (walking, running, paddling) or by their beasts of burden. As they note, humans can only travel a certain distance within a day, creating boundedness on what can make an urban boundary (Lobo et al., 2019; Marchetti, 1994). Cities, both historic and modern, can be defined as a space a person can get to within about a day, though the distance traveled can, of course, change as new types of movement are introduced. So, a final definition includes not only the physical representation of a social network, the property that people are highly aggregated and frequently interact with strangers, but also the property that a city's boundaries should only extend to where an individual can move within a day.

Taking this definition to the extreme, the UN defines settlements known as megacities that comprise 10 million people or more to differentiate them from regular cities (UN, 2018). As of 2016 there were 31 megacities, with 24 of these in the less developed global south. The UN projects that an additional ten cities will join the ranks of megacities based on demographic projections, all within developing countries (Table 2.1). Due to the constraints of the frontal cortex, it would be physiologically impossible for a person to recognize more than approximately 0.015 percent of the inhabitants of a megacity, allowing for the definition of frequent interaction with strangers to be clear in the definition of a megacity. The physical boundaries of megacities, such as Tokyo or São Paolo, may also stretch the limits of a daily commute and are only possibly with modern infrastructure.

TABLE 2.1 Populations of megacities in 2016 in millions and projected population of megacities in 2030. Note that while Tokyo is projected to have a decline, all other cities are projected to increase

Rank	City, Country	Population in 2016 (millions)	City, Country	Projected Population in 2030 (millions)
1	Tokyo, Japan	38.1	Tokyo, Japan	37.2
2	Delhi, India	26.5	Delhi, India	36.1
3	Shanghai, China	24.5	Shanghai, China	30.8
4	Mumbai, India	21.4	Mumbai, India	27.8
5	São Paulo, Brazil	21.3	Beijing, China	27.7
6	Beijing, China	21.2	Karachi, Pakistan	24.8
7	Ciudad de México, Mexico	21.15	Cairo, Egypt	24.5
8	Osaka, Japan	20.3	Lagos, Nigeria	24.3
9	Cairo, Egypt	19.1	Ciudad de México, Mexico	23.9
10	New York-Newark, USA	18.6	São Paulo, Brazil	23.4

This shift to modern city dwelling is strongly tied to economic development (Bettencourt, 2013). More opportunities for cash-paying jobs entice people to urban centers, often eschewing traditional land-based jobs. Though with the concentration of people into dense urban areas, this can also leave them prone to economic losses related to disasters (UN, 2018). These losses can be sudden and catastrophic, such as with the earthquake that impacted Haiti in 2010, forcing approximately 1.5 million people into makeshift internally displaced rescue camps (World Vision, 2021). Urbanization can also create challenges for the adaptation of the human body; urban heat island effects (Kalnay and Cai, 2003) can be proximal causes of mortality, as seen in the summer 2003 European heatwave that killed up to around 70,000 people (Robine et al., 2008). These impacts may become more frequent, as more people move into cities and as climate change strains the environment and creates greater challenges to an ever-increasing number of people, though these challenges likely impacted people in the archaeological past as well.

These potential losses, however, may be offset by the benefits from living in cities. Education, medical care, governance, cash-paying jobs, and social services like the number of restaurants or the possibility of attending operas or ballets are more easily reached in the city (Bettencourt, 2013; Bettencourt et al., 2007). Cities are "social reactors" providing engines for economic growth and innovation, allowing citizens a disproportionate access to these services in comparison to their rural counterparts.

Thinking through Modern Cities

While cities have their own unique character, certain properties link them and seem to be invariant whether in a smaller settlement or a megacity. From Spokane, WA to the megalopolis of Tokyo, each city is subject to scaling laws. First is the suggestion that social innovation scales with cities. We may predict that as population doubles, the number of patents doubles, since the number of individuals increased the same. This would suggest a log-linear (also known as log-normal) relationship. Log-normal or log-linear distributions mean that for every increase in one dimension of 1 there is an equal increase in another dimension. Log-normal distributions are classically produced by something that can be called the law of proportionate effect (Aitchison and Brown, 1958, p. 1).

Gross domestic product (GDP) in modern cities, one would think, should increase in a similar way. Yet, when subjected to a scaling analysis, these are seen to increase super-linearly. With more people come a disproportionate quantity of patents as well as wages. Within cities, a "rich get richer" dynamic emerges, as it seems that people benefit from close living quarters, deriving substantial gains from social contact.

However, there is a dark side to this rich get richer dynamic. Along with increasing numbers of patents, GDP, and other social gains indicative of an increase in creativity comes a disproportionate increase in crime, infectious disease, and the negative aspects of urban living. When cities grow quickly, slums develop quickly to provide housing for the urban poor, often with poor sanitation, no utilities, and little oversight to how individuals should heat their homes. Aggregation comes at a cost. Along with rich get richer it seems there may be a "sick get sicker" dynamic in modern cities.

Yet the benefits for a city may, indeed, outweigh the costs at the individual level (often felt by the urban poor) for the costs of creating infrastructure decrease in aggregated cities. As a city increases in size, the space-saving metrics of building new main roads, adding sewer pipes, power lines, or telecommunications lines makes cities more efficient. Often, these can just be "tacked on" to the original infrastructure, allowing for cost saving at the urban level (Bettencourt et al., 2007).

Taking a closer look at the scaling relationships discussed by Bettencourt, we can examine how these things scale together. We can see that both the benefits of urban living are seen as being subject to an increasing economy of scale of about 1.15. So, as a city doubles in size, its number of patents, GDP, and wages increase by not double, but increase with an exponent of $n + .15$. Unfortunately, crime and infectious disease also increase at the same rate. With a fair amount of accuracy, given the population of one city versus another you could estimate the GDP, the number of patents, and the number of violent crimes (West, 2018).

On the other side, the scaling exponent of $n-.15$ seems to explain the growth of infrastructure. On this side it seems an increasing economy of scale is felt as a city increases in size. Proportionally less investment in infrastructure is required to build a city as it grows than one may expect. This property seems similar between ancient and modern cities. This suggests that the principle that as a city grows, it does not have to invest heavy amounts in its infrastructure, is potentially time invariant; roads that radiate out from a city, gas stations, temples, and other services, can be created without the 1:1 ratio. This holds true in antiquity as much as it does today, as we shall see in the following.

Ancient Cities, Ancient Scaling

We took a detour through scaling of modern systems to get to understanding of ancient scaling. As with much archaeological science, the techniques are calibrated on modern methods. First came the sequencing of DNA, and then we were able to understand ancient DNA. First came remote sensing for modern landscapes, and then it was used to understand landscapes of the past. So, we calibrate our understanding of scaling laws on modern cities and now turn the lens to ancient cities.

We know cities are millennia old, and so the origins of scaling in cities should also have deep roots. While working at the Santa Fe Institute, Scott

Ortman, an archaeologist working in the American Southwest, teamed up with Luis Bettencourt, the originator of the work on the scaling of cities. Bettencourt's work identified the economies of scale governing infrastructure in modern cities; the question was whether comparable patterns could be observed in archaeological settlements or whether such features were unique to contemporary urbanism.

The first paper within the origins of scaling work examines settlement scaling in the Basin of Mexico (Ortman et al., 2014). Analyzing approximately 1400 settlements in varying timescales (230 sites in the earliest period, and 546 settlements in the latest period), they show that despite changes in political centralization and differences in urbanism, that as urban boundaries and population increase, these ancient cities conform to a scaling relationship with an exponent of between 2/3 and 5/6. Even though transportation has changed dramatically since these ancient cities were built and we now can harness fossil fuels for our movement, we still see similar scaling powers to the work by Bettencourt.

What was most striking from this work was the fact that these scaling relationships developed independently in the Pre-Hispanic Basin of Mexico long before European Colonists arrived in the Americas. Ortman and colleagues suggest that this may mean that there is an underlying principle that unifies the scaling of settlements worldwide.

In follow-on work, Ortman and his team further examined data from the Basin of Mexico, including both size of settlements and size of population from the original study with the growth of monuments and the size of houses (Ortman et al., 2015). They suggest that larger political units produced monuments at faster rates than smaller political units. They also find that the sizes of houses are larger on average in more populous settlements and suggest that the scaling exponents they discover are indistinguishable from modern cities. This work ties into settlement scaling theory, which suggests that measurements of infrastructure, of measurable socioeconomic outputs, and of social network connectivity can be detected via aggregate measures and that there are underlying principles that link with an understanding of social networks that drive the scaling of these measures.

Smith et al. (2021b) applied settlement scaling theory among Mesoamerican sites, including sites from the Classic period Maya, to examine the extent to which these settlements could be classified as "urban." They found that while the population structure is markedly different from that of many other agrarian settlement systems, the low-density settlements in their study region conformed to some definitions of urbanism but not to others. Interestingly, while they find low settlement densities, their work finds that Mesoamerican settlements generated economies of scale and increasing returns to scale via political centers that provided gathering places for many people to come together. In this way, scaling theory provides a way to detect patterns of interaction in the past, something that would not be made possible via traditional analyses.

Several other projects from the Social Reactors Project applied settlement scaling theory to other archaeological cases worldwide (e.g., Hanson, 2024; Klassen et al., 2022; Ortman et al., 2015; Ortman et al., 2016; Ortman and Coffey, 2017; Ossa et al., 2017; Smith et al., 2021a, 2021b). Generally, within these studies the authors find that infrastructure scales with increasing economies of scale with an exponent between 2/3 and 5/6. They also find that there are likely increasing returns to scale via the social opportunities that cities provide.

Conclusions

What this chapter provided is an introduction to scaling theory, from the foundations of understanding metabolic scaling to understanding cities as large-scale metabolisms that people live within. Via examining the archaeological record with tools from scaling theory, we can better detect hidden patterns of order in the complex world of archaeology. Scaling theory provides a method for doing just this—for telescoping between how people experience the city (increasing returns to scale) and how the city itself is organized.

What is perhaps most remarkable is that the principles of settlement scaling appear to transcend both time and geography. Despite the immense variation in social structure, economy, and political organization across ancient civilizations, the repeated emergence of similar scaling exponents across datasets suggests there may be universal principles guiding how human societies aggregate, interact, and build their environments. In this way, cities become more than physical containers—they become structured reflections of the social networks and energetic flows that constitute human life. By seeing cities as both infrastructure and interaction, as physical space and social system, we gain a lens for recognizing ancient urbanism as part of a continuous trajectory of human collective behavior.

The ability to identify increasing returns to scale in ancient cities offers an archaeological pathway to detecting forms of urbanism that may not resemble modern cities in form or function but nonetheless perform similar social roles. The presence of gathering places, monumental construction, and house size differentials in the past are not only empirical signals—they are manifestations of underlying processes. This reframing allows archaeologists to think beyond traditional typologies of urban versus rural, or centralized versus dispersed, or "more complex" to more simple, and instead focus on how energy, information, and social connectivity scale with population in patterned ways.

Moreover, scaling theory gives us a common vocabulary for comparing past and present, opening up new avenues for cross-disciplinary dialogue between archaeologists, physicists, urban theorists, and complexity scientists. By calibrating our methods on modern cities and applying them to ancient contexts, we blur the lines between the "then" and the "now" and begin to see the human settlement as part of a much longer story of adaptation, innovation, and transformation.

In Chapter 5, we will turn to a case study of using methods from scaling theory within my own work in the Ancestral Pueblo Southwest. This work employs agent-based modeling to understand the past but then leverages scaling theory to examine whether or not settlements exhibited hierarchical organization. However, before we can fully engage with that case study, we must take a deeper dive into agent-based modeling itself. So, in the next chapter, we explore how agent-based modeling functions as a methodological bridge between individual decision-making and emergent social patterns, revealing new insights into the ways relationships formed among archaeological societies and how those relationships shaped the spaces people built and inhabited.

Works Cited

Aiello, L.C., and Dunbar, R.I.M., 1993. Neocortex Size, Group Size, and the Evolution of Language. *Current Anthropology* 34, 184–193.

Aitchison, J., and Brown, J. A. C., 1958. The Lognormal Distribution, with Special Reference to Its Uses in Economics. *Economic Review* 9(2), 185–187.

Bettencourt, L.M.A., 2013. The Origins of Scaling in Cities. *Science* (1979) 340, 1438–1441. https://doi.org/10.1126/science.1235823

Bettencourt, L.M.A., Lobo, J., Helbing, D., Kühnert, C., and West, G.B., 2007. Growth, Innovation, Scaling, and the Pace of Life in Cities. *Proceedings of the National Academy of Sciences* 104, 7301–7306. https://doi.org/10 1073/pnas.0610172104

Bird, M.I., Crabtree, S.A., Haig, J., Ulm, S., and Wurster, C M., 2021. A Global Carbon and Nitrogen Isotope perspective on Modern and Ancient Human Diet. *Proceedings of the National Academy of Sciences of the United States of America* 118, 1–17. https://doi.org/10.1073/pnas.2024642118

Crabtree, S.A., Dunne, J.A., and Wood, S.A., 2021. Ecological Networks and Archaeology. *Antiquity* 95, 812–825. https://doi.org/10.15184/aqy.2021.38

Crane, P., and Kinzig, A., 2005. Nature in the Metropolis. *Science* (1979) 308, 1225.

Dunbar, R., 1992. Neocortex Size as a Constraint on Group Size in Primates. *Journal of Human Evolution* 22, 469–493.

Dunbar, R., 2016. Do Online Social Media Cut through the Constraints that Limit the size of Offline Social Networks? *Royal Society Open Science* 3, 150292. https://doi.org/10.1098/rsos.150292

Dunbar, R., Baumard, N., Hamilton, M.J., Hooper, P., Finkel, D.N., and Gintis, H., 2012. Networking Past and Present. *Cliodynamics* 3, 344–362.

Dunsworth, H.M., 2016. Thank your Intelligent Mother for your Big Brain. *Proceedings of the National Academy of Sciences of the United States of America* 113, 6816–6818. https://doi.org/10.1073/pnas.1606596113

Fitzhugh, B., Phillips, S.C., and Gjesfjeld, E., 2011. Modeling Hunter-Gatherer Information Networks: An Archaeological Case Study from the Kuril Islands. In *The Role of Information in Hunter-Gatherer Band Adaptations*. Cotsen Institute of Archaeology, edited by R. Whallon, W. Lovis and R. Hitchcock. University of California, Los Angeles, CA, pp. 85–115.

Hanson, J.W., 2024. Scaling in Pompeii: Preliminary Evidence for the Occurrence of Scaling Phenomena Within an Ancient Built Environment. *Journal of Archaeological Method and Theory* 31, 448–472. https://doi.org/10.1007/s10816-023-09604-x

Hill, R.A., and Dunbar, R.I.M., 2003. Social Network Size in Humans. *Human Nature* 14, 53–72. https://doi.org/10.1007/s12110-003-1016-y

Hodder, I., 2012. *Entangled: An Archaeology of the Relationships between Humans and Things*. Wiley-Blackwell, Malden, MA.

Kalnay, E., and Cai, M., 2003. Impact of Urbanization and Land-Use Change on Climate. *Nature* 423, 528–531. https://doi.org/10.1038/nature01675

Klassen, S., Ortman, S.G., Lobo, J., and Evans, D., 2022. Provisioning an Early City: Spatial Equilibrium in the Agricultural Economy at Angkor, Cambodia. *Journal of Archaeological Method and Theory* 29, 763–794. https://doi.org/10.1007/s10816-021-09535-5

Kleiber, M., 1947. Body Size and Metabolic Rate. *Physiological Reviews* 27, 511–541.

Kostof, S., 1991. *The City Shaped: Urban Patterns and Meanings Through History*. Bullfinch, Boston, MA.

Lewis, P.A., Rezaie, R., Brown, R., Roberts, N., and Dunbar, R.I.M., 2011. Ventromedial Prefrontal Volume Predicts Understanding of Others and Social Network Size. *Neuroimage* 57, 1624–1629. https://doi.org/10.1016/j.neuroimage.2011.05.030

Lobo, J., Bettencourt, L.M.A., Smith, M.E., and Ortman, S., 2019. Settlement Scaling Theory: Bridging the Study of Ancient and Contemporary Urban Systems. *Urban Studies* 57, 731–747. https://doi.org/10.1177/0042098019873796

Marchetti, C., 1994. Anthropological Invariants in Travel Behavior. *Technological Forecasting and Social Change* 47, 75–88. https://doi.org/10.1016/0040-1625(94)90041-8

Nature Portfolio, 2021. Scaling Laws [WWW Document].

Ortman, S.G., Cabaniss, A.H.F., Sturm, J.O., and Bettencourt, L.M.A., 2014. The Pre-History of Urban Scaling. *PLoS One* 9, e87902.

Ortman, S.G., Cabaniss, A.H.F., Sturm, J.O., and Bettencourt, L.M.A., 2015. Settlement Scaling and Increasing Returns in an Ancient Society. *Science Advances* 1, e1400066. https://doi.org/10.1126/sciadv.1400066

Ortman, S.G., and Coffey, G.D., 2017. Settlement Scaling in Middle-Range Societies. *American Antiquity* 82, 662–682. https://doi.org/10.1017/aaq.2017.42

Ortman, S.G., Davis, K.E., Lobo, J., Smith, M.E., Bettencourt, L.M.A., and Trumbo, A., 2016. Settlement Scaling and Economic Change in the Central Andes. *Journal of Archaeological Science* 73, 94–106. https://doi.org/10.1016/j.jas.2016.07.012

Ossa, A., Smith, M.E., and Lobo, J., 2017. The Size of Plazas in Mesoamerican Cities and Towns: A Quantitative Analysis. *Latin American Antiquity* 28, 457–475.

Robine, J.-M., Cheung, S.L.K., Le Roy, S., Van Oyen, H., Griffiths, C., Michel, J.-P., and Herrmann, F.R., 2008. Death Toll Exceeded 70,000 in Europe during the Summer of 2003. *Comptes Rendus Biologies* 331, 171–178. https://doi.org/10.1016/j.crvi.2007.12.001

Romanowska, I., Gamble, C., Bullock, S., and Sturt, F., 2017. Dispersal and the Movius Line: Testing The Effect of Dispersal on Population Density through Simulation. *Quaternary International* 431, 53–63. https://doi.org/10.1016/j.quaint.2016.01.016

Sennett, R., 1977. *The Fall of Public Man*. Knopf, New York.

Smith, M.E., Lobo, J., Peeples, M.A., York, A.M., Stanley, B.W., Crawford, K.A., Gauthier, N., and Huster, A.C., 2021a. The Persistence of Ancient Settlements and Urban Sustainability. *Proceedings of the National Academy of Sciences* 118, e2018155118. https://doi.org/10.1073/pnas.2018155118

Smith, M.E., Ortman, S.G., Lobo, J., Ebert, C.E., Thompson, A.E., Prufer, K.M., Liendo Stuardo, R., and Rosenswig, R.M., 2021b. The Low-Density Urban Systems of the Classic Period Maya and Izapa: Insights from Settlement Scaling Theory. *Latin American Antiquity* 32, 120–137. https://doi.org/10.1017/laq.2020.80

UN, 2018. *World Urbanization Prospects: The 2018 Revizion*. United Nations, New York.

West, G., 2018. *Scale: The Universal Laws of Life, Growth, and Death in Organisms, Cities, and Companies*. Penguin Random House, New York.
Wirth, L., 1938. Urbanism as a Way of Life. *American Journal of Sociology* 44, 1–24.
World Vision, 2021. 2010 *Haiti Earthquake: Facts, FAQs, and How to Help* [WWW Document]. World Vision From the Field.
Zhou, W.-X., Sornette, D., Hill, R.A., and Dunbar, R.I.M., 2005. Discrete Hierarchical Organization of Social Group Sizes. *Proceedings: Biological Sciences* 272, 439–444. https://doi.org/10.1098/rspb.2004.2970

3
AGENT-BASED MODELING AND ARCHAEOLOGY

One of the greatest challenges facing archaeology is that we want to understand the ways that people lived in the past based mostly on the detritus that they left behind. We may find potsherds, or we may find lithics, or we excavate a midden to be able to see the animal bones and plant remains that people had discarded into the trash. From these remains we attempt to understand the ways that societies changed over time, how individuals were connected to each other and to their ecosystems, and perhaps the ways societies grew and then societies collapsed. The archaeological record itself is the accumulation of the detritus of past societies, from which we reconstruct the intricate histories of ancient civilizations, and ultimately the end point that we archaeologists observe.

In recent decades, scientists from a diverse set of disciplines have developed theoretical frameworks and sophisticated hypotheses by testing them against available data using advanced computational techniques, particularly a technique called agent-based modeling (e.g., Hammond and Barkin, 2024). In archaeology as well as other historical disciplines, agent-based modeling allows us to explore the possible lives of people in the past and analyze our theories about them via a principled and systematic approach (Romanowska et al., 2021). These *in silico* experiments enable us to test and refine hypotheses, investigate the causal mechanisms behind societal transformations, and refine data collection to address key questions.

What Are Agent-Based Models?

Agent-based models are a type of computer simulation that enables investigation of phenomena from the bottom up. These phenomena are shaped by individual actions and interactions, but they are constrained by larger overarching

DOI: 10.4324/9781003585251-3

structures. In agent-based models the agents are the individual entities themselves, be they cells in a body, individual people, families, or cities. The agents follow user-defined rules and behavior and may interact with one another and the environment at each time step; these models are then run for multiple timestep to analyze the emergent way that the actions and interactions of the agents can lead to larger overarching structures. Critically, agent characteristics mediate the interaction effects which can be at varying spatial scales.

For example, an agent-based model could be built to look at how a virus could invade a person's body and how differing levels of immune capability could allow the virus to take hold over time or not. The model then could be extended to look at how person-to-person contact could help a virus spread through a community and what behaviors would be best for stopping spread. An agent-based model could also look at how individual people adopt altruistic behaviors or become selfish cheaters, and how the behaviors of the individuals influence society (Crabtree et al., 2024).

Within archaeology, agent-based models have been leveraged to understand intractable aspects of prehistory. Agent-based modeling and other types of simulation (such as network models, see Chapter 4 in this book, or settlement scaling models, see Chapter 2) can be viewed as a type of Binfordian middle-range theory, bridging empirical data-based research and theory-building exercises (Romanowska et al., 2021). While a full review of agent-based models in archaeology is beyond the scope of this book, there are other publications that both summarize and reproduce agent-based models (e.g., see Romanowska et al., 2021). Here I will focus on foundational models, as well as models that have directly impacted my own work.

While there are some published models before this, agent-based modeling began its revolution in archaeological work in the late 1990s and early 2000s. The book *Dynamics in Human and Primate Societies: Agent-Based Modeling of Social and Spatial Processes* by Kohler and Gumerman, published in 2000 by the Santa Fe Institute Press, grew out of a workshop at the Santa Fe Institute in 1997 (Kohler and Gumerman, 2000). That volume works as a launching point for agent-based modeling in archaeology.

Two large-scale projects aiming to understand the ways that climate, food production, and population interacted in two distinct parts of the American Southwest were presented at the 1997 meeting, and early publications were written up in the volume. The first, known as *Artificial Anasazi*, examined the way that the Kayenta Ancestral Pueblo people of the Longhouse Valley lived and farmed between A.D. 800 and A.D. 1350 (Dean et al., 2000). The thrust of the model was seeing whether or not climate variables, specifically availability of water, could reproduce the pattern of population growth and decline observed archaeologically. Via a simple model the authors were able to demonstrate that population could be tied to agricultural productivity, which was in-turn tied to water availability and climatic fluctuation over time, but these variables alone could not explain the rapid depopulation of Longhouse Valley (Axtell et al., 2002). There have been several reproductions of this model (Janssen, 2009; Stonedahl and Wilensky, 2010), most notably the one by Janssen that has become part of the NetLogo Models Library, demonstrating the importance of replicating models built by other teams.

The second of these early projects published in this volume (Kohler et al., 2000) was developed around the same time, but continued to produce research well into the late 2010s (e.g., Crabtree et al., 2017). The Village Ecodynamics Project also leveraged the well-studied record of the Ancestral Pueblo, but this time focused on the Central Mesa Verde region of southwestern Colorado, the most densely inhabited part of the Ancestral Pueblo world. This project was interested in developing a testbed that had realistic GIS dataplanes of the landscape as well as realistic climate hindcasts spanning the 700 years of Pueblo occupation of the Four Corners region of southwest Colorado from A.D. 600 to A.D. 1280. Upon this testbed the researchers could ask questions about farming (Kohler et al., 2012), hunting (Bocinsky et al., 2012), specialization (Cockburn et al., 2013), conflict (Crabtree et al., 2017), and many other research questions. The Village Ecodynamics Project agent-based model, known colloquially as Village, showed that by leveraging high-quality data to create a baseline agent-based model, and then building upon that base, we could better understand the archaeological past of not only that region but also fundamental aspects of human culture.

Artificial Anasazi and Village were large, complex models, with dynamically interacting systems, aligning with data-driven models that aimed to reproduce and understand observed archaeological trends. Other types of models developed at the time include more stylized models that tend to be simpler and deploy theory as a means to refine understandings of human behavior. Within the same volume, Lake presented his MAGICAL model (Multi-Agent Geographically Informed Computer AnaLysis) of Mesolithic foraging (Lake, 2000). Within this model, agents slowly built up their mental map of an abstract resource landscape, allowing the agents to refine their decisions about mobility on the landscape in relation to foraging patches. Other early models included models of cooperation (Lansing, 2000), models of state formation processes (Reynolds and Lazar, 2002), and human social organization (Read, 2002). A pair of simulations led by Brantingham (Brantingham, 2003; Brantingham et al., 2007) developed around this time that examined processes related to the formation of the archaeological record and lithic materials. The model of lithic material procurement takes a simple model of foraging (similar to the mushroom foraging model in Railsback and Grimm (2011)) and allows the agent to pick up lithics it comes across, hold onto them, and discard them when it acquires more than it can carry and has been recreated multiple times (Crabtree et al., 2019; Davies et al., 2019; Oestmo et al., 2016; Romanowska et al., 2019). In another early agent-based model, Brantingham and colleagues used both mathematical and agent-based models to look at sediment mixing in post-depositional processes of archaeological deposits (Brantingham et al., 2007).

With the aim of teaching agent-based modeling to large numbers of practitioners, Romanowska, Wren, and Crabtree et al. (2021) recreated 58 models in their book, organizing them into models of subsistence, models of migration, and models of exchange. Many archaeological models seem to fit in these three camps, though Cegielski and Rogers note a larger array of types, dividing models into six types: (1) historical, (2) social complexity, (3) formation processes, (4) human ecology, (5) evolutionary processes and (6) complexity science (Cegielski and Daniel Rogers, 2016). Yet even with this wider array of types, each of these models generally corresponds to models of migration, exchange, or subsistence at the core level.

In separate commentaries, Lake (2014) and Cegielski and Daniel Rogers (2016) suggest that a growing cadre of archaeologists have been calling for the use of agent-based models to become more mainstream, but that they have been stymied by three main challenges: (1) agent-based models were seen as understandable in theory, but the methodology was too complex, requiring a background in computer science, to wield directly by many archaeologists. (2) the methodological and theoretical underpinnings of agent-based modeling were seen as underdeveloped for questions in social science, and (3) the rise of post-processual critiques in the 1980s, when approaches like individual-based modeling were being adopted in ecology, made computational approaches less likely to take hold in archaeology.

One of the aims of "Agent-based Modeling for Archaeology" (Romanowska et al., 2021) was to address challenges 1 and 2. They suspected that the root of these critiques was due to a lack of formalized training in agent-based modeling in social science at higher education institutions. An increase in workshops and formal classes, as well as this open-source textbook, have aimed to augment general understanding of the technique as well as to increase the number of practitioners. Yet, even with these challenges, agent-based models have become more frequently used to test hypotheses and refine understanding of past societies in recent years. The flexibility of the tool to study such varied systems and model counterfactual histories are especially useful for studying archaeology.

One of the ways that agent-based modeling addresses key gaps in archaeological research is by providing a clear way to examine the palimpsest nature of the archaeological record. Taphonomic processes, human reuse, natural environmental factors, and more all contribute to the wiping away of traces from the past, making it difficult to interpret. Agent-based modeling, however, is unique in that it allows practitioners to build hypothesis-driven models that can be run hundreds to thousands of times to examine how well (or how poorly) the output conforms to what we observe in the archaeological record. These models directly allow us to examine the ways that the past formed, by simulating counterfactuals to help us refine our understanding of the past. Further, many different models can be built that specifically examine competing scenarios and hypotheses, further helping us to refine our understanding of the past by allowing us to discard those hypotheses that are the least likely.

When Are Agent-based Models the Best Approach?

Agent-based models are a highly flexible tool that can help to understand key aspects of the past. But when are they the most appropriate tools to be used?

First, agent-based models are useful when there is a spatial component to the problem. While real physical geography may or may not be important, there at least needs to be a spatial dimension that impacts the problem.

Second, agent-based models are useful when there is a temporal dimension to the problem. If we care how things unfold over time, then agent-based modeling may be the right approach to the problem.

Third, agent-based models are appropriate when the population has a heterogenous structure to it and you care about how the different agents may act and interact with each other.

While there are no hard and fast rules for when exactly to build an agent-based model, generally we look to whether there is spatial structure, temporal dimensions, and a heterogenous population.

As an example, one of the models that did not begin as an agent-based model but quickly has been adapted to the library of agent-based models is Thomas Schelling's model of segregation (Schelling, 1969). Within this model, agents belong to one of two types, agents that are a dark color or agents that are a light color. The agents have two states, being happy or unhappy which has to do with how many of the neighboring agents are the same color as they are. While this heterogeneity is quite basic, it still fulfills the need for heterogeneous agents within an agent-based model: the agents can be one of two colors and one of two states, allowing for four possible agent types (dark happy, dark unhappy, light happy, light unhappy).

These agents then live on a grid with no real geographic features. All that is represented is the location of the pixel. However, it is critical that the agents are represented at different points in space because the happiness state for the agents depends on who their neighbors are. Thus, space is a general term and is used to house the grid that agents can live in.

At the beginning of every timestep agents look at how many agents who look like them are nearby and how many agents in the neighboring cells are of the opposite color. They then compare this number and see if it is below their threshold for happiness, which is a parameter that can be set by the user. For the case of explanation, let's say that agents want 2/3 of their neighbors to be the same color as them. If 2/3 of the neighbors are the same color, the agent is happy and stays put. If there aren't 2/3 of their neighbors the same color, the

FIGURE 3.1   The "Segregation" model in the NetLogo library, an agent-based model version of Schelling's model of segregation (1969). In this model agents are one of two colors, light or dark, and they are either happy or unhappy based on the percent of neighbors who are the same color as them. Agents move until they are "happy." Schelling showed that with agents only wanting 2/3 out of their neighbors the same color as themselves that there would be system-wide segregation.

agent is then unhappy and decides to move to a new space. Every timestep this evaluation takes place, and the simulation keeps advancing until all agents are happy. The temporal dimension in this simulation is also fairly stylized, as it doesn't represent real minutes, months, or years (Figure 3.1).

While this model is quite simplified, it still offers real insights into how segregation in cities can occur. If an individual wants only a small majority of its neighbors to look like them, then neighborhoods of one color tend to form.

Importantly for our discussion, this model illustrates why an agent-based model is helpful, in that this highly simple model still uses simplified space, simplified heterogeneity, and simple time.

In agent-based models of archaeology, often these dimensions are much richer. Space will often be represented by realistic geography by using digital elevation models. Time will often represent a real measure of time, such as days, seasons, months, or years. Heterogeneity in agents may be different species, such as humans and their domesticated animals, or perhaps different sexes or genders of agents, as well as agents of different age structures.

Beyond encapsulating temporal and spatial dimensions as well as heterogeneity, agent-based models are useful for two types of prediction: predicting based on known knowledge of past events and looking at counterfactuals from the past.

For prediction I mean that when an agent-based model can take into account data from the past as a calibration dataset, the model can then predict future outcomes. For example, let's suppose we have high-resolution data from historical archaeology of the extent of certain species, be they plants or animals. Now let's suppose we have highly resolved precipitation data and temperature data over decades, which we can then tune to our model of species distribution in the past. We then could use these data to *project forward* under different climate and precipitation scenarios to suggest what that landscape will look like in the future.

By counterfactuals what I mean is running experiments of *what if?* What would have happened if there was no "Great Drought" impacting the American Southwest? What would have happened if Chinggis Khan had not died when he did and the Mongols had continued to sweep west into Europe? What would have happened if the bubonic plague had not occurred? With appropriate parsimony these questions can be examined via an agent-based model. In fact, counterfactuals are frequently employed in the field of public health. Agent-based modeling has been successfully used to examine the COVID-19 Omicron wave and look at which measures, such as masking, isolation, and testing, could have reduced the number of infected and the number of casualties (O'Gara et al., 2023).

When Are Other Approaches Better?

Agent-based models can help to answer many questions, but sometimes are not the right tool for the job. Because they can take a long time to develop, have to be examined well, and must adhere to the principals of parsimony, sometimes they are more *computationally expensive* than is necessary.

There are other tools at an archaeologist's disposal that can complement building an agent-based model or be more appropriate to the question than spending time building a complex computational model from the ground up. For example, Bayesian statistics are a fantastic way to use information to calibrate predictive models. While Bayes' theorem was developed in the 1800s, it has become *de rigeur* in the past few decades for predicting an outcome based on prior information, most notably with advances in the technique beginning in the 1990s. Bayesian inference takes the data at hand and, so as to not bias the end-resulting hypotheses, assigns vague probabilities to all possible prior data giving equal probability to every possible state of the estimated parameters. Bayesian statistics allow scientists to assess each of these competing hypotheses, weighing them against the evidence at hand (Otárola-Castillo and Torquato, 2018).

In Otárola-Catillo and Torquato's helpful review, they use the example that an archaeologist may have an assemblage of projectile points and want to assess whether they are arrow points or not. They may have three Bayesian hypotheses that they can evaluate against the data: that the points are arrow points, that the points are spear points, and that the points are dart points. By establishing these competing hypotheses and then analyzing these data, allowing probabilities that each of these statements are true, we can come to a conclusion statistically about the use of these projectile points.

Bayseian statistics are incredibly useful for the kinds of questions where we may have data that can help us make an unbiased prediction, but more often than not do not have a specific spatial structure (though we do use Bayesian statistics to infer population structures, which are inherently spatial). Often, when there is a spatial element to the data, we will deploy Geographic Information Systems (GIS) to both understand the spatial structure of the data and to predict spatial locations of items.

We could take the same example as above, but instead of just having one type of projectile point, perhaps we have a large geographic area and many mixed projectile points. While we could break the problem up spatially to predict the types of projectile points using Bayesian statistics, we could also then map these points onto the landscape, which could lend us more information. In our imaginary landscape, perhaps there is an area in the northwest quadrant that is mountainous with predominately spear points. Perhaps in the northeast in an area where it is mostly flat we mostly find arrow points. And perhaps in the southeast where it is mostly wooded we find only dart points. Now as we look to the rest of the map there may be other areas that are wooded, mountainous, or flat but they don't correspond nicely to northeast, northwest, and southeast. However, we can input all of this information and use a predictive model (Verhagen, 2018) which will give us greater information about the likely whereabouts of these archaeological materials.

Both Bayesian statistics and GIS predictive models are models themselves and tell us a lot of information that perhaps we could glean from an agent-based model but in a simpler manner. There are other types of models that are a step toward an agent-based model but require fewer moving parts.

One example of these is when spatial structure and time are incorporated, but the agents are not necessarily heterogenous nor do they require movement. For example, often when trying to understand the ways that populations expanded, researchers will deploy a cellular automaton, a type of simulation that does incorporate spatial structure and does have a time dimension, but often the individual people are not modeled. Instead, what is modeled is the carrying capacity of individual cells to see the likely speed and direction that populations would spread. Cellular automata are very similar to agent-based models, but they do not take into account agent heterogeneity. Rather, they are simplified to geographic and temporal attributes (i.e., occupied and non-occupied), as well as exogenous factors such as extreme weather events, to simulate a process of spread.

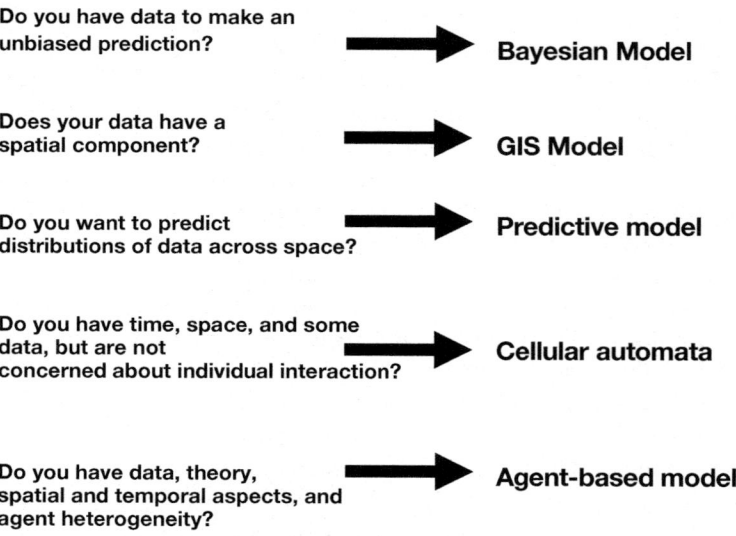

FIGURE 3.2   Simple decision tree of data types on the left and types of models on the right. There are, of course, many other types of models but this is a basic way of thinking through which type of model to pursue.

Yet if we wanted to know how individuals impacted the spread of a population we could move beyond the cellular automata and make an agent-based model with many similar features of the original cellular automata simulation. In Figure 3.2, I illustrate these different modeling pathways. These are by no means the only types of models and simulations there are, but they serve as an example of how to determine when to build an agent-based model and when other approaches may be better suited to the problem at hand.

The strength in agent-based modeling lies in its flexibility. It is up to the developer of the model to choose defensible parameters for their model. This requires an in-depth knowledge of the system they are studying as well as good hypotheses for what the model may help them understand about their system. Yet, because of this flexibility, agent-based modeling has been subjected to many criticisms. In the following I outline many of the criticisms of agent-based modeling I have heard in the process of using this technique in my own work.

Critiques of Agent-based Models

Critiques of techniques can be field specific—that is, critiques in physics are likely to be different from critiques of models in ecology. I have found that critiques of agent-based models in archaeology generally fall into three camps. (1) The "manipulatable model": (a) that practitioners can make the model do anything they want; and (b) the phrase "garbage in garbage out"; (2) The "too complex" model: (a) that the model itself is so complex you cannot understand anything from the system you are studying, and (b) that humans as a species are too complex to model; and (3) The "reductionist" model, that agent-based models can be "dehumanizing" and must oversimplify complexities of human behavior in order to computerize them.

The "Manipulatable Model"

Can Agent-Based Models Do Whatever You Want Them To?

One benefit of agent-based modeling is its inherent flexibility in that you can model any system, as long as you are looking at the interactions of heterogeneous individuals and incorporate spatial and temporal dimensions. However, a critique of agent-based models (usually by other types of sophisticated computer modelers) is that because ABMs are so flexible, a practitioner can include any variables they want and tune the model to get the output they desire. In effect, you can ask a question and then reify your own hypothesis by adjusting the model code until the results match your expectations.

This is a serious concern, but I believe this critique can be leveled against any type of scientific tool, especially as the tool is adopted more broadly and as standards are set within science. Let's look to critiques of other types of model building first, to then look at how these would or would not apply to agent-based modeling.

Principal Components Analysis is a statistical technique that reduces the dimensionality of a large complex dataset to be able to understand the interactions of different components. While used broadly in the sciences, it is generally accepted in many social sciences, such as psychology, sociology, and anthropology, as well as being a primary analytical technique in things like randomized control trials in medicine. In principal components analysis, generally, a scientist has created a study, such as a large questionnaire, that has many possible responses. From the questionnaire, you as the scientist get a large data table and you want to understand some type of structure for this data. This large multivariate data table is then subjected to projections that can take the large datasets and compress them to summary indices so that you can observe trends in the data, how different data points cluster together, or which data points are outliers. Principal components analysis is a highly flexible tool that can allow for analyzing data that may have missing values or have colinear variables, it can handle categorical data, imprecise data as well as more precise measurements. Because it was invented in the early 1900s and has become *de rigeur* in many sciences (Pearson, 1901), it isn't subject (as frequently) to the same critiques as agent-based models are.

However, like any scientific technique it is incumbent upon the scientist to know how to use the technique before deploying it. One major challenge with principal components analysis is the portability of the same components onto new datasets. If a scientist uses large survey data to then try to understand the system, identifies those first components, then uses a brand new dataset but the same derived axes from the first component, the ensuing interpretation may not make any sense and the results may be a completely new model (Leek and Peng, 2015). In this way a principal component analysis could "do anything a researcher wanted it to" by identifying those first components then forcing every model into those derived axes.

For example, perhaps a researcher wanted to understand how people's buying habits were impacted by awareness of climate change due to the prevalence of extreme weather events. This researcher might send a survey to 1000 households in early July to ask them what they bought, whether there were any local extreme events (fires, heatwaves), and whether or not they have read news on climate change of late. They might then find that those who experienced extreme events and were aware of climate change bought things like air purifiers in their homes, while people who didn't experience extreme events did not. Now let's hypothesize that this researcher had the exact same survey to be sent out every 3 months, but perhaps it's difficult to get the same households to reply, perhaps because of turnover of individuals in the same houses that are targeted. Now let's also assume that during month 2 of the third survey a new invention came out that dramatically improved the quality of life of people, but this invention was not something you had to buy but was given by the government, such as the free air purifier program in Utah. Let's also imagine those folks in Utah that were surveyed did not experience the same extreme event but experienced something like extreme air pollution from the refineries there. The new survey may not capture the changes that happened between the old surveys and the new, and it may not account for these latent variables (given versus bought products). Yet, the narrative that prevalence of extreme events and awareness of climate change on buying habits is such a compelling narrative, that perhaps this researcher decided to push the same variables despite the changes that occurred in the system. The researcher could be unscrupulous and throw out additional data, or could simply be ignorant of the changes in the system.

However, we generally expect scientists to know to rerun their analyses on new data (or new respondents) to determine new axes. Because the technique has been around for a long time, we trust the process of training researchers, and generally trust that researchers won't fit a model to give them compelling results. Though cases of scientific fraud do happen (Kozlov, 2022), we blame the unscrupulous researcher and not the technique.

Agent-based modeling is similar to any other scientific technique in that it can be abused. Yet with standardization and training it can be a powerful tool, just like PCA can. When a modeler builds an agent-based model they need to build it from simplicity to complexity and test every new parameter addition to ensure that the modeler understands the simulation. Going back to Chapter 1, this integrates with the principle of parsimony—only include the things that are necessary and no more.

What is different about agent-based modeling is that it is a much newer technique than principal components analysis, training in agent-based modeling is less common than in various types of factor analysis, and models *can* investigate any scenario (though so can a factor analysis, but perhaps less flexibly). It is incumbent upon the scientist to make sure that they understand the technique they are using and understand the model they have produced.

Several projects have been aiming to create high-quality training in agent-based modeling for archaeologists. First is the open-access book published by myself, Iza Romanowska, and Colin Wren that reproduces 58 models from archaeology and other social sciences and provides a way to teach students agent-based modeling from first lines of code to running a fully-fledged model.

The second initiative is the Network for Agent-Based Modeling of Socio-ecological Systems in Archaeology. This project has been curating tried and tested algorithms used in archaeological agent-based models to help lead toward consistency in code writing. (https://archaeology-abm.github.io/NASSA-hub/). This project can help to reduce error when modeling, say, algorithms of subsistence farming since tested algorithms will be reproduced instead of having to write all aspects of the code *de novo*. In this way it helps to create simple models that can provide the backbone for more complex questions.

A third example is the CoMSES Network program (comses.net), formerly known as OpenABM, which published code of agent-based models that anyone can download and examine. This program creates an ethic of openness around modeling, which allows transparency in science and creates the expectation that code will be reviewable by others.

Finally, training programs at conferences, such as at CAA (Computational Approaches and Quantitative Methods in Archaeology) and SAA (Society for American Archaeology), as well as sessions dedicated to communicating agent-based modeling, have helped to increase literacy in agent-based modeling. All of these together will continue to help agent-based modeling grow as a standard tool in the social sciences.

Garbage in Garbage Out

A subset of the idea of the manipulatable model is the oft-repeated phrase "garbage in, garbage out" or "rubbish in rubbish out," which comes from the early days of computing (Demming, 2019). What this phrase means in the context of agent-based modeling is that if you build your model around poor data, poorly developed theories, or poor assumptions, then the results you will get will also be poorly reflecting the reality. Any conclusions you draw from a model built on rubbish will, necessarily, be rubbish. This of course is true of any archaeological interpretations made from garbage data, theories, and assumptions and is not particular to agent-based models.

Just as with the criticisms for a manipulatable model, to avoid "garbage in garbage out" it is incumbent upon the modeler to build a model from simplicity to complexity, to work with appropriate theoretical backgrounds, to collect as much data as is appropriate, and to parsimoniously build a model to address the questions at hand. To avoid this problem, it is best to work early and often with collaborators to ensure you are collecting the right data or building on the right theoretical models. The review process, also, can help avoid this challenge, but hopefully by the time a model is written up for publication you have rooted out the "garbage"' and have built a model that is strong and adds to the intellectual merit of the subject at hand.

The Complex Model

Are Agent-Based Models Too Complex to Understand Anything?

Because of the inherent flexibility of agent-based models, in that they can be built to examine a multitude of questions, there can be a tension between building a model that is parsimonious and a model that overreaches and includes too much. Many early agent-based models made use of many parameters (such as my own early work, see: (Crabtree, 2015); *mea culpa*) causing scientists to have to investigate the impact of every parameter, often leading to long and challenging discussions. This criticism usually comes in tandem with the previously stated, that an agent-based model can do anything a scientist wants it too. Often, the critique that ABMs are too complex to understand anything comes from a place of misunderstanding how models are built.

However, this critique is still alive and well. In a recent review of a paper I coauthored, Reviewer 2 stated "agent-based models necessarily need a lot of parameters" in their review (Reviewer 2, personal communication), questioning why we fixed parameters in the run. ABMs don't necessarily need a lot of parameters. While some do have many parameters, others do not. What is critical is that the quantity of parameters chosen make sense for the model and that the scientist spends time building the model to do exactly what is to be analyzed.

A good agent-based modeler will build the model up from the simplest possible form to its most complex form and describe along the way how each of the parameters interact. One of the ways to most easily confront this critique is to provide an extensive supplement to your analyses that shows the full analysis of one parameter before adding another one.

Are Humans Too Complex to Understand via Models?

The Nobel Prize winning physicist Murray Gell-Mann, who discovered and documented the quark, famously said "think how hard physics would be if particles could think." While a similar quote is attributed to his colleague Richard Feynman, Gell-Mann was a huge admirer of archaeology as well as other social sciences. In my opinion, this quote encapsulates how difficult it can be for archaeologists and anthropologists to understand their own species, with its myriad ways of expressing itself.

Within ecology individual-based modeling has been employed for decades to understand things as varied as predator-prey cycles and species migration. While wolves, for example, are complex creatures that live in hierarchical societies, few critiques of the predator-prey dynamics model (Lotka, 1925; Volterra, 1926) have focused on how these models failed to model the age structure of wolf packs or the complex ways that wolves migrate throughout seasons. Moreover, these models use a simple probability for reproduction rather than true sexual reproduction. The model focuses on the simple interactions of probabilistic reproductive dynamics and food availability and it demonstrates that equilibrium *can* be achieved, but that it is difficult, and that when a system is moved from that equilibrium it quickly collapses.

Yet, frequently criticisms of agent-based models of human systems suggest that the model didn't take into account some facet of human culture that is likely not related to the model. It is doubtless that wolves exhibit complex behaviors related to hierarchy, reproduction, migration, and feeding that would not be encapsulated in a model that looks at Lotka-Volterra dynamics; however, the wolves themselves do not get to criticize the agent-based model. Much like Gell-Mann's quote on how difficult physics would be if particles could talk back, models of nonhuman animal systems also do not get to talk back.

Human systems are not too complex to model, but rather we are more aware of—and possibly sensitive to—the complexities of human cultures. Because of this we may be tempted to add more and more parameters to a model to encapsulate the complexity of the culture we are trying to study. Many of these parameters may not actually be necessary for understanding the system, and they may be included only to assuage the fears of the researcher (or their critics) that leaving out a particular parameter would reduce the complexity of the human culture to something much too simple. Remember Chapter 1; we do not want to model ladies' hats.

Humans, I would argue, are not inherently more complex than wolves or particles, but humans can critique the models of themselves in a way that wolves or particles cannot. What matters for building an agent-based model is that it adheres to the principles of parsimony, that we simplify as much as we can to model the aspects of the culture we find the most salient for what we are studying, and that we clearly communicate the aspects of that society that we are studying.

The Reductionist Model

Are Agent-based Models Dehumanizing and Computerize the Complexities of Culture?

The first time I received this criticism I was surprised by it. I am a trained anthropologist, so I think of myself as understanding and being sensitive to the myriad ways culture can express itself. Agent-based modeling is a tool by which we can understand certain phenomena. It can augment our understanding of societies through other ways, be that through participant observation, survey, excavation of archaeological sites, or other methods familiar to traditional anthropological and archaeological work.

The critique that agent-based models can be dehumanizing I believe comes from a dual-sided place, one of misunderstanding by those leveling the critique and one that should be a point of caution for those using agent-based modeling.

On the side of caution, the idea that agent-based models can be dehumanizing puts the responsibility on the researcher to ensure that their research is grounded in the culture they are studying and that inappropriate analogies are not made between the computerized humans in the models and real humans. For example, in building the digitized humans in the models of migration into Sahul (the supercontinent of Australia, New Guinea, and Tasmania) (Crabtree et al., 2021) we were careful to use information from ethnographic work from Australia as well as information on average body size in Binford's "Constructing Frames of Reference" (Binford, 2001). However, we do not imply that our digital people are the same as real people, nor that the cultures that migrated into Sahul 70,000 years ago were the same as the rich cultures that live in Australia both today and in the ethnographic present. Instead, we ground our models on real-world data and define our digital people based on characteristics that real people in this region exhibit. This allows the model to be truer to the particular system we were studying, allowing the results to be more comparable to the real data that we gathered to examine the performance of the models.

It is incumbent upon researchers to ensure that when they are making decisions in building their agents that the researchers use the most realistic data possible, and that they ground their agents in that data to reflect the reality of people in those cultures as parsimoniously as possible. However, it is also incumbent upon researchers that they do not equate their agents with the actual people. The agents are merely computerized individuals who are built on realistic characteristics that help us refine our hypotheses about the real archaeological record and the real people who lived in the past.

On the side of misunderstanding, this critique may stem from a misinterpretation of what an agent-based model actually does. An agent-based model doesn't try to reduce all of human complexity into bits of code. Rather, what it tries to do is look at *specific questions* of how societies in the past functioned and leverage advances in computer science as a tool to understand those societies. Archaeology has long adopted techniques from other sciences to better understand the past, for example geoarchaeology leverages advances in soil science to understand the interaction of geological formative processes and cultures. Agent-based modeling is just one way by which computer science has been integrated into understanding the past, just as approaches from other sciences have been integrated into archaeology for decades.

Confronting the Critiques

So, if you are critiqued for using a flexible tool, how can you confront the types of critiques that suggest it can be molded to do anything? First off, open source and open access code is critical for these kinds of critiques. If others can view your model, often this will help them to be able to "look under the hood" and understand that you have built a parsimonious model.

Second, often publishing agent-based modeling results requires a minimal descriptor in the text, but a massive online supplemental information. Frequently as we are building our models, we are testing how certain parameters interact before we fix values for parameters, and you will need to describe those early experiments in detail to show that you accounted for everything as you build your model.

Finally, when scientists have verbally said to me that one can put anything they want into an agent-based model, I remind them that that is true for almost any model, such as PCA, but that we learn how to build the most parsimonious models through good training. And while early agent-based models may have been enthusiastic about how many parameters were included and sparse in how they were written up, that standards such as the ODD Protocol (Grimm et al., 2010; Müller et al., 2013) have helped immeasurably in ensuring clear descriptions of how the models are built.

Agent-Based Models: Final Thoughts

Agent-based models allow archaeologists to explore how the actions and interactions of individuals may have unfolded, offering a dynamic means to compare simulated scenarios with the fragmentary snapshots preserved in the archaeological record. Through these simulations, we can gain insights into the underlying processes that shaped the world we inhabit today, enriching our understanding of the deep past. By enabling the systematic examination of historical contingencies, agent-based models provide a framework to test past evidence and evaluate how well streamlined simulations align with archaeological patterns. Although traditional approaches, like empirical experimentation, present challenges for investigating hypotheses about the deep past, simulation offers a robust alternative for studying the processes that influenced past societies.

Because of this, as well as efforts to teach larger groups of social scientists, agent-based models have begun to be adopted by more and more practitioners. As agent-based modeling becomes more common in archaeology it likely will become more well accepted, just like principal components analysis is.

Agent-based modeling of archaeological systems not only enhances our ability to quantify and understand the dynamics of past societies but also serves as a bridge between historical insights and the challenges of the present. By using the past as a calibration dataset, we gain a clearer picture of our current societal trajectories and potential future pathways. The record of past human experiences—how individuals and groups responded to myriad environmental and social pressures—acts as a valuable archive of "experiments" with sustainability, offering insights into the diverse solutions that societies have devised over millennia to confront adversity and change. These historical "experiments" are among the most reliable references we have as we try to anticipate the societal shifts that lie ahead.

Central to these investigations is the enduring human element: our shared capacities, motivations, and ways of making sense of the world, which connect past populations with present and future societies. Through modeling the decisions and actions of people from the archaeological past, we deepen our understanding of human behavior, examining the varied ways in which individuals and communities have adapted to their circumstances and navigated their lives. This approach has the potential to inform decision making on contemporary issues, demonstrating that the study of our past is not only about knowledge for its own sake but also about empowering society today with lessons drawn from the human story. Agent-based modeling can help in this endeavor by systematically examining the ways that people lived in the past and helping to understand how these lessons from the past can apply today.

Works Cited

Axtell, Robert L., Joshua M. Epstein, Jeffrey S. Dean, George J. Gumerman, Alan C. Swedlund, Jason Harburger, Shubha Chakravarty, Ross Hammond, Jon Parker, and Miles Parker. 2002. Population Growth and Collapse in a Multiagent Model of the Kayenta Anasazi in Long House Valley. *Proceedings of the National Academy of Sciences* 99(suppl 3): 7275–7279. https://doi.org/10.1073/pnas.092080799

Binford, Lewis. 2001. *Constructing Frames of Reference: An Analytical Method for Archaeological Theory Building Using Ethnographic and Environmental Data Sets.* University of California Press, Berkeley.

Bocinsky, R. Kyle, Jason A. Cowan, Timothy A. Kohler, and C. David Johnson. 2012. How Hunting Changes the VEP World, and How the VEP World Changes Hunting. In *Emergence and Collapse of Early Villages*, edited by Timothy A. Kohler and Mark D. Varien, pp. 145–152. University of California Press, Berkeley.

Brantingham, P. 2003. A Neutral Model of Stone Raw Material Procurement. *American Antiquity* 68(3): 487–509.

Brantingham, P. Jeffrey, Todd A. Surovell, and Nicole M. Waguespack. 2007. Modeling Post-depositional Mixing of Archaeological Deposits. *Journal of Anthropological Archaeology* 26(4): 517–540. https://doi.org/10.1016/j.jaa.2007.08.003

Cegielski, Wendy H., and J. Daniel Rogers. 2016. Rethinking the Role of Agent-Based Modeling in Archaeology. *Journal of Anthropological Archaeology* 41: 283–298. https://doi.org/10.1016/j.jaa.2016.01.009

Cockburn, D., S.A. Crabtree, Z. Kobti, T.A. Kohler, and R.K. Bocinsky. 2013. Simulating Social and Economic Specialization in Small-scale Agricultural Societies. *JASSS* 16(4) https://doi.org/10.18564/jasss.2308

Crabtree, S.A., K. Harris, B. Davies, and I. Romanowska. 2019. Outreach in Archaeology with Agent-Based Modeling: Part 3 of 3. *Advances in Archaeological Practice* 7(2): 194–202. https://doi.org/10.1017/aap.2019.4

Crabtree, Stefani A. 2015. Inferring Ancestral Pueblo Social Networks from Simulation in the Central Mesa Verde. *Journal of Archaeological Method and Theory* 22(1): 144–181. https://doi.org/10.1007/s10816-014-9233-8

Crabtree, Stefani A., R. Kyle Bocinsky, Paul L. Hooper, Susan C. Ryan, and Timothy A. Kohler. 2017. How to Make a Polity (in the Central Mesa Verde Region). *American Antiquity* 82(1): 71–95. https://doi.org/10.1017/aaq.2016.18

Crabtree, Stefani A., Devin A. White, Corey J. A. Bradshaw, Frédérik Saltré, Alan N. Williams, Robin J. Beaman, Michael I. Bird, and Sean Ulm. 2021. Landscape Rules Predict Optimal Superhighways for the First Peopling of Sahul. *Nature Human Behaviour* 5: 1303–1313. https://doi.org/10.1038/s41562-021-01106-8

Crabtree, Stefani A., Colin D. Wren, Avinash Dixit, and Simon A. Levin. 2024. Influential Individuals can Promote Prosocial Practices in Heterogeneous Societies: A Mathematical and Agent-based Model. *PNAS Nexus* 3(7): 224. https://doi.org/10.1093/pnasnexus/pgae224

Davies, B., I. Romanowska, K. Harris, and S.A. Crabtree. 2019. Combining Geographic Information Systems and Agent-Based Models in Archaeology: Part 2 of 3. *Advances in Archaeological Practice* 7(2): 185–193. https://doi.org/10.1017/aap.2019.5

Dean, Jeffrey S., George J. Gumerman, Joshua M. Epstein, Robert L. Axtell, Alan C. Swedlund, Miles T. Parker, and Steven McCarroll. 2000. Understanding Anasazi Culture Change through Agent-based Modeling. In *Dynamics in Human and Primate Societies: Agent-based Modeling of Social and Spatial Processes*, edited by Timothy A. Kohler and George J. Gumerman, pp. 179–205. Oxford University Press, Inc., USA.

Demming, Anna. 2019. Machine Learning Collaborations Accelerate Materials Discovery. *Physics World* 30. Retrieved from https://physicsworld.com/a/machine-learning-collaborations-accelerate-materials-discovery/

Grimm, Volker, Uta Berger, Donald L. DeAngelis, J. Gary Polhill, Jarl Giske, and Steven F. Railsback. 2010. The ODD Protocol: A Review and First Update. *Ecological Modelling* 221(23): 2760–2768. https://doi.org/10.1016/j.ecolmodel.2010.08.019

Hammond, Ross A., and Shari Barkin. 2024. Making Evidence Go Further: Advancing Synergy Between Agent-based Modeling and Randomized Control Trials. *Proceedings of the National Academy of Sciences* 121(21):e2314993121. https://doi.org/10.1073/pnas.2314993121

Janssen, Marco A. 2009. Understanding Artificial Anasazi. *Journal of Artificial Societies and Social Simulation* 12(4): 13.

Kohler, Timothy A., R. Kyle Bocinsky, Denton Cockburn, Stefani A. Crabtree, Mark D. Varien, Kenneth E. Kolm, Schaun Smith, Scott G. Ortman, and Ziad Kobti. 2012. Modelling Prehispanic Pueblo Societies in their Ecosystems. *Ecological Modelling* 241: 30–41. https://doi.org/10.1016/j.ecolmodel.2012.01.002

Kohler, Timothy A., and George J. Gumerman (Eds.). 2000. Dynamics in Human and Primate Societies: Agent-Based Modeling of Social and Spatial Processes. In *Santa Fe Institute Studies in the Sciences of Complexity*. Oxford University Press, Santa Fe, NM.

Kohler, Timothy A., James Kresl, Carla van West, Eric Carr, and Richard H. Wilshusen. 2000. Be There Then: A Modeling Approach to Settlement Determinants and Spatial Efficiency among Late Ancestral Pueblo Populations of the Mesa Verde Region, U.S. Southwest. In *Dynamics in Human and Primate Societies: Agent-Based Modeling of Social and Spatial Processes*, pp. 145–178. Oxford University Press, Inc., USA.

Kozlov, Max. 2022. How a Scandal in Spider Biology Upended Researchers' Lives. *Nature* 608: 658–659.

Lake, Mark Winter. 2014. Trends in Archaeological Simulation. *Journal of Archaeological Method and Theory* 21(2): 258–287. https://doi.org/10.1007/s10816-013-9188-1

Lake, Mark Winter. 2000. MAGICAL Computer Simulation of Mesolithic Foraging. In *Dynamics in Human and Primate Societies: Agent-Based Modeling of Social and Spatial Processes*, pp. 107–143. Oxford University Press, Inc., USA.

Lansing, J. Stephen. 2000. Anti-chaos, Common Property, and the Emergence of Cooperation. In *Dynamics in Human and Primate Societies: Agent-Based Modeling of Social and Spatial Processes*, pp. 207–223. Oxford University Press, Inc., USA.

Leek, Jeffrey T., and Roger D. Peng. 2015. Statistics: P Values Are Just the Tip of the Iceberg. *Nature* 520(7549): 612. https://doi.org/10.1038/520612a

Lotka, Alfred J. 1925. *Elements of Physical Biology*. Williams and Wilkins Co, London.

Müller, Birgit, Friedrich Bohn, Gunnar Dreßler, Jürgen Groeneveld, Christian Klassert, Romina Martin, Maja Schlüter, Jule Schulze, Hanna Weise, and Nina Schwarz. 2013. Describing Human Decisions in Agent-based Models – ODD + D, an Extension of the ODD Protocol. *Environmental Modelling & Software* 48: 37–48. https://doi.org/10.1016/j.envsoft.2013.06.003

Oestmo, Simen, Marco A. Janssen, and Curtis W. Marean. 2016. Testing Brantingham's Neutral Model: The Effect of Spatial Clustering on Stone Raw Material Procurement. In *Simulating Prehistoric and Ancient Worlds*, edited by Juan A. Barceló and Florencia Del Castillo, pp. 175–188. Computational Social Sciences, Springer International Publishing.

O'Gara, David, Samuel F. Rosenblatt, Laurent Hébert-Dufresne, Rob Purcell, Matt Kasman, and Ross A. Hammond. 2023. TRACE-Omicron: Policy Counterfactuals to Inform Mitigation of COVID-19 Spread in the United States. *Advanced Theory and Simulations* 6(7): 2300147. https://doi.org/10.1002/adts.202300147

Otárola-Castillo, Erik, and Melissa G. Torquato. 2018. Bayesian Statistics in Archaeology. *Annual Review of Anthropology* 47: 435–453. https://doi.org/10.1146/annurev-anthro-102317-045834

Pearson, Karl. 1901. LIII. On Lines and Planes of Closest Fit to Systems of Points in Space. *The London, Edinburgh, and Dublin Philosophical Magazine and Journal of Science* 2(11): 559–572. https://doi.org/10.1080/14786440109462720

Railsback, Steven F., and Volker Grimm. 2011. *Agent-based and Individual-based Modeling: A Practical Introduction*. Princeton University Press.

Read, Dwight W. 2002. A Multitrajectory, Competition Model of Emergent Complexity in Human Social Organization. *Proceedings of the National Academy of Sciences* 99(suppl_3): 7251–7256. https://doi.org/10.1073/pnas.072079999

Reynolds, R.G., and A. Lazar. 2002. Simulating the Evolution of Archaic States. In *Proceedings of the 2002 Congress on Evolutionary Computation. CEC'02 (Cat. No.02TH8600)*, 1: 861–866.

Romanowska, I., S.A. Crabtree, K. Harris, and B. Davies. 2019. Agent-Based Modeling for Archaeologists: Part 1 of 3. *Advances in Archaeological Practice* 7(2). https://doi.org/10.1017/aap.2019.6

Romanowska, Iza, Colin D. Wren, and Stefani A. Crabtree. 2021. *Agent-based Modeling for Archaeology: Simulating the Complexity of Societies*. SFI Press, Santa Fe, NM.

Schelling, Thomas C. 1969. Models of Segregation. *The American Economic Review* 59(2): 488–493.

Stonedahl, Forrest, and Uri Wilensky. 2010. Evolutionary Robustness Checking in the Artificial Anasazi Model. In *Complex Adaptive Systems—Resilience, Robustness, and Evolvability: Papers from the AAAI Fall Symposium (FS-10-03)*, pp. 120–129. Association for the Advancement of Artificial Intelligence.

Verhagen, Philip. 2018. Predictive Modeling. *The Encyclopedia of Archaeological Sciences*, pp. 1–3.

Volterra, Vito. 1926. Variazioni e fluttuazioni del numero d'individui in specie animali conviventi. *Mem. Acad. Lincei Roma*. 2: 31–113.

4
NETWORK ANALYSIS AND ARCHAEOLOGY

Sometimes it's easy to look at how interconnected the modern world is, with our telephones, airplanes, trains (or high-speed rail if you're lucky enough to read this in a country that has it!), emails, and social networks, and forget that the past was also extremely interconnected. People communicated across great distances in the past (Eğilmez and Kalkan, 2023), they exchanged goods across vast spaces (Watson et al., 1983), they told stories that connected them in networks of shared beliefs (Fitzhugh et al., 2011), and powerful ideas diffused through cultural groups (VanPool and Savage, 2009), knitting different—and disparate—people together. People in the past also experienced constraints and opportunities from their environments, embedding themselves in their food webs (Dunne et al., 2016), exchanging nutrients across long distances (Crabtree, 2015), hunting and gathering in different ecosystems (Crabtree et al., 2019), or bringing domesticated species to new environments they hadn't lived in before (da Fonseca et al., 2015). Each of these represents the ways that humans were connected to multiple networks in the past, and why network analysis has been embraced with such vigor in the archaeological community.

How Network Science Is One of the Complex Systems Approaches in Archaeology

While complex adaptive systems science approaches vary, network science is perhaps the most firmly adopted and normalized method into archaeology from the complex systems science toolkit. Recall that complex adaptive systems aim to understand how the actions and interactions of individuals can lead to larger, overarching structures. These systems express nonlinearities and cannot be understood merely by understanding the individual strategies of

DOI: 10.4324/9781003585251-4

each individual in the system. Rather, we need to understand the ways that individuals interact to be able to understand the whole. Network science provides a way to telescope between the interactions of individuals and the interactions of the whole, allowing researchers to not have to choose between individual interactions and larger structures, but allowing a comprehensive understanding of the system and all of its parts (Romanowska, 2023).

Because network science provides a means for understanding these interactions—as well as the system as a whole—it is a particularly useful method from complex adaptive systems for understanding the archaeological past.

Euler, Bridges, Parsimony

Now, how did network science come to be, and how can we learn from the beginnings of network science to understand how archaeology and network analysis merge?

In the early 1700s, in the city of Konigsberg, Prussia, a fashionable pastime by many of the city's denizens was to walk across the city, traversing the river that divided the city and housed its two islands (named Kneiphof and Lomse), while attempting to cross each of the seven bridges only once. Yet, try as they might the ability to traverse the city while passing each bridge only once seemed impossible. Local academics, frustrated by being unable to solve this practical problem, wrote to one of the most famous mathematicians of the day, Leonhard Euler (Euler, 1953).[1]

Euler approached the problem by simplifying the extraneous information and applying the principle of parsimony to find the answer. Like any good modeler he realized that things like the length of the bridges, the characteristics of the islands or shores that they connected, and even the aspects and orientations of the bridges did not matter to the question at hand. Instead, he realized that what was germane was how many different pieces of land were connected (two islands, two banks on either side of the river, so four landmasses total) and how many bridges there were (seven). This simplification became the first network and provided the answer to the first network problem (Euler, 1953) (Figure 4.1).

Euler found that it was actually impossible to traverse the city by walking across each bridge only once. He found that there needed to be two bridges emanating from either every single landmass, or from every single landmass except for two of them, and those two could have an odd number of bridges (one or three). Because three of the landmasses had only one bridge it would necessitate someone walking over at least one bridge twice, making it impossible to solve the challenge that the fashionable set of Konigsberg set for themselves.

The way Euler approached the problem is rather similar to how many archaeological modelers approach their problems. While he may have talked to

Network Analysis and Archaeology 55

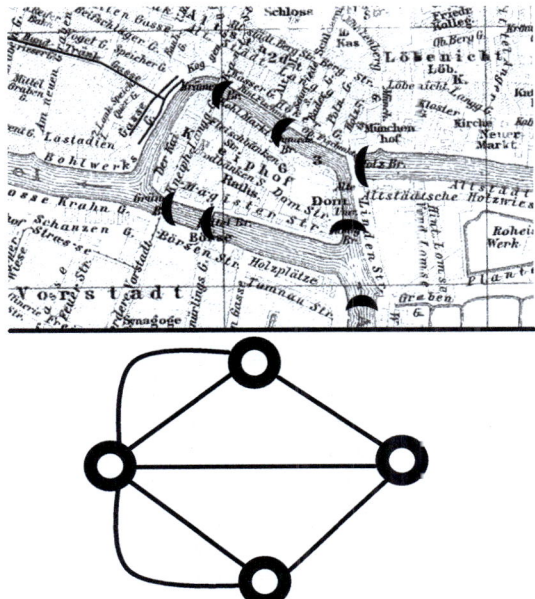

FIGURE 4.1 A map of Konigsberg, Prussia and the islands that the city's citizens would try to reach by crossing the seven bridges, juxtaposed with a network that would be required to solve the problem. Here the circles are the littorals and the edges are the bridges.

individuals who thought the characteristics of the bridges or of the islands and littorals were important, he broke the problem down into its simplest, most parsimonious parts. Certainly, information is lost when it is done this way, but it can enable the archaeologist (or mathematician) to focus on the germane aspects of the problem, moving science forward.

Euler, by breaking the problem down to its most parsimonious parts and determining how many bridges would be needed to solve the problem, invented graph theory—the mathematical field that network analysis is based on.

In network analysis we would call the bits of the islands and shores the "nodes" and we call bridges the "edges." The answer to the problem, that the nodes needed an even number of edges, could also be explained in network parlance that the nodes needed an even "degree." In network analysis the degree of a node is how many edges it has. This simplification of the system from bridges and islands to nodes and edges enables a mathematical calculation of the problem. And it turns out that simplifying some archaeological problems into the ways that certain entities are connected can help us to learn quite a bit about the system.

A Brief History of Network Analysis

Social network science as it is understood today is essentially the marriage of tools and concepts from mathematics, statistics, sociology, anthropology, and more recently computer science. While Euler is most frequently seen as the founder of the mathematics of graph theory, other scientists brought their own expertise to the development of the field.

One of these early scientists, working at the turn of the 19th to 20th centuries, was Georg Simmel, a sociologist who approached understanding society with a neo-Kantian view, asking the question "what is society?" in a way similar to Kant's question "what is nature"? Simmel's work aimed to quantify social interactions within groups, looking at how society emerges from the layered interactions between individuals (Hollstein, 2021).

The development of formal quantitative methodologies in social network analysis began in earnest during the 1930s, led by pioneering researchers such as Jacob Moreno, William Lloyd Warner, Allison Davis, Burleigh Gardner, and Mary Gardner. Their early work focused on the visual analysis of systematic relational data but lacked computational tools for network analysis. It was not until the 1940s that significant progress toward quantification was made when Eliot Chapple, Conrad Arensberg, and Willard Quine introduced an algebraic model that allowed for the calculation of relative relationships between individuals who were not directly observed to interact. This approach laid the groundwork for a more rigorous, mathematically driven exploration of social networks, opening new avenues for analyzing indirect interactions in a structured manner. Their work, while initially limited by the computational constraints of the era, provided an essential foundation that influenced later advancements in social network analysis, particularly with the advent of digital computational methods in the latter half of the 20th century (Freeman, 2004).

Two decades later, in the 1960s, psychologist Stanley Milgram set out to understand how connected American society was. He gave letters to several people in the Midwest asking them to get a letter to a specified individual in Boston, MA. They could not mail that letter directly to the person in Boston. Rather, they had to find an individual they knew personally who they thought could get the letter closer to the end recipient in Boston. That person would then forward the letter to someone they knew, and on until the letter arrived in Boston. After analyzing the dozens of letters, Milgram found that the letters would then follow a path that on average took about six steps, coining the term "six degrees of separation." This work showed that most likely America was characterized by a "small-world" network, meaning that everyone was tightly knit and could be connected via 5 or 6 edges (Travers and Milgram, 1977).

Only a decade after this work, Granovetter's influential paper entitled "The Strength of Weak Ties" suggested that those individuals that were less strongly connected to someone—an acquaintance rather than a close friend—would potentially provide richer connections and opportunities than a close connection would (Granovetter, 1973).

These studies helped elucidate the ways that modern human groups are connected. In all likelihood, most humans are connected via a small number of individuals, and those individuals who we don't know as well can provide important avenues for us for connectivity to other groups. But do these patterns hold when we look at people who lived before modern times?

Capturing the intricate interplay between humans, their societies, and their environments presents a significant challenge, as individual specializations—such as lithic analysis or palynology—tend to focus on a limited set of variables, often overlooking the complex interconnections between and among them. Consequently, these disciplinary approaches frequently fall short of offering a comprehensive explanation of the multifaceted relationships that shape human-environment interactions. The beauty of social network analysis is that it provides a toolset that can be applied to any type of data that contains entities and connections. This is likely what attracted the first researchers to bring social network analysis to archaeological data. Often, we are confronted with datasets that give us unique entities—say, potsherds—and interesting, sometimes tenuous, connections—say the distance a sherd traveled from its original clay source.

Each of these studies exhibits key properties of social network analysis. There are nodes—the individuals themselves—and edges—the connections between each node. By looking at the density of connections or how many edges each node has we can examine certain characteristics of the overall network.

In archaeology, the 1970s marked the emergence of some of the first formal applications of social network analysis, with pioneering contributions by researchers such as Irwin, Irwin-Williams, Terrell, and White (Brughmans, 2013). These early studies laid a conceptual foundation, but the full potential of network analysis was limited by the computational resources available at the time. By the 1990s, however, the rise of personal computing facilitated more sophisticated analyses. Researchers began to apply formal centrality measures to investigate the geographical distribution of architecture within settlements like Cahokia, a key Mississippian cultural center, using these measures to argue for its role as a primary node in a broader network of regional interaction (Peregrine, 1991). Another early use of network analysis with direct input from complex adaptive systems is the work by Kohler et al. (2000), building upon work by Stuart Kauffman (1969), to examine reciprocal exchanges between nodes (see Romanowska, 2023). These early network analyses, however, typically focused only on the most proximate connections between nodes, often neglecting the full spectrum of possible interactions within the network. As computing power continued to grow, the application of network studies within archaeology also increased (Brughmans, 2013).

In recent years, several comprehensive volumes have examined the role of networks in archaeology, making a full-scale review unnecessary for the present work (Brughmans et al., 2024; Brughmans and Peeples, 2023). Instead, this chapter focuses on the specific contributions of network analysis and complex adaptive systems to understanding the past, with an emphasis on both social network analysis and ecological network analysis—two approaches that have been widely adopted within archaeology.

Modern network approaches offer archaeologists a multi-scalar framework to explore individuals within communities and situate those communities within broader landscapes and cultural systems. These methods bridge empirical data with established theoretical models, formalizing long-standing hypotheses about past human interactions. The integration of network analysis in archaeology has expanded rapidly, serving as both the primary focus of research (Brughmans and Peeples, 2023; Giomi and Peeples, 2019; Mills et al., 2013) and as an analytical tool that strengthens interpretations (Brughmans et al., 2024; Crabtree et al., 2017; Peeples and Randall Haas, 2013). This increasing adoption reflects both the utility of network-based approaches in illuminating past social and material connections and the growing computational expertise within the discipline. As methodological advancements continue and more datasets are incorporated, network analysis is poised to play an even greater role in archaeological inquiry.

The study of food webs also has deep roots. The earliest graph of a food web is attributed to Lorenzo Camerano (1880), with similar work from Shelford (1913), and Summerhayes and Elton (1923, discussed in Egerton 2007). Many decades later, Yodzis and Inness (1992) formalized how producers and consumers relate to one another in trophic networks via relationships between creation of biomass and predation upon biomass. In 1998, Estes et al. created the first food web model of nearshore and oceanic systems by looking at the functional response of killer whale predation on sea otters—a study seen as a landmark for modern food web approaches.

Links are always directed in food webs, since one species consumes the other. Although there are instances of reciprocation in which a species will both prey on and be prey to another species (wolves and cougars, for example, might each opportunistically eat each other), the key characteristic of food webs is the directionality of the feeding links. Common analyses of these networks include removing species to see how resilient the network is to extinction (e.g., Binzer et al., 2011; Brose, 2011), examining the effects of diet shifts by key species (e.g., Ramos-Jiliberto et al., 2011), examining declines (or increases) in species richness (e.g., Murphy and Romanuk, 2014; Romanuk et al., 2009), and examining how different functional types of species, like parasites, affect networks (Dunne et al., 2013).

Social networks, unlike food webs, can have directed links (unreciprocated friendships, or donations) or undirected links (reciprocated friendships and gifts). Some of the most common measures in social network approaches to archaeological data are centrality measures: degree centrality, betweenness centrality and eigenvector centrality (Brughmans, 2013: 14). Such measures have been used to argue for the importance of specific sites in migration events (Mills et al., 2013), the evolution of Cahokia as a major political center (Peregrine, 1991: 68), or the spread and diffusion of pottery through sites in the Roman world (Brughmans 2013: 635). Centrality measures are useful for archaeology because they reveal which nodes are the most important for the functioning of the network, with implications for the size or the location of sites. Or, reversing the logic, such measures might help explain how or why certain locations became important through historical contingencies.

Network science thus acts as a bridge between the local details of the nodes and the overall structure of a system, recalling the discussion earlier in this book of agent-based modeling, which honors both the agency of actors and the structure of the system. Brughmans argues that "it is a combination of SNA and complex network simulation techniques that seems to hold the true potential of networks for archaeology" (Brughmans 2013: 642).

In one study that exemplifies the use of social networks in archaeology, Collar (2007) explores religious innovation in the form of the invention of monotheism in the Roman Empire. She examines how religious ideas flowed in the network of the cult of Theos Hypsistos, and how Christian orthodoxy came to become dominant. She finds that small-world theory or "innovation cascade" (Collar 2007: 150) helps explain why monotheism so successfully spread in the declining Roman Empire. Collar's work demonstrates how to explore archaeological data with network science, using complexity theory to help us understand how a complicated observed phenomenon (the dominance of Christianity) can result from simple actions of key individuals (influential nodes that affect the system).

The benefits to archaeology of network approaches include at least that they analyze and display the connectivity among nodes in ways that lend themselves to comparisons among different networks providing intuitively understandable and analytically useful translations of abstract concepts such as centrality, and that they can reveal the vulnerability of systems. One can see exactly how the network responds to removal of nodes, and one can predict how the system would rearrange itself due to external perturbations.

Archaeological Network Approaches

This book explores how techniques from complex adaptive systems can be applied to the archaeological record, revealing aspects of past societies that might be otherwise intractable. Among these, network analysis is particularly powerful, offering novel ways to reconstruct human interactions from material culture.

From spatial reconstructions of site interactions (Peregrine, 1991) to the examination of trade routes, migration pathways (Crabtree et al., 2021a), and the diffusion of ideas across space and time (Mills et al., 2013), network-based approaches have become increasingly central to archaeological research (Brughmans, 2013; Brughmans and Peeples, 2017, 2023).

Historically, archaeologists have relied on visual network representations to explore spatial and social relationships. For instance, researchers analyzing movement within architectural spaces have employed space syntax, a network-based methodology for modeling accessibility and connectivity (Wilson, 2018). Likewise, kinship diagrams—a long-standing tool in anthropology—are inherently network-based visualizations, where individuals function as nodes and relationships as edges (Wilson, 2018). These networks can be enriched with additional attributes, allowing for more sophisticated analyses of social structures.

Consider, for example, a kinship network of a foraging community. Beyond mapping familial ties, researchers might incorporate data on resource acquisition and redistribution. Who gathers the most resources? Who shares the most? Who receives the most? By modeling these interactions, archaeologists can identify central actors in subsistence networks, elucidating patterns of cooperation, social cohesion, and resource management. This fusion of kinship analysis with social network methods provides a quantitative framework for examining social organization in the past (Crabtree and Borck, 2019).

While space syntax and kinship analysis are among the most widely recognized applications of network analysis—likely because they feature prominently in introductory anthropology courses—archaeologists now employ network science in far more diverse ways. Broadly speaking, two dominant strands have emerged: social network analysis and ecological network analysis. Both derive from graph theory but differ in their conceptual foundations, methodological approaches, and the types of interactions they examine.

Both social network analysis and ecological network analysis offer powerful tools to investigate the structure and dynamics of networks, but they differ significantly in their focus, the types of entities they examine, and the nature of the interactions they analyze. These differences extend to the types of questions that each method can address, particularly in archaeological contexts. Since archaeology is the study of past human societies and their environments, both social network analysis and ecological network analysis can be valuable methodologies for uncovering the social and ecological dimensions of ancient communities. Each approach, though distinct, operates on a fundamental understanding of network theory. As such, mastery of one method can often facilitate an understanding of the other.

Social network analysis is a quantitative and qualitative framework for examining the structure, relationships, and dynamics within networks of interconnected entities, such as individuals, groups, or organizations. In social network analysis, actors are represented as "nodes," while the connections between them—such as collaborations, communications, or shared resources—are depicted as "edges" or "links." This method allows researchers to explore how network structures shape behavior, influence, power dynamics, and the flow of information or resources.

Ecological networks, like social networks, consist of nodes and edges, where nodes represent taxa—species or groups of functionally similar species—linked by their interactions. Food webs form a particular class of ecological networks that emphasize consumer–resource, or trophic, interactions. Other ecological network types, such as mutualistic networks (e.g., Bascompte and Jordano, 2013), are also widely studied. Ideally, food webs capture the entire spectrum of co-occurring taxa within a defined ecosystem, spanning plants, bacteria, fungi, invertebrates, and vertebrates, along with the links between them representing feeding relationships. These links denote the transfer of biomass across different trophic levels, including detritivory (the consumption of decaying organic matter), herbivory, predation, cannibalism, and parasitism. At the foundation of every food web are one or more autotrophic taxa, such as plants or chemoautotrophic bacteria, as well as dead organic material. The flow of organic matter through trophic interactions supplies the energy, carbon, and essential nutrients that sustain the metabolic processes of all heterotrophic organisms within the network. Tracing the food chains connecting consumers to these foundational autotrophic nodes enables the calculation of each taxon's trophic level, providing insights into ecosystem structure and energy flow (Dunne, 2006).

Food webs can be quantitatively described using similar metrics that are used in social networks, enabling the comparison of shared patterns, the integration of theoretical frameworks, and the transfer of analytical methodologies across these domains. Connectivity patterns within networks—ranging from sparse to highly interconnected—yield valuable information about both social and ecological systems (Crabtree et al., 2021b). For instance, in social networks, understanding connectivity patterns can elucidate how certain communities strategically exploit their physical or social positions to act as power brokers (Peeples and Randall Haas, 2013). Similarly, in ecological networks, examining the role of highly connected nodes can reveal insights into the consequences of species loss, such as the cascading effects that lead to secondary extinctions. Additionally, high levels of connectance, or the number of links per species, may confer greater resilience to ecological communities, enhancing their robustness against the removal of key species (Dunne et al., 2002a, 2002b; Pocock et al., 2012). By understanding these interconnected patterns, researchers can better predict the dynamics of complex systems and their responses to perturbations.

Focus and Subject Matter

The primary distinction between social network analysis and ecological network analysis lies in their focus. Social network analysis is concerned with the relationships and interactions among human actors or organizations. In social network analysis, nodes represent individuals, groups, households, or larger units such as cities, while the edges, or connections, represent a wide range of social interactions. These might include friendships, alliances, economic trade, political ties, or shared information. Archaeologists often apply social network analysis to infer social behaviors and structures from material culture, using artifacts such as pottery, tools, or architectural styles as proxies for human interaction (Mills et al., 2013). For example, the distribution of a particular type of pottery across different archaeological sites might be analyzed to trace trade networks, suggesting that the people in these sites had social or economic exchanges. In some cases, however, social network analysis can draw on more direct evidence, such as written records from literate societies like ancient Egypt (Yeakel et al., 2014) or Rome (Brughmans and Poblome, 2016). In such instances, archaeologists and historians can use social network analysis to mathematically reconstruct historical social networks, analyzing how individuals or groups were connected through kinship, politics, or economic relations.

In contrast, ecological network analysis focuses on the interactions within biological and ecological systems. Here, nodes typically represent species, populations, or functional groups, such as all carnivores or all detritivores within an ecosystem (Dunne, 2006). The edges in ecological networks represent ecological interactions such as predation, competition, mutualism (e.g., pollination), or the flow of nutrients through food webs. Ecological network analysis is particularly useful for examining the structure of ecosystems, the flow of energy or nutrients, species interactions, and ecosystem resilience. By analyzing ecological networks, archaeologists can investigate how past societies interacted with their environments and how these past ecosystems may have responded to human activities. For example, ecological networks can be used to model how ancient agricultural practices might have affected local biodiversity or how the collapse of a keystone species could have led to broader ecosystem shifts, as I show in the next chapter.

Types of Interactions

The nature of interactions within social and ecological networks is fundamentally different. Social networks often involve both direct and indirect relationships that can be either material or nonmaterial. For example, archaeologists can trace the exchange of goods between two cities based on the presence of similar artifacts in both locations, but they may also be interested in less tangible interactions, such as the spread of social influence, ideas, or political power. Measuring the impact of one person on another, or the diffusion of cultural norms through a community, often requires the analysis of nonmaterial aspects of relationships, such as trust, prestige, or social capital. These intangible connections are central to understanding how human societies function and change over time (Crabtree, 2015).

In contrast, ecological networks are more focused on physical and biological interactions, often involving the flow of energy, matter, or nutrients. Ecological interactions are almost always material, involving processes such as predation (the transfer of biomass from prey to predator), parasitism, or nutrient cycling. For instance, the analysis of an ecological network might track the flow of energy from plants (autotrophs) to herbivores and then to carnivores, analyzing how changes at one trophic level can cascade through the ecosystem. These material flows are critical for understanding the balance and resilience of ecosystems, including how they may respond to environmental disturbances such as climate change or human exploitation. Even things that may seem immaterial come from a material interaction; for example, competitive exclusion is related to two species competing over a niche, with one species winning out. The interactions could be seen as competition, so even though it may look immaterial, they do come from material interactions.

Metrics and Objectives

Given the different types of interactions in social networks and ecological networks, the metrics and objectives employed in each approach also diverge. In social network analysis, the primary goal is often to understand the structure of relationships influencing social processes, such as decision making, social cohesion, or power dynamics. Metrics commonly used in social network analysis include centrality (which measures the influence or importance of a node within the network), betweenness (which identifies nodes that act as gatekeepers between different parts of the network), and degree (the number of connections a node has). These metrics help researchers identify key individuals or groups that may play pivotal roles in the network, such as political leaders, trade brokers, or influential families. For instance, an analysis of trade networks in the ancient Mediterranean might reveal how certain cities, such as Lattara, France, acted as central hubs (Crabtree, 2016), facilitating the exchange of goods and ideas across wide geographical areas.

In ecological network analysis, the focus shifts toward understanding how energy, matter, or information flows through ecological systems. Key metrics in ecological networks include trophic level (the position of a species in a food web), connectance (the proportion of possible interactions that actually occur within the network), and ecosystem robustness (a measure of how resilient an ecosystem is to species loss and other perturbations). The objectives of ecological network analysis are often ecological in nature, such as modeling how energy flows through a food web, understanding species interdependencies, or assessing how the loss of one species might lead to cascading effects throughout an ecosystem. In archaeological contexts, ecological network analysis can be particularly useful for studying the long-term impacts of human activity on ecosystems, such as the introduction of new species via domestication or the over-exploitation of natural resources, leading to ecological collapse.

Theoretical Foundations

The theoretical underpinnings of social networks and ecological networks also differ, reflecting the distinct intellectual traditions from which these methods emerged. Social network analysis is deeply rooted in sociology, anthropology, and related fields that focus on human social behavior. As a result, social network analysis can draw on social theories that emphasize power, influence, and social capital. For example, theories of social capital suggest that individuals or groups with more connections in a network can access more resources, wield more influence, and achieve greater success in social or economic endeavors. In archaeology, this theoretical framework can help explain how certain groups or individuals rose to power or how innovations spread through ancient societies.

By contrast, ecological network analysis is grounded in ecological theory and systems biology. These theoretical frameworks emphasize the interconnectedness of species and the flow of energy and nutrients within ecosystems. Employing ecological network analysis helps researchers, understand how ecosystems function as integrated systems and how changes in one part of the network can affect the whole. For example, in studying past human–environment interactions, leveraging ecological network approaches can reveal how agricultural intensification or deforestation might have disrupted local ecosystems, leading to long-term environmental degradation.

In sum, social network analysis and ecological network analysis offer complementary yet distinct approaches to studying networks in archaeological systems. Social network analysis focuses on human relationships, both material and nonmaterial, and is useful for analyzing social structures, power dynamics, and the diffusion of ideas or goods. Ecological network analysis, on the other hand, is concerned with biological interactions and material flows within ecosystems, providing insights into energy transfer, species interdependencies, and ecological resilience. Both methods are valuable for understanding the complexities of past societies and their environments, and each draws on its own theoretical and methodological traditions. By integrating these approaches, archaeologists can gain a more holistic understanding of the past, uncovering the intricate web of social and ecological interactions that shaped ancient human societies and their environments.

When Should Networks Be Used

One challenge with much network analysis in archaeological research is that it can veer into the descriptive. For example, while it's useful to understand how individuals could be connected in the past, it may be tempting to stop at creating the interesting graphics that show how people were connected. In a way, this is a "cart before the horse" problem, because archaeology is often concerned with understanding how people lived in the past, and leveraging any type of tool necessary to understand that can be useful. To move beyond the mere description requires delving deeper into the mechanisms that created these networks in the first place. So, using network analysis as a tool can help elucidate the connections, which then may require greater research to understand how and why those connections formed. In this way network analysis can be an iterative process, where first the description of the network can be made and then an analysis of how it formed can be aided by further network analysis.

Once again, we will take the example of ceramics. Social network analysis can help us understand where a ceramic came from by looking at the composition of the clay and linking the location of the pot to the location of the clay source. But is that enough to create the one link? What if we find *many* pots and link them to the *many* sources? Then we have a descriptive network. But perhaps we can go farther and look at how the connections change over time. Or we can look at the costs for traveling across the landscape with the clay or the pots to use networks to move beyond the mere descriptive. Once we have multiple nodes and edges we can leverage the strengths of network analysis and move beyond describing "this pot came from here" but "the collection of pots came from these places, likely traded across space and through time."

So, network analysis should be used when we have a comprehensive account of entities and the way they were connected, be those connections social or ecological in nature. We should deploy network analysis when we want to move beyond the mere description of connection and understand the ways the connections shaped the overall system. And we should use network analysis when we are unsure how the interactions of two individuals shaped the full network as a whole. In these ways network analysis can help us to understand the connectivity of people in the past, or people and their environments, in ways that move beyond mere description.

Challenges in Network Analysis and Addressing the Critiques

While network analysis is a flexible tool that can help us understand intractable aspects of the past, there are challenges when using network analysis in archaeology. Here I suggest some of the main critiques and ways to address those critiques as well.

The idea that "pots are people" has underlaid archaeological interpretations for decades, hinging on the premise that material artifacts (in this case, pottery) directly reflect the populations responsible for their creation and use. However, this assumption is increasingly contested for a variety of reasons. A striking example is known as the Bell Beaker phenomenon, which may suggest that the distribution of pottery styles often occurred without significant human migration. Recent ancient DNA studies have provided compelling evidence that, while Beaker pottery diffused widely across Europe, the genetic makeup of the associated populations remained distinct. This suggests that the transmission of material culture often occurred independently of population movement, possibly through trade, imitation, or the use of social networks though there is also, of course, evidence for population movement as well (Olalde et al., 2018).

This evidence underscores a broader methodological challenge: the simplistic association of artifacts with ethnic or cultural identities is inadequate for understanding complex processes of cultural transmission. Pottery and other artifacts can act as agents within dynamic social and economic networks, disseminating technologies, ideas, and practices across regions. Recognizing the role of social networks in shaping material culture provides a more nuanced framework for interpreting archaeological evidence, moving beyond deterministic models of cultural diffusion based solely on migration.

Network analysis offers a solution to this challenge by shifting the focus from static associations between artifacts and people to dynamic relationships within social systems. Instead of seeing pots as passive indicators of identity or group movements, network analysis allows archaeologists to explore the connections and interactions that underpin material culture. By mapping the distribution of artifacts and tracing their relationships across sites and regions, network approaches can reveal the complex pathways through which ideas, technologies, and social practices travel. This moves beyond simplistic correlations between material culture and ethnicity, providing a more nuanced understanding of how social networks facilitate cultural exchange.

Through network analysis, archaeologists can uncover how different communities interact with pottery, not just in terms of its production but also its exchange, use, and deposition, helping to reconstruct the social dynamics of past societies. This approach offers a richer, multilayered understanding of material culture that accounts for both human and nonhuman actors in the construction of social networks (Knappett, 2011).

The "pots are people" challenge presents an important critique of traditional archaeological approaches. Network analysis, by focusing on relationships rather than objects as fixed symbols of identity, offers a way to transcend the limitations of this model. It opens up new possibilities for understanding how material culture, people, and social structures are interconnected in the archaeological record. Through this lens, pots become part of a broader network of social and cultural relationships, allowing for a more comprehensive interpretation of the past.

The second main challenge in network analysis for archaeological systems is that we seldom have a full suite of data that represents everything we are studying. Archaeological data itself is inherently fragmentary. While other disciplines such as sociology or epidemiology often collect data through direct observation, archaeologists work retrospectively, relying on what survives from the past. Artifacts must endure through time and be discovered, and those artifacts that are not discovered cannot lend evidence to our understanding of the past. As a result, the networks we attempt to reconstruct are often built on incomplete evidence; we have connections that we know existed, we often have connections we know didn't exist, but there is gray area in between. This missing data problem limits the ability to reconstruct the full range of social relationships, economic exchanges, ecosystems, and political alliances that shaped past societies.

The incomplete nature of archaeological datasets creates uncertainty in how representative these samples are of the entire system. For example, if we find a certain type of pottery at several sites, we can infer connections between these sites. However, we do not know if we have recovered all the relevant pottery at that site, nor are we certain that we have a full suite of every site represented. This uncertainty raises several critical questions: are we observing the full network, or only a fragment? How can we account for missing data? Are the patterns we observe reflective of broader structures, or merely random distributions?

The missing data challenge also impacts how we interpret the structure of past networks. Archaeological data tends to be clustered in areas where preservation conditions are favorable or where excavations have been conducted, leading to geographical biases. Consequently, some places and some data types may be overrepresented, while others are entirely absent. The observed network, even the observed archaeological record, could be a misleading representation of the reality.

Given the challenges posed by incomplete data, archaeologists have turned to statistical models to make inferences about past networks. Exponential random graph models (ERGMs) are one such approach used for social networks (Amati et al., 2020), which are similar in many ways to niche models which are used for understanding food webs (Williams and Martinez, 2000). ERGMs allow researchers to model the likelihood of observed relationships in a network while accounting for missing or incomplete data. This makes them particularly suited for archaeology, where the dataset is always partial.

ERGMs work by comparing the observed network to a set of random networks generated from a similar data structure, allowing the model to assess the likelihood that specific network features (e.g., the presence of certain connections or clustering) are statistically significant rather than random artifacts. By iteratively fitting the model to the data, researchers can identify patterns of relationships that are likely to reflect real world processes.

Let's look at archaeological examples of ERGMs and niche models in practice. In a study leveraging ERGMs to examine the trade networks of the Bronze Age in Southern Spain, researchers were able to model the likelihood of connections between various archaeological sites based on the intervisibility of these sites. Despite incomplete data, the ERGM helped to identify that intervisibility shaped the persistence of settlements through time, which would have otherwise been difficult to infer from the available evidence alone (Brughmans et al., 2015). This illustrates how ERGMs can help archaeologists move beyond the limitations of incomplete datasets and reconstruct more robust networks.

In a study that leveraged niche models to examine the ways that food webs changed over time, researchers were able to examine observed food webs from the 1960s as well as observed food webs today, and assess how impactful human roles were in the food web (Crabtree et al., 2019). Because there were both invasive species and species that went extinct it was not a simple task of just looking at the older web and comparing it to the new web. Rather, researchers were able to leverage niche models to simulate the natural fluctuations in the food web and examine if the modern web's statistics fell within or outside of the natural fluctuations. Crabtree et al. (2019) were able to demonstrate that humans were critical for knitting the food web together, and with their removal the food web began unravelling.

These types of statistical models are especially useful when studying archaeological networks because they explicitly model network formation processes under conditions of uncertainty. In archaeological contexts, these models allow for hypothesis testing about how networks may have been structured in the past. By incorporating probabilities into the network reconstruction, archaeologists can evaluate the likelihood that a given network pattern is representative of the broader system, rather than being an artifact of incomplete data.

For example, in network studies of prehistoric societies, certain nodes (e.g., settlement sites) might have a higher likelihood of forming connections due to their geographic location or access to resources. These types of statistical models can quantify this by examining the attributes of nodes (like site size or material culture richness) to determine if certain sites are more likely to have participated in exchanges or alliances. Thus, even if some sites or artifacts are missing from the archaeological record, the exponential random graph model can offer insights into the broader structure of the network by modeling the probable connections based on observed patterns. Deploying these kinds of advanced statistical models can help us get beyond the critique that archaeology never has enough data; mathematical models can help us quantify the likely variance and help us make predictions about the past based on principles of graph theory.

Wrapping Up

The study of the archaeological past leveraging both social network analysis and ecological networks has yielded remarkable insights into the complexity and resilience of societies and ecosystems, offering models that elucidate the dependencies and vulnerabilities in societies in the past. Moreover, network analysis has enabled us to move beyond simplistic views of artifacts as representing societies, instead looking at networks as the relationships between people and their material culture as traces of these past relationships. This work is perhaps the first step in leveraging archaeological datasets as calibration datasets for understanding the present and future. Can we understand modern political economies by looking at the interconnections of those in the past? Can our understanding of modern ecosystems be built on a synthetic understanding of past ecosystems, leading to more robust models of the human place within them?

Looking forward, the potential for leveraging network approaches with archaeological data is vast. As datasets from archaeological studies grow and become more interconnected with studies from ecology, sociology, geography, and other disciplines, they can allow for systematic comparisons of human interactions across diverse ecosystems and time periods. This future direction promises a more synthetic understanding of humanity's place from our evolutionary origins through to modern industrial societies. By embracing the methodologies of both ecological and social network analysis, we can move beyond disciplinary silos to generate a unified perspective on the ways humans naturally interconnect, emphasizing the enduring influence of human networks in shaping both social and ecological landscapes.

This synthesis will enhance our ability to trace the human trajectory and its environmental impacts, providing a framework for understanding socio-ecological interdependence. In doing so, networked approaches in ecology and archaeology promise not only to advance their respective fields but also to contribute valuable insights for addressing contemporary environmental challenges and fostering sustainable human–ecosystem interactions for the future.

Note

1 Euler is pronounced "Oy-ler" like the Edmonton Hockey Team the Oilers. Not yoo-ler.

Works Cited

Amati, Viviana, Angus Mol, Termeh Shafie, Corinne Hofman, and Ulrik Brandes. 2020. A Framework for Reconstructing Archaeological Networks Using Exponential Random Graph Models. *Journal of Archaeological Method and Theory* 27(2):192–219. https://doi.org/10.1007/s10816-019-09423-z

Bascompte, Jordi, and Pedro Jordano. 2013. *Mutualistic Networks*. Princeton University Press, Princeton, NJ.

Binzer, A., U. Brose, A. Curtsdotter, A. Eklöf, B. C. Rall, J. O. Riede, and F. De Castro. 2011 The susceptibility of species to extinctions in model communities. *Basic and Applied Ecology* 12(7):590–599.

Brose, U. 2011. Extinctions in complex size-structured communities. *Basic and Applied Ecology* 12(7):557–561.

Brughmans, T. 2013. Networks of Networks: A Citation Network Analysis of the Adoption, Use, and Adaptation of Formal Network Techniques in Archaeology. *Literary and Linguistic Computing* 28(4):538–562. https://doi.org/10.1093/llc/fqt048

Brughmans, Tom 2013 Connecting the dots: towards archaeological network analysis. *Oxford Journal of Archaeology*, 29(3): 277–303.

Brughmans, Tom 2013 Thinking Through Networks: A Review of Formal Network Methods in Archaeology. *Journal of Archaeological Method and Theory*, 20:623–662. https://doi.org/10.1007/s10816-012-9133-8

Brughmans, Tom, Simon Keay, and Graeme Earl. 2015. Understanding Inter-Settlement Visibility in Iron Age and Roman Southern Spain with Exponential Random Graph Models for Visibility Networks. *Journal of Archaeological Method and Theory* 22(1):58–143. https://doi.org/10.1007/s10816-014-9231-x

Brughmans, Tom, Barbara J. Mills, Jessica Munson, and Matthew A. Peeples. 2024. *The Oxford Handbook of Archaeological Network Research*. Oxford University Press, Oxford.

Brughmans, Tom, and Matthew A Peeples. 2017. Trends in Archaeological Network Re-Search: A Bibliometric Analysis. *Journal of Historical Network Research* 1:1–24.

Brughmans, Tom, and Matthew A. Peeples. 2023. *Network Science in Archaeology*. Cambridge University Press, Cambridge.

Brughmans, Tom, and Jeroen Poblome. 2016. Roman Bazaar or Market Economy? Explaining Tableware Distributions in the Roman East through Computational Modelling. *Antiquity* 90(350):393–408. https://doi.org/10.15184/aqy.2016.35

Camerano, Lorenzo 1880 Dell' equilibrio dei viventi mercè la reciproca distruzione. *Atti della Reale Accademia delle Scienze du Torino* 15:393–414.

Collar, A. C. F. 2007 Network theory and religious innovation. *Mediterranean Historical Review*, 22(1), 149–162.

Crabtree, Stefani A. 2015. Inferring Ancestral Pueblo Social Networks from Simulation in the Central Mesa Verde. *Journal of Archaeological Method and Theory* 22(1):144–181. https://doi.org/10.1007/s10816-014-9233-8

Crabtree, Stefani A. 2016. Simulating Littoral Trade: Modeling the Trade of Wine in the Bronze to Iron Age Transition in Southern France. *Land* 5(1):5. https://doi.org/10.3390/land5010005

Crabtree, Stefani A., Douglas W. Bird, and Rebecca Bliege Bird. 2019. Subsistence Transitions and the Simplification of Ecological Networks in the Western Desert of Australia. *Human Ecology* 47: 165–177. https://doi.org/10.1007/s10745-019-0053-z

Crabtree, Stefani A., and Lewis Borck. 2019. Social Networks for Archaeological Research. *Encyclopedia of Global Archaeology* (Peregrine 1991): 1–12. https://doi.org/10.1007/978-3-319-51726-1_2631-2

Crabtree, Stefani A., Lydia J. S. Vaughn, and Nathan T. Crabtree. 2017. Reconstructing Ancestral Pueblo Food Webs in the Southwestern United States. *Journal of Archaeological Science* 81:116–127. https://doi.org/10.1016/j.jas.2017.03.005

Crabtree, Stefani A., Jennifer A. Dunne, and Spencer A. Wood. 2021a. Ecological Networks and Archaeology. *Antiquity* 95(381):812–825. https://doi.org/10.15184/aqy.2021.38

Crabtree, Stefani A., Devin A. White, Corey J. A. Bradshaw, Frédérik Saltré, Alan N. Williams, Robin J. Beaman, Michael I. Bird, and Sean Ulm. 2021b. Landscape Rules Predict Optimal Superhighways for the First Peopling of Sahul. *Nature Human Behaviour* 5: 130–131. https://doi.org/10.1038/s41562-021-01106-8

da Fonseca, Rute R, Bruce D Smith, Nathan Wales, Enrico Cappellini, Pontus Skoglund, Matteo Fumagalli, José Alfredo Samaniego, et al. 2015. The Origin and Evolution of Maize in the Southwestern United States. *Nature Plants* 1(1):14003. https://doi.org/10.1038/nplants.2014.3

Dunne, J. A., K. D. Lafferty, A. P. Dobson, R. F. Hechinger, A. M. Kuris, N. D. Martinez, J. P. McLaughlin, K. N. Mouritsen, R. Poulin, K. Reise, D. B. Stouffer, D. W. Thieltges, R. J. Williams, and C. D. Zander 2013 Parasites affect food web structure primarily through increased diversity and complexity. *PLoS Biology* 11:e1001579.

Dunne, Jennifer A. 2006. The Network Structure of Food Webs. In *Ecological Networks: Linking Structure to Dynamics in Food Webs*, edited by Mercedes Pascual and Jennifer A. Dunne, pp. 27–86. Oxford University Press Oxford.

Dunne, Jennifer A., Herbert Maschner, Matthew W. Betts, Nancy Huntly, Roly Russell, Richard J. Williams, and Spencer A. Wood. 2016. The Roles and Impacts of Human Hunter-Gatherers in North Pacific Marine Food Webs. *Scientific Reports* 6:21179.

Dunne, Jennifer A., Richard J. Williams, and Neo D. Martinez. 2002a. Network Structure and Biodiversity Loss in Food Webs: Robustness Increases with Connectance. *Ecology Letters* 5(4):558–567. https://doi.org/10.1046/j.1461-0248.2002.00354.x

Dunne, Jennifer A., Richard J. Williams, and Neo D. Martinez. 2002b. Food-Web Structure and Network Theory: The Role of Connectance and Size. *Proceedings of the National Academy of Sciences* 99(20):12917–12922. https://doi.org/10.1073/pnas.192407699

Egerton, F. N. 2007 Understanding food chains and food webs, 1700–1970. *Bulletin of the Ecological Society of America* 88: 50–69.

Eğilmez, Savaş, and Gönül Bayram Kalkan. 2023. Yam (Post/Communication) Organization in Mongols. *Turcology Research* 77(1):164.

Euler, Leonhard. 1953. Leonhard Euler and the Koenigsberg Bridges. *Scientific American* 189(1):66–72.

Fitzhugh, Ben, S. Colby Phillips, and Erik Gjesfjeld. 2011 Modeling Hunter-Gatherer Information Networks: An Archaeological Case Study from the Kuril Islands. In *The Role of Information in Hunter-Gatherer Band Adaptations*, edited by R. Whallon, W. Lovis, and R. Hitchcock, pp. 85–115. Cotsen Institute of Archaeology, University of California, Los Angeles, CA.

Freeman, Linton C. 2004. *The Development of Social Network Analysis: A Study in the Sociology of Science*. Empirical Press, BookSurge.

Giomi, Evan, and Matthew A. Peeples. 2019. Network Analysis of Intrasite Material Networks and Ritual Practice at Pueblo Bonito. *Journal of Anthropological Archaeology* 53:22–31. https://doi.org/10.1016/j.jaa.2013.10.002

Granovetter, Mark S. 1973. The Strength of Weak Ties. *American Journal of Sociology* 78(6):1360–1380.

Hollstein, Betina. 2021. Georg Simmel's Contribution to Social Network Research. In *Personal Networks: Classic Readings and New Directions in Egocentric Analysis*, edited by Mario L. Small, Brea L. Perry, Bernice Pescosolido, and Edward B. Smith, pp. 44–59. Structural Analysis in the Social Sciences. Cambridge University Press, Cambridge.

Kauffman, Stuart A. 1969. Metabolic Stability and Epigenesis in Randomly Constructed Genetic Nets. *Journal of Theoretical Biology* 22(3):437–467.

Knappett, Carl. 2011. *An Archaeology of Interaction: Network Perspectives on Material Culture and Society*. Oxford University Press.

Kohler, Timothy A., Matthew Van Pelt, and Lorene Yap. 2000. Reciprocity and Its Limits: Considerations for the Study of the Prehispanic Pueblo World. In *Alternative Leadership Strategies in the Prehispanic Southwest*, edited by Barbara J. Mills, pp. 180–206. University of Arizona Press, Tucson, AZ.

Mills, Barbara J., Jeffery J. Clark, Matthew A. Peeples, W. R. Haas, John M. Roberts, J. Brett Hill, Deborah L. Huntley, et al. 2013. Transformation of Social Networks in the Late Pre-Hispanic US Southwest. *Proceedings of the National Academy of Sciences* 110(15):5785–5790. https://doi.org/10.1073/pnas.1219966110

Murphy, G., and T. N. Romanuk 2014 A meta-analysis of local declines in species richness from human disturbances. *Ecology and Evolution* 4:91–103.

Olalde, Iñigo, Selina Brace, Morten E. Allentoft, Ian Armit, Kristian Kristiansen, Thomas Booth, Nadin Rohland, et al. 2018. The Beaker Phenomenon and the Genomic Transformation of Northwest Europe. *Nature* 555(7695):190–196. https://doi.org/10.1038/nature25738

Peeples, Matthew A., and W. Randall Haas. 2013. Brokerage and Social Capital in the Prehispanic U.S. Southwest. *American Anthropologist* 115(2):232–247. https://doi.org/10.1111/aman.12006

Peregrine, Peter. 1991. A Graph-Theoretic Approach to the Evolution of Cahokia. *American Antiquity* 56(1):66–75. https://doi.org/10.2307/280973

Pocock, Michael J. O., Darren M. Evans, and Jane Memmott. 2012. The Robustness and Restoration of a Network of Ecological Networks. *Science* 335(6071):973–977. https://doi.org/10.1126/science.1214915

Ramos-Jiliberto, R., F. S. Valdovinos, J. Arias, C. Alcaraz, and E. García-Bertho 2011 A network-based approach to the analysis of ontogenetic diet shift: an example with the endangered fish Aphanius iberus. *Ecological Complexity* 8:123–129.

Romanowska, Iza. 2023. Complexity Science and Networks in Archaeology. In *The Oxford Handbook of Archaeological Network Research*, edited by Tom Brughmans, Barbara J. Mills, Jessica Munson, and Matthew A. Peeples, pp. 265–279. Oxford University Press, Oxford, UK.

Romanuk, T. N., B. E. Beisner, A. Hayward. L. J. Jackson, J. R. Post, and E. McCauley. 2009 Processes governing riverine fish species richness are scale-independent. *Community Ecology* 10:17–24.

Shelford, V. 1913 *Animal Communities in Temperate America as Illustrated in the Chicago Region*. University of Chicago Press. Chicago, Illinois.

Summerhayes, V. S.; C. S. Elton 1923 Contributions to the Ecology of Spitsbergen and Bear Island. *Journal of Ecology* 11: 214–286.

Travers, Jeffrey, and Stanley Milgram. 1977. An Experimental Study of the Small World Problem. In *Social Networks*, edited by Samuel Leinhardt, pp. 179–197. Academic Press.

VanPool, Todd L., and Chet Savage. 2009. War, Women, and Religion: The Spread of Salado Polychrome in the American Southwest. In *Innovation in Cultural Systems: Contributions from Evolutionary Anthropology*, edited by Michael J. O'Brien and Stephen J. Shennah.

Watson, P. L., O. Luanratana, and W. J. Griffin. 1983. The Ethnopharmacology of Pituri. *Journal of Ethnopharmacology* 8(3):303–311. https://doi.org/10.1016/0378-8741(83)90067-3

Williams, Rich, and Neo D. Martinez. 2000. Simple Rules Yield Complex Food Webs. *Nature* 404(6774):180–183. https://doi.org/10.1038/35004572

Wilson, Ara. 2018. Visual Kinship. *History of Anthropology Review* 42. Retrieved from https://histanthro.org/clio/visual-kinship/

Yeakel, Justin D., Mathias M. Pires, Lars Rudolf, Nathaniel J. Dominy, and Paul L. Koch. 2014. Collapse of an Ecological Network in Ancient Egypt. *Proceedings of the National Academy of Sciences* 111(40):14472–14477. https://doi.org/10.1073/pnas.1408471111

Yodzis P, S. Innes 1992 Body size and consumer-resource dynamics. *American Naturalist* 139:1151–1175.

5
SETTLEMENT SCALING AND AGENT-BASED MODELING

The next chapter turns to a case study from my own research that applies agent-based modeling to long-standing archaeological questions about the origins and persistence of sociopolitical hierarchy. This case study operates along two intersecting axes central to the application of complex adaptive systems methods in archaeology: the formal analysis of settlement scaling and the dynamic exploration afforded by agent-based simulations. By integrating scaling theory with archaeological data, we developed a simulation model to test hypotheses about the organizational principles underlying ancient settlement systems (Crabtree et al., 2017; Kohler et al., 2018). This approach allows us to move beyond static snapshots of the past and instead interrogate the generative processes through which small, seemingly autonomous households could aggregate into nested polities—systems marked by emergent order, enduring hierarchy, and expansive social networks. In doing so, the work illuminates how subtle constraints and local interactions may give rise to macroscale patterns of governance and social differentiation that persisted across space and through time.

This is precisely where the tools of complex adaptive systems science become invaluable (Mitchell, 2009). Complexity science approaches allow us to scale between the micro-level interactions of individual agents and the macro-level structures that emerge from them—offering a framework to explore how something greater than the sum of its parts can take shape. For archaeology, this is especially powerful. We often see the terminus of a process—the point of site abandonment, architectural collapse, or the end of artifact deposition. Complexity science frameworks, particularly when operationalized through simulation, help us probe the pathways that might have produced those endpoints, allowing us to theorize backwards from the traces we find to the behaviors that generated them.

DOI: 10.4324/9781003585251-5

The question of whether the Ancestral Pueblo people were hierarchical or egalitarian has been hotly debated, particularly since the 1980s (Crabtree et al., 2017). Some scholars, noting that descendant communities like the Hopi are egalitarian and eschew hierarchy, have argued that Ancestral Pueblo societies must have also been egalitarian—why would a hierarchical society become acephalous? Others, particularly those studying Chaco Canyon, have pointed to prestige goods like turquoise, macaw feathers, and cacao as evidence of inequality. Further, burials at Aztec, NM, which fluoresced after the decline of Chaco Canyon, suggest powerful individuals. Most strikingly, recent evidence indicates that burials deep in Chaco Canyon itself, where much of the prestige goods were found, belonged to a single matriline, suggesting matrilineal inheritance over time (Kennett et al., 2017). In contrast, areas far from Chaco Canyon do not exhibit prestigious burials or evidence of differential household wealth, suggesting that many settlements remained egalitarian. To reconcile the opposing viewpoints of egalitarian or hierarchical, we hypothesized that if hierarchy were to develop, it would develop as most things in the US Southwest seemed to develop—as a means to control productive yields of maize and arable land. To examine whether hierarchy could emerge from egalitarian antecedents, we built an agent-based model where we knew the mechanisms for hierarchy to compare against the empirical archaeological record to examine the ways that groups could connect into larger entities (Kohler et al., 2018).

To better understand how hierarchy may have emerged, we examined two key archaeological datasets for hierarchical organization: (1) the possible size of maximal groups using kivas and great kivas during Pueblo II and Pueblo III times in the Northern San Juan, Middle San Juan, and the Chacoan core and periphery; and (2) momentary household population data from the Northern San Juan region. Both datasets were subjected to power-law analyses, as power-law distributions often indicate uneven distributions of wealth and power (Bettencourt et al., 2007). The results showed that Pueblo II kiva data exhibited the strongest evidence for hierarchical organization, while Pueblo III data indicated a decline in hierarchy (Kohler and Higgins, 2016). The household population data mirrored this trend, suggesting that hierarchy was strongest in Pueblo II and that it weakened in Pueblo III.

Of course, patterns alone do not explain process. To explore how hierarchy might have emerged from more egalitarian origins, we developed an agent-based model—"Polity"—rooted in the Village Ecodynamics Project's earlier "Village" model. This simulation tracks the behavior of individual households as they form groups, compete for resources, engage in conflict, and navigate shifting political relationships. Each household in the model represents a multigenerational family that farms maize, hunts, and domesticates turkeys for protein. Agricultural productivity is governed by a paleoproductivity model derived from reconstructed precipitation and soil data, allowing environmental variability to drive agent decision making.

Group formation in the model is based on relatedness, with territories delineated using minimum-bounding polygons. Households respond to changes in local productivity by migrating to more favorable locations, leading to shifting territorial boundaries and periodic group realignments. When territories begin to overlap, the simulation evaluates whether groups choose to enter into conflict or establish alliances. To simulate warfare, we adapted Lanchester's Laws—originally developed during World War I to model battle outcomes based on relative force size (Lanchester, 1956). In our version, combatants are male individuals between the ages of 15 and 50, and outcomes are calculated stochastically. If a group loses a battle, it may be absorbed into the winning polity and required to pay tribute—creating a hierarchical relationship. However, political flux is also built into the system: groups can secede from larger polities if environmental or social conditions shift, introducing a dynamic balance between centralization and fragmentation.

Simulation results were revealing. During periods of high productivity—when rainfall was abundant and maize yields strong—larger, more hierarchical polities tended to form. As productivity declined, these structures collapsed into smaller, more localized groupings. This pattern aligns with the archaeological record: hierarchy appears to have been most pronounced during the Pueblo II period, when environmental conditions were relatively favorable, and to have diminished during the Pueblo III period as Ancestral Pueblo people adapted to environmental degradation and social instability.

To validate the model's output, we compared simulated distributions of settlement and kiva sizes to empirical data, focusing on whether those distributions aligned more closely with log-normal or power-law curves. Power-law distributions suggest a rich-get-richer dynamic—a centralization of power—while log-normal distributions indicate a more equitable organization. In the early simulation phases, both modeled and empirical data followed log-normal distributions, consistent with egalitarian social organization. However, during the apex of the Chacoan system, the distributions shifted toward power-law patterns, suggesting increasing social stratification. As the Chacoan system waned, these patterns once again softened, pointing to a re-localization of authority.

Additional evidence for hierarchy emerges from the spatial design of ceremonial architecture. We estimated the number of decision makers involved in Chacoan governance by calculating the carrying capacity of Casa Rinconada, the largest great kiva in the region. With a capacity of roughly 130 individuals, and drawing on Hamiltonian nestedness logic (Hamilton et al., 2007), we estimate that decisions made in Rinconada could have influenced the lives of approximately 2,900 individuals across the region. This spatially nested form of governance offers a plausible mechanism for coordinating social and political activity across great distances—without the need for bureaucratic infrastructure in the modern sense.

Ultimately, our findings suggest that hierarchy in the Ancestral Pueblo Southwest was neither permanent nor ubiquitous. Rather, it emerged episodically—in response to environmental, social, and demographic pressures—and receded when the conditions that supported it disappeared. While many communities remained resolutely egalitarian, the Chacoan system created opportunities for political centralization, especially during the climatically favorable Pueblo II period. This research underscores the power of combining settlement scaling theory with agent-based modeling to illuminate the hidden architectures of past societies. By simulating plausible pathways of development and disintegration, we gain not only explanatory leverage but also a deeper appreciation for the complexity of social organization in deep time.

Works Cited

Bettencourt, Luís M. A., José Lobo, Dirk Helbing, Christian Kühnert, and Geoffrey B. West. 2007. Growth, Innovation, Scaling, and the Pace of Life in Cities. *Proceedings of the National Academy of Sciences* 104(17):7301–7306. https://doi.org/10.1073/pnas.0610172104

Crabtree, Stefani A., R. Kyle Bocinsky, Paul L. Hooper, Susan C. Ryan, and Timothy A. Kohler. 2017. How to Make a Polity (in the Central Mesa Verde Region). *American Antiquity* 82(1):71–95. https://doi.org/10.1017/aaq.2016.18

Hamilton, Marcus J., Bruce T. Milne, Robert S. Walker, Oskar Burger, and James H. Brown. 2007. The Complex Structure of Hunter–Gatherer Social Networks. *Proceedings of the Royal Society B: Biological Sciences* 274(1622):2195–2203. https://doi.org/10.1098/rspb.2007.0564

Kennett, Douglas J., Stephen Plog, Richard J. George, Brendan J. Culleton, Adam S. Watson, Pontus Skoglund, Nadin Rohland, et al. 2017. Archaeogenomic Evidence Reveals Prehistoric Matrilineal Dynasty. *Nature Communications* 8(1):14115. https://doi.org/10.1038/ncomms14115

Kohler, Timothy A., Stefani A. Crabtree, R. Kyle Bocinsky, and Paul L. Hooper. 2018. Sociopolitical Evolution in Midrange Societies. In *The Emergence of Premodern States*, edited by Jeremy A Sabloff and Paula Sabloff. SFI Press.

Kohler, Timothy A. and Rebecca Higgins. 2016. Quantifying Household Inequality in Early Pueblo Villages. *Current Anthropology* 57(5):690–697. https://doi.org/10.1086/687982

Lanchester, F. W. 1956. Mathematics in Warfare. In *The World of Mathematics, Volume 4*, edited by J. R. Newman, pp. 2138–2157. Simon and Schuster.

Mitchell, Melanie. 2009. *Complexity: A Guided Tour*. Oxford University Press, Oxford.

CASE STUDY: HOW TO MAKE A POLITY (IN THE CENTRAL MESA VERDE REGION)*

The causes of the growth and spread of hierarchical societies, so common in the post-Neolithic world, still deserve more exploration. It is perhaps curious that southwestern archaeology, which has made so many other contributions to finely resolved culture history and process, has on offer no general model explaining how such societies can emerge and be maintained. Indeed, for the last decade of the 20th century and the first decade of the next, most southwestern archaeologists (with a few notable exceptions such as Feinman et al., 2000, Plog, 1995, and Sebastian, 1992) pursued other problems.

This likely reflects not just fashion in archaeology; the extent to which village-spanning political hierarchies and regional social stratification existed among Ancestral Pueblo societies remains controversial among southwestern archaeologists three decades after a wrenching debate on this very subject (e.g., Cordell and Plog, 1979; Lightfoot and Feinman, 1982; Reid and Whittlesey, 1990). That is, for some archaeologists there is little to no sociopolitical complexity to be explained. Characterization of ethnographically documented Pueblos as peaceful and egalitarian invited interpretations of their ancestors as adhering to similar norms. Indeed, examining household-level distributions of storage and living areas on the northern edge of the Pueblo world, one of us has recently argued that ritual in Pueblo I (PI) societies[1] had a leveling effect among households, limiting the accumulation of wealth differences to no more than expected in a typical horticultural society (Kohler and Higgins, 2016). But to infer a history free of hierarchy from arguments for relatively egalitarian societies in contemporary and recent times, even bolstered by archaeologically

---

* Reprinted from Stefani A. Crabtree, R. Kyle Bocinsky, Paul L. Hooper, Susan C. Ryan, and Timothy A. Kohler. (2017). How to Make a Polity (in the Central Mesa Verde Region). *American Antiquity* 82(1): 71–95. DOI:10.1017/aaq.2016.18.

derived inferences for leveling of wealth accumulation in some early Pueblo societies, is possibly too facile. What happened in between?

One does not have to maintain that states were ever present in the prehispanic Southwest to see the potential relevance of the claim that

> nowhere in the world did the development of a state equipped with impersonal, pragmatic bureaucracy and coercive, disciplinary force happen overnight, leaping directly from a small autonomous village, the integration of which was based primarily on face-to-face contacts among its members.
>
> *(Inomata and Coben, 2006: 11)*

We will argue that Chaco represented a complex hierarchical society—an example of a society in the gap identified by Inomata and Coben. We will first show why this is likely, and then we will demonstrate how it could have happened from non-hierarchical (indeed, probably anti-hierarchical) precedents.

The most well-known archaeological complex in the Pueblo Southwest, which began to form in Chaco Canyon during late PI times, displays clear aggrandizement and evident consolidation of power if we interpret great houses to be "palaces" of nobles and view the nearby, less labor-intensive contemporaneous habitations to be commoners' residences, as argued by Lekson (2015: 37–38). Chacoan influence spread over most of the Pueblo Southwest by the mid-to-late Pueblo II period (PII: 890–1145), as established beyond reasonable doubt by a number of shared features (including great houses) discussed in contributions to Lekson (2006b).

The interpretation of these societies as hierarchical (or at least non-egalitarian) is strengthened by the two exceedingly rich burials from Room 33 in Pueblo Bonito, the largest and one of the oldest great houses in Chaco Canyon (Plog and Heitman, 2010). The two males in Room 33 were interred in the ninth-century A.D. with the largest assemblage of ritual paraphernalia known from the Pueblo Southwest: intricately carved wooden sticks; wooden flutes with decorative designs; a shell trumpet; nearly 25,000 pieces of turquoise including beads, mosaic pieces, inlays, and carved ornaments; shell bracelets and beads; abundant ceramics including several unusual forms; a cylindrical basket covered in a mosaic of turquoise; several human skulls; and a formalized cache of arrows and wooden staffs in the adjacent Room 32 (Pepper, 1909)—all or most interpreted as curated heirlooms and ritual sacra (Heitman, 2015).

The next-largest set of great houses, in the Chaco-derived Aztec complex north of Chaco Canyon, also contained an unusually rich burial—an exceptionally tall male buried with a number of items (a coiled basketry shield, a wooden sword, a knife, and hafted axes or mauls) suggesting his nickname "the Warrior" (Morris, 1924: 193–195). The burials at Pueblo Bonito were likely emulated elsewhere on the Chacoan periphery, including the 12th-century burial of "the Magician" in the Sinagua area at Ridge Ruin (Gruner, 2015; McGregor, 1943).

Gruner (2015) argues that the ritual paraphernalia associated with the Magician burial signals a common material identity between the occupants of Ridge Ruin and Pueblo Bonito. The burials in Room 33 at Pueblo Bonito, the Magician, and the Warrior are strikingly unusual among prehispanic Pueblo burials and imply heightened wealth and status of the interred individuals, perhaps in part derived from several ritual roles. Direct evidence from burial assemblages for similar hierarchy is generally lacking or is at least much more muted within the Pueblo world before PII and after Pueblo III (PIII: A.D. 1145–1285).

But how much weight should we place on hidden and rare features, such as these burials, in inferring social hierarchy that (were it fundamental) must have benefitted from widespread support and participation that should be visible in more mundane features? Here we offer a generalizable approach to examining hierarchy by describing transitions in site- and structure-size distributions through time for portions of the northern Southwest at three spatial scales—the simulation boundary, the greater VEPIIN boundary which encompasses much of the central Mesa Verde region, and the greater Southwest which incorporates the Northern San Juan, the Middle San Juan, and the Chacoan core and periphery (Figure 5.1).

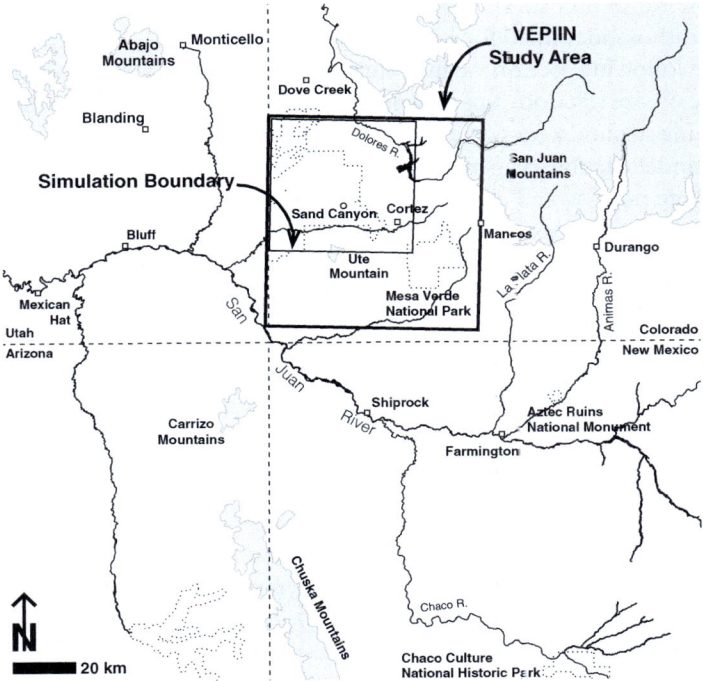

FIGURE 5.1 Location of the VEP I study area (shown by simulation boundary) within the VEPIIN area, which encompasses the most populous portion of the central Mesa Verde region.

Abundant, well-preserved archaeological traces in the Southwest enable us to examine final products of years of planning and group cooperation, as materialized in great kivas, for example. Such data form *patterns* to be explained, yet they are more or less silent on the *processes* creating those patterns. We must turn to models as descriptions of—and potential generative explanations for—those processes, and then return to the archaeological record to determine whether the models are capable of generating patterns more or less similar to those we encounter. We build on the Village Ecodynamics Project's (VEP) simulation "Village" to explore the consequences of hypotheses about the process of hierarchy formation. The processes on which we focus are the collaboration of households within groups, the growth of leadership within groups in tandem with the growth of groups, and the formation of groups-of-groups (polities) in the context of competition over arable land. We then compare the demographic patterns and the distribution of polity sizes generated by the simulation with the empirical evidence presented here on characteristics of size distributions for kivas and settlements. The thread connecting these disparate datasets will be an *inference* of generating process from the nature of the size distributions, and an *explicit definition* of (what we claim to be) the same process in the simulation, which generates size distributions similar to those identified for kivas and settlements.

In the following section we introduce useful concepts for characterizing the structure of size relationships among kivas and settlements. In the third section we examine site and kiva size distributions using these concepts. Then we introduce a model capable of generating similar size relationships among growing inter-village polities and explore its behavior using various parameterizations on virtual landscapes resembling a 1,817 km^2 portion of southwestern Colorado between 600 and 1280. Harmonies between the empirical record and the simulation results suggest that sociopolitical processes in large portions of the Pueblo world during the PII and portions of the PIII periods were substantially different from both earlier and later times, indicating the development, and eventual partial dissolution, of village-spanning political hierarchies.

Nestedness, Hierarchy, Log-Normality, and Power Laws

Whether or not they exhibit hierarchies in power or wealth, human societies typically exhibit a nested structure that may be termed "hierarchical" in the more limited sense that units at each scale are nested within units at more inclusive scales (Randall Jr. et al., 2015; Johnson, 1982). For example, group size of ethnographic hunter-gatherer societies scales from individuals to families, bands, villages, and large aggregates (Hamilton et al., 2007). This scaling, or nesting, may enable efficient movement of information among all members of the group (Bernardini, 1996; Kosse, 2000; Lekson, 1990) though several other possible functions for the larger scales (beyond those that are typically co-resident) have been proposed (Lehman et al., 2014; Kosse, 1994; Lekson, 1990). The concept of "Horton orders" describes the scaling constant relating the numbers of groups of similar sizes that participate in or belong to groups of the next larger size, which in turn nest within yet larger groups. In many cases the larger groups encompass 3–4 (Hamilton et al., 2007; Zhou et al., 2005) of the next-smaller-size groups, and if this ratio is constant as the scale increases, it is said to be self-similar. (The term "Horton order" commemorates Horton's (1945) calculations of the average number of streams flowing into ever larger streams.)

Many archaeologists have suggested that during the PII and PIII periods one or more regional system(s) featuring at least three tiers of site sizes can be discerned in many portions of the Pueblo region, with the largest great house sites (community centers) at the top, followed by significantly smaller sites with more modest great houses, and the vernacular "Prudden unit" hamlets at the bottom. Powers et al. (1983): Table 41; see also Judge, 1989:222) recognized three site-size tiers within just great house floor-area estimates, implying a four-tiered hierarchy overall if small villages and hamlets without a great house were part of the same system. Some (e.g., Lekson, 2006a:32–33; Lekson et al., 1984:267) see this site-size hierarchy—with the great houses in Chaco Canyon at the top of the pyramid and sites outside the canyon as second or third tier— as evidence for sociopolitical hierarchy. Others (e.g., Johnson, 1989) propose that the observed distribution of site sizes can be explained by the concept of "sequential hierarchy," a relatively egalitarian organizational alternative to elites, forming in response to increasing group membership generating "scalar stress" and driving group fission.

Alberti (2014) recognizes that change from simple nesting of group sizes as a result of decision making via a sequential hierarchy—in which no differential power may be implied—to a site-size hierarchy that implies power differentials will take multiple steps. In general, it is reasonable to presume that sequential hierarchies may constitute a "middle stage between fission and the emergence of non-consensual (i.e., hierarchical) decision-making bodies" in a growth process (Alberti, 2014:3). Fissioning might be the immediate group response to scalar stress in contexts where that is possible (Lyman, 2009) and such processes might not generate group integrative facilities and would also not imply hierarchies.

In more densely occupied landscapes, fission might not be possible, or easy, and we might expect ritual facilities to appear, providing locations for "sequences of redundant and invariant acts ... [which] can ameliorate scalar stress by promoting an effective communication flow and by fostering in-group consensus and cohesion" (Alberti, 2014: 2; see also Adler and Wilshusen, 1990). Coward and Dunbar (2014: 388) suggest that more-or-less universal appearance of such structures is due to the fact that "elaborating the 'settings' for social interaction [with ritual facilities for example] simplifies social interactions and performance by off-loading the social information necessary for effective interactions from human memory into the material environment."

Such facilities are likely to become necessary as community sizes exceed ~150 members and are likely locations for religious practices that require investment of time, currency, or adherence to various forms of self-denial, making participation costly enough to deter fakers (Coward and Dunbar, 2014: 390). Performances are likely to include rhythmic dancing, chanting, and even laughter, triggering the release of endorphins, enhancing group solidarity and encouraging pro-social tendencies within the group (Coward and Dunbar, 2014: 392–393). By themselves, the presence of such facilities need not indicate significant power differentials, though if further growth eventually prompted the emergence of doctrinal religions, development of religious hierarchies might be expected. We will suggest that analysis of the size distributions of some of these facilities (kivas and great kivas) provides insight into the processes that generate them and that in turn are relevant to questions of differential social power.

We acknowledge that what we call kivas here likely had multiple functions, often quotidian but occasionally sacred. Our concern is for the capacity for social integration that these structures embodied at the scales of organization for which they were intended and their ability to reinforce social integration (and potentially hierarchy) through their use.

Turning to the question of site sizes, Duffy (2015) identified at least five processes other than regional political hierarchy capable of generating site size hierarchies in the archaeological record. Three of these result from time-averaging effects that are minimized by the relatively fine dating employed here (anchored by tree-ring dating, extended to ceramic depositional signatures). One of the other processes Duffy mentions, however—growth differentials due to differences in catchment productivity—must be considered before interpreting hierarchies in site-size histograms as possible evidence for regional functional specialization. Glowacki and Ortman (2012) examined potential maize productivity (derived as explained by Kohler, 2012) for the 90-some community centers in the study area within which the simulation is set (see Figure 5.1). Community centers are the largest sites in their neighborhoods, usually contain civic-ceremonial architecture, and tend to be occupied longer than is typical for smaller habitations. Glowacki and Ortman showed that the peak population of centers is only weakly associated with the estimated mean maize productivity of their surrounding 2-km catchments ($r^2 = 0.07$; $p = 0.02$). As maize constitutes 70 percent or more of the local diet its productivity is highly relevant (Coltrain et al., 2006; Matson, 2016). This suggests that variability in community center size was greatly influenced by factors other than catchment productivity, though catchment productivity is *not* irrelevant.

Following Duffy (2015), this suggests that the community-center size differentials we see in this area represent regional functional specialization, for example as the outcome of a political/economic structuring process. This also appears likely based on what we know about differential representation of structure types through time. Group-assembly features such as great kivas and plazas are present in most of the pre-980 community centers. In the 1000s, restricted-use features (especially great houses) become the most common civic-ceremonial architecture, replaced in turn after 1140 by controlled-access features such as towers and enclosing walls until regional abandonment in the mid-to-late 1200s (Glowacki and Ortman, 2012: Table 14.2). By the mid-1100s, great kivas become characteristic of only the largest centers, suggesting that they served as periodic group-assembly points for a number of surrounding smaller centers, defining a hierarchy that was simultaneously geographic, ritual, and size based.

Two previous studies have characterized site-size hierarchies in this region. For the central Mesa Verde region (an area larger than—though encompassing—the areas for which we have settlement-size data and simulation results), Lipe (2002: 217–220) studied habitation sites with an inferred momentary population of 50 or more. On the basis of a rank-size analysis he determined that from 1150–1225, sites exhibit a "well-integrated settlement system" in which the ranks plotted against the sizes approximate the expected diagonal (log-normal distribution) very closely. For the 1225–1290 period, however, the ranks plotted against the sizes deviate convexly upward from the diagonal, usually interpreted as indicating the presence of several competing systems.

For the same region examined in the simulations reported here, Kohler and Varien (2010) characterized the distributions of all sites with more than one household for 14 periods from 600 to 1280; their figure 3.5 displays rank-size graphs for four of these periods. Generally, their results echoed those of Lipe (2002) where their periods overlapped, although they additionally recognized a slight tendency for the largest site (which after 1060 is Yellow Jacket Pueblo) to be larger than expected (until at least 1140) by the rank-size metric. They suggested that this tendency toward primacy for Yellow Jacket Pueblo measured "the degree to which it drew benefits—unknown in nature—from other settlements through processes that remain to be defined" (Kohler and Varien, 2010: 54).

Here we will apply recent advances in characterizing scaling relationships to sharpen these arguments, using empirical estimates of kiva sizes (and the groups they could accommodate), momentized site populations, and territory sizes for groups of sites generated by the simulation. To shed light on the processes that generate such distributions, we focus on whether these correspond more closely to a log-normal or to a power-law distribution. Although these distributions look somewhat similar (both have long tails to the right and so exhibit positive skew in which, for example, small sites are common but large sites rare) they differ in their generating processes in ways that relate to the equality of their constituents.

If the size of some variate (e.g., settlement population) is graphed against its frequency, and the distribution is normal (Gaussian) when the logarithm of the size is used, the distribution is said to be log-normal (Aitchison and Brown,

1957: 1). Log-normal distributions are classically produced by something which can be called the law of proportionate effect (Aitchison and Brown, 1957: 1) or the multiplicative process (Mitzenmacher, 2004: 235). If settlements grow (or shrink) in response to a number of unrelated processes, each of which is proportionate in its effect to the size of the settlement in the previous time step, the expected result is a log-normal distribution of settlement sizes.

If settlement sizes (or kiva sizes) conform to a log-normal distribution, we will argue that this implies the outcome of a number of unrelated processes, but importantly *not* including a process in which largeness itself was disproportionately rewarded. Power-law distributions, on the other hand, are classically generated by preferential attachment. An example would be a case in which the largest existing settlement is also the preferred target for migration (Mitzenmacher, 2004: 233–235) also mentions optimization as a possible process leading to power-law distributions, though its efficacy has been debated. Some variate x, obeys a power-law distribution if it is drawn from the probability distribution $p(x) \propto x^{-\alpha}$, where α is a scaling exponent typically taking on a value between 2 and 3. We have known since Albert et al. (1999) that the in-degrees and out-degrees of nodes in the worldwide web are commonly power-law distributed and the reasons that more popular nodes will be preferential targets for new links seem obvious in this case.

Power-law-like distributions frequently indicate the outcome of processes such as consolidation of power and growth of hierarchy (Grove, 2011). Modern city population sizes follow a power-law distribution (e.g., Auerbach, 1913; Bettencourt, 2013; Bettencourt et al., 2007) because large aggregates create increasing returns in wealth and innovation, in turn attracting to themselves a growing number of people. In our data, we will argue that settlement-size distributions matching power laws suggest that the largest settlements were benefitting the most from the ritual or political system. To strengthen this inference we will present model results in which larger groups come to have a power advantage over smaller groups as regional population size and density increase and demonstrate that this produces power-law-distributed territory sizes. Beyond the factors considered in the simulation, larger settlements would likely have served as engines of innovation and attracted more residents (Bettencourt et al., 2007), more wealth (Brown et al., 2012), more ritual (Glowacki and Ortman, 2012) and more feasting (Mills, 2007).[2] These benefits will in the event be balanced against the social and economic costs of being large, including alleviating size-induced social frictions, as well as traveling greater distances to fields and slowly renewable resources such as deer and firewood.

With these ideas in mind, we begin by examining data on kiva sizes for the large portion of the Pueblo Southwest studied by Ryan (2013: Figure 2.1). We then turn to estimated population sizes for habitations (including community centers) in the VEPIIN area (Figure 5.1). Using these two datasets may allow us to profit from convergence of semi-independent lines of evidence. In both cases we attempt to determine whether their size distributions through time correspond to a power law, which might suggest the development of supravillage polities, or exhibit log-normality, which suggests a variety of non-hierarchical generating processes. After introducing the simulation model, we will also compare the distributions of territory size generated by the simulation to these two theoretical distributions.

Scaling Relationships in Archaeological Data

Kiva Sizes

For the last three decades archaeologists in the central Mesa Verde region have identified small kivas (with diameters less than 10 m) as serving a domestic function in addition to focusing some ritual activities at the level of the household, extended household, or lineage group. Larger structures such as great kivas (10 m or larger) focused nondomestic ritual activities for one or more communities (Adler and Wilshusen, 1990). If we grant that kiva sizes are related to the sizes (and types) of the groups they served, and if settlements have fairly discrete hierarchical size categories (e.g., hamlets and villages), we might also expect kiva dimensions to exhibit fairly discrete size classes. Further, if either of these size distributions appears more likely to have been drawn from a power law than a log-normal distribution, that will be taken as evidence for some type of reward for largeness—such as the processes we define for the simulation—in and of itself.

Susan Ryan (2013) compiled data on 407 fully excavated kivas of all sizes during PII and PIII periods within three large subregions of the prehispanic Pueblo Southwest: the Northern San Juan (NSJ), centered on, though larger than, the central Mesa Verde region; the Middle San Juan (MSJ), centered on the Aztec area; and the Chaco Core and Periphery (CCP), centered on Chaco Canyon. Of those 407 structures, we used the 248 having bench widths, and added 224 kivas to her dataset, mostly in the NSJ, whose diameters could be estimated accurately, even if they were not fully excavated. Diameters in Ryan's data were computed from bench-face to bench-face (Ryan, 2013: 133, 136); diameters for additional pit structures we added here were computed by measuring the interior of kiva-circles on maps. Our total sample of 472 structures represents an unknown proportion of the total population of PII–PIII–period preserved kivas in these regions. It is highly probable that our sample is over-weighted toward larger size classes since they are more noticeable and more likely to have been investigated.

Of greater interest than the diameters of kivas, however, are the group sizes that they could accommodate. One approach to estimating these is simply to assume that each person needs a square meter of space, so that a 7-m–diameter kiva (with a floor area of 38 m^2) could accommodate a group of 38 (Van Dyke, 2007a: 119). Alternatively, one might partition the space into spectator and performance space.

Of course, "performance space" means different things for great kivas and household kivas, and here we use the term broadly to incorporate both spectacles and performances, as defined by Inomata and Coben (2006). *Spectacles* are "gatherings linked around theatrical performance of a certain scale in clear spatial and temporal frames, in which participants witness and sense the presence of others and share a certain experience" (Inomata and Coben, 2006: 16). This assumes an audience and an emotional response, includes props, and incorporates a great deal of symbolic material. Events performed in great kivas would be spectacles typically witnessed by a group of people and incorporating many props such as foot drums and elaborate costumes laden with symbolic associations. Spectacles also incorporated participants outside the confines of the kiva walls through sound, adding to their scope.

Performance, on the other hand, includes "informal daily activities as forms of human interactions and self-presentations" (Inomata and Coben, 2006: 14). A performance, then, is any activity that can affect the life of the performer as well as a potential observer (Inomata and Coben, 2006; Goffman, 1959). Grinding maize, weaving a blanket, and teaching a child all fall within its scope. Such "performances" could have incorporated other people performing complementary tasks related to the activity at hand (e.g., preparing the kernels for grinding). We assume that each spectator (or maize-grinding helper) needs one linear meter around the circumference, and each "performer" needs 4 m^2 (a generous figure allowing for presence of floor features).

A kiva with a diameter of 7 m has a circumference of ~22 m and an area of ~38 m^2, allowing for 22 spectators and 38/4 = ~9 performers, or a total group size of 31. For pit structures more than 4 m in diameter, this method yields lower group-size estimates than assuming 1 m^2/person. Even though we acknowledge that the activities in small and great kivas were typically different, we use the same formula to estimate the probable group size in both.

Using this approach we translate diameters into expected group sizes for kivas in the PII and PIII periods (Figure 5.2). The most dramatic feature in this figure is the loss of most large kivas (groups) in the two southern areas in the PIII period, with the exception of the Salmon Ruins great kiva (dated to PII–PIII by Windes and Bacha, 2008: 130) and the Chacra Mesa great kiva (dated to PII–PIII by Van Dyke, 2007b: 123). Multiple modes can be seen in most of these histograms.[3] In both the NSJ and MSJ during the PII period, modes occur around 15 and 25 participants, with possible larger modes in the 60–70 and the 80–90 range. Pueblo II CCP sites also exhibit modes around 15, 25, and 90, but unlike those to the north there is apparently an additional mode around 45 participants (most of these appear to be what Windes, 2015 calls court kivas), and the unique great kiva, Casa Rinconada (Vivian and Reiter, 1965: 9–26), which, according to our (possibly conservative) rules, would have accommodated some 130 participants (Figure 5.2).

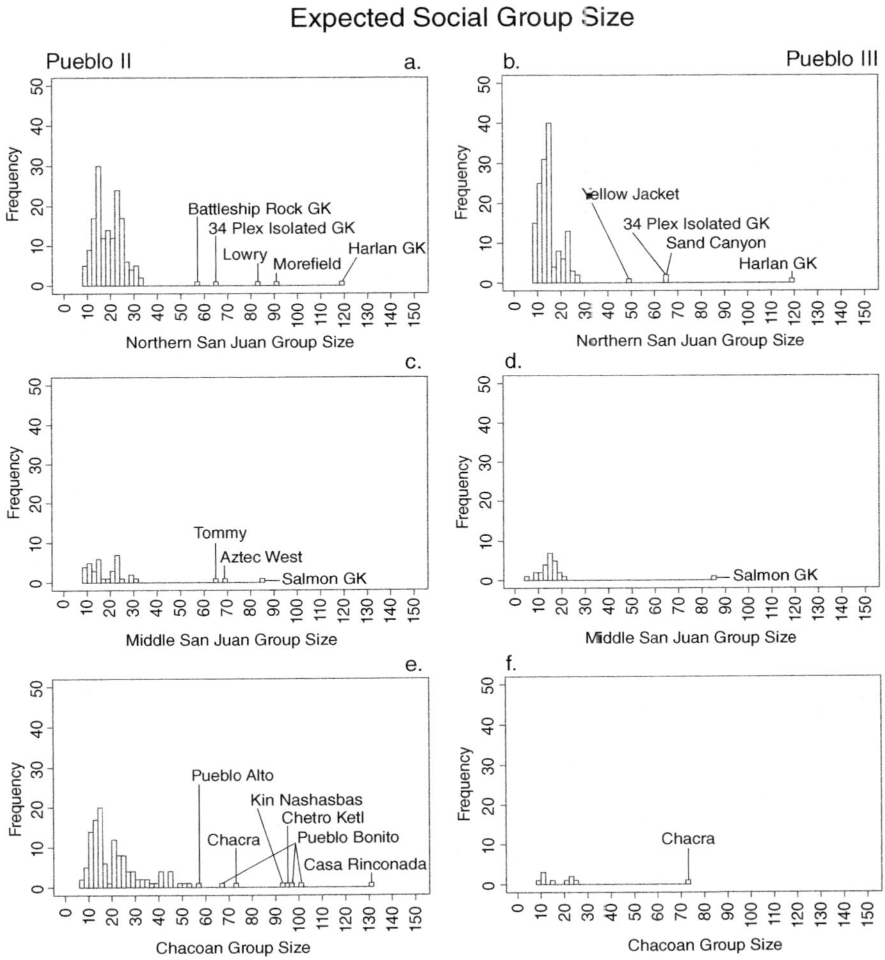

FIGURE 5.2 Expected social group sizes represented by kiva floor areas, calculated from kiva diameters assuming circular shape; PII, left column; PIII, right column. NSJ data are in the top row, MSJ data in the second row, and the CCP in the third row. Axes are standardized.

During Pueblo III the NSJ and CCP both retain modes around 10–15 and 25 participants, though the MSJ seems to retain only the smallest size class. In the NSJ there continues to be a possible mode in the 48–65 participant range, whereas the long-lived Harlan Great Kiva (Coffey, 2014) in the Goodman Point community fills a Casa Rinconada–like role as the largest integrative structure in the region. Yet there seem to be fewer kivas overall, and fewer kivas in the middle-range of sizes, during the PIII period, although we know that open-air plazas, or common areas, as well as biwall and triwall structures increased in frequency (Glowacki, 2015: 69). Such spaces may have reduced the need to invest in costly and complicated kivas and perhaps substituted in particular for kivas serving ~40–50 people. However, the functions of the multi-walled structures are uncertain, and plazas presumably served a variety of purposes. For these reasons we focus on kivas.

For these we can suggest a scaling parameter on the order of 1.7–2 (15 people × 1.67 = 25 people; 25 people × 1.8 = 45 people; 45 people × 2 = 90), suggesting that as ritual moved beyond the household, each larger structure might accommodate 1 or 2 of the people participating in the rituals in the next–smaller-size kiva. (This argument does not abandon the point of view that all non-great kivas had residential functions; it merely recognizes that such kivas also likely had ceremonial functions.) If we assume strict nestedness we can express the same result slightly differently. Kivas in the 25-participant size range should be aggregating their participants from about (25/1.67=) 15 of the 15-participant-size kivas; each kiva in the 45-participant size range should be drawing participants on average from about (45/1.8=) 25 of the 25-participant-size structures; and great kivas in the 90-participant size range should be drawing on about (90/2=) 45 kivas in the 45-participant size range. By this logic a "standard" great kiva accommodating about 90 people could serve representatives of (25 × 45=) 1125 of the social units represented by the smallest kivas—an interestingly high number which either suggests that strict nestedness did not apply, or that such great kivas could easily accommodate participants from two very large communities of >500 households each.

The relationship between the 90-participant great kivas and the 130 we estimate for Casa Rinconada has a somewhat lower scaling parameter (90 × 1.44 = 130), but if we nevertheless use the same logic it may have been drawing its 130 participants at the rate of 1 or 2 representatives each from about (130/1.44=) 90 of the 90-participant size great kivas. This might be plausible; the Chaco Research Archive[4] lists 106 outliers with great kivas, not all of which may have been in use at once.

Although these numbers might seem to suggest an implausibly high number of households represented in increasingly large structures, Windes (2015) does argue that court kivas at Chaco were in many cases used by non-residents, and if the distance traveled to Chaco Canyon was great it is reasonable to expect that only one or two representatives of kivas in the 25-participant class might have made the journey. Van Dyke (2007a): 119) likewise suggests that great kivas accommodated only a "small fraction of the resident or visiting population," intentionally (one presumes) restricting access to that segment.

Chaco researchers are increasingly embracing regional analyses that imply a broad spatial scope for Chacoan social integration, if not explicitly arguing for a Chacoan polity. Van Dyke et al. (2016) demonstrate that shrines, stone circles, and herraduras enhanced visibility between great houses, and created a network of visual dominance over the landscape that seems to peak after AD 1000. Chacoan road systems betray regional-scale planning (if not functional economic integration; Kantner and Hobgood, 2003), and roads and directional alignments between outlier great houses in the middle San Juan suggest subregional coordination for the observation of celestial events (Coffey, 2016:14). It remains to be seen whether these systems evidence coordination and unity at the scale of the Chaco world, or merely a shared subregional identity that is undoubtedly influenced—but not controlled—by Chaco (Kantner, 2003:218). Here, we argue that a regional system with Chaco at its core need not have its origins in a unified system but instead can emerge from hierarchical power relationships that form at a local scale. As we shall see, kiva size distributions across the Pueblo Southwest reify and likely served to reinforce hierarchy at multiple scales of Pueblo society.

Analysis of Kiva Size Distributions

Now we examine these kiva data from the perspective of whether (and when) their size distributions fit those expected by a power law, using the log-linear distribution as an explicit comparison given the ease with which these two distributions can be confused. Many studies (e.g., Brown et al., 2012) identify the fingerprints of power laws based solely on visual inspection of distributions. Here we use the poweRlaw package (Gillespie, 2015) which implements procedures suggested by Clauset et al. (2009) with results displayed in Figure 5.3. Since log-normal and power-law distributions differ primarily in their extreme right tails, Gillespie (2015) employs a Kolmogorov-Smirnov test to locate the minimum value in an empirical distribution at which a power law ought to apply, setting that as the x_{min} value for the test. We imposed the same x_{min} value on the log-normal distribution to facilitate comparison of the two.

Table 5.1 summarizes the results of this examination. The *alpha parameter* reports the slope of the best-fit power-law line; note for example in Figure 5.3 that the power-law-fit line slopes down more rapidly for NSJ PIII (alpha=2.9, Figure 5.3d) than it does for CCP PII (alpha=1.8, Figure 5.3g). Then we tabulate the results of several complementary tests that do not always deliver precisely the same conclusions. The *power-law probability* reports the probability that the empirical data could have been generated by a power law; the closer that statistic is to 1, the more likely that is. We consider values below 0.1 as rejecting the hypothesis that the distribution was generated by a power law (Clauset et al., 2009: 16). The *test statistic* indicates how closely the empirical data match the log normal. Negative values indicate log-normal distributions, and the higher the absolute value, the more confident the interpretation. However, it is possible to have a test statistic that indicates a log-normal distribution in addition to a power-law probability that indicates a power-law, so we employ the *compare distributions* test to compare the fit of the distribution to a

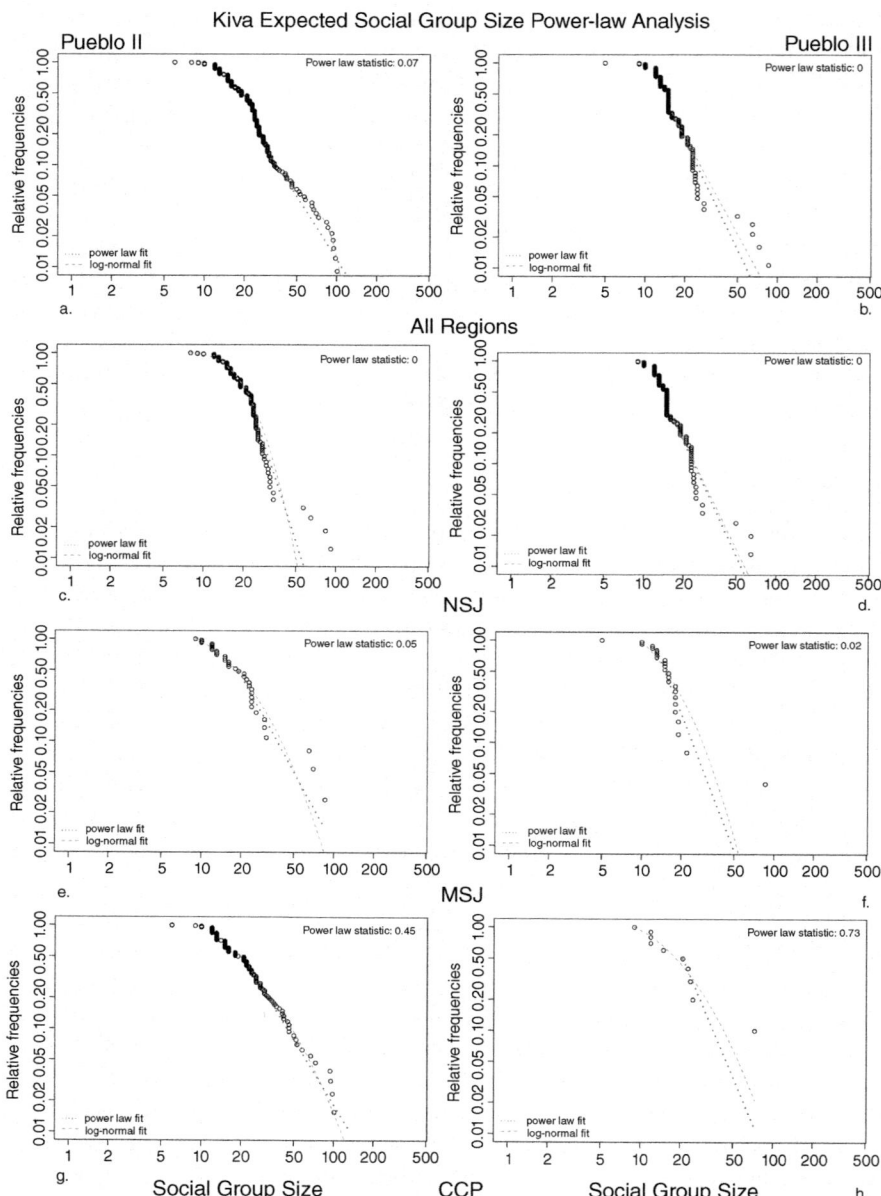

FIGURE 5.3 Power-law analysis of the expected social group sizes represented by kivas of various sizes, by period and region. Power-law probability values from Table 5.1 are reported in the upper right-hand corner of each panel.

TABLE 5.1 Summary of conformity of kiva-size distributions to power-law expectations. "Power-law probabilities" between 0.1 and 1 indicate inability to reject the hypothesis that the data could have been generated by a power law. "Compare distributions" values of 0.6 to 1 indicate a power law; values from 0 to 0.4 indicate a log-normal distribution; intermediate values are ambiguous. Positive values for the "Test statistic" indicate power-law distributions; negative values indicate log-normal distributions

Area and period	Alpha	Power-law probability	Compare distributions	Test statistic
All PII	1.828	0.07	0.541	0.104
All PIII	1.881	0	0.669	0.440
NSJ PII	2.115	0	0.671	0.443
NSJ PIII	2.868	0	0.562	0.153
CCP PII	1.780	0.45	0.604	0.265
CCP PIII	2.378	0.73	0.566	0.166
MSJ PII	2.325	0.05	0.577	0.193
MSJ PIII	1.885	0.02	0.651	0.699

power-law and to the log-normal distribution. Values below 0.4 indicate a better fit to the log-normal; those above 0.6 favor a power-law; intermediate values are ambiguous (Table 5.1 and Figure 5.3).

Discussions with the developer of the procedure implemented in the poweRlaw package lead us to suggest that over-sampling of the larger kivas, in the NSJ in particular, is likely responsible for the somewhat contradictory results in Table 5.1, where "power-law probability" (when it rejects a power law) is often at odds with the "compare distribution" and "test statistic" indicating power laws. Clauset (personal communication 6/10/2016) suggests our results may indicate that the NSJ and PII–PIII kiva data represent weak power laws (see Supplemental Text: Detecting Outliers in Kiva Size Distributions in this issue of *American Antiquity*). Grove's analysis of ritual centers in Ireland (2010: Figure 5) showed that the largest stone circles in his sample also tended to weaken what appeared from the body of the distribution to be a power-law distribution.

With that in mind, the results from Table 5.1 generally support the inference that kiva sizes in Chaco Canyon and its periphery in PII and probably PIII times were generated by a power-law–like process. Elsewhere, this is slightly less clear, although in all three regions and in both periods power-law distributions fit the kiva data better than log-normal distributions do.

Analysis of Settlement Population Distributions

We now turn to the results of the same analysis based on estimates for the number of households in habitation sites by period, as compiled by Schwindt et al. (2016) for the sub-portion of the NSJ studied by VEP II, using only those sites assigned one or more households for that period. The site-size estimates used here were generated by steps 1–4 in Schwindt et al. (2016:78–80) which were then momentized by multiplying by the mean occupation span in each period from Varien et al. (2007: Table 3) divided by the length of each period. The histograms of site size (Supplemental Figures 4.1 and 4.2) show the expected pattern of many small sites and decreasing numbers of sites of larger sizes through all periods. Populations of the largest sites, however, tend to increase through time. Discrete modes are less visible in the settlement-size distributions than for the kivas; although the case for the presence of modes is visually stronger in the later periods (Supplemental Figure 2), we do not pursue their identification here.

In general, the site-size distributions are more clearly power-law-distributed than are the kiva sizes (Supplemental Figures 4.3 and 4.4; Table 5.2). Exceptions are the periods 1020–1060, 1060–1100, 1180–1225, and 1225–1260, all of which have one or two ambiguous indicators, although the "test statistic" in each case points to a power law. Rather surprisingly, the two earliest periods appear to correspond to a power law, though the results may be spurious since nearly their entire distribution after momentizing is composed of many one-household settlements (Table 5.2).

TABLE 5.2 Summary of degree of conformity of VE PII N settlement-size distributions to power-law expectations. "Power-law probabilities" between 0.1 and 1 indicate inability to reject the hypothesis that the data could have been generated by a power law. "Compare distributions" values of 0.6 to 1 indicate a power law; values from 0 to 0.4 indicate a log-normal distribution; intermediate values are ambiguous. Positive values for the "Test statistic" indicates power-law distributions; negative values indicate log-normal distributions

Years AD	Alpha	Power-law probability	Compare distributions	Test statistic
600–725	5.57	0.3	0.991	2.385
725–800	2.23	0.3	0.672	0.445
800–840	3.21	0.22	0.672	0.445
840–880	3.14	0.55	0.623	0.331
880–920	3.59	0.43	0.835	0.975
920–980	3.11	0.46	0.591	0.230
980–1020	4.49	0.46	0.942	1.575
1020–1060	2.80	0.03	0.568	0.171
1060–1100	2.80	0.08	0.568	0.171
1100–1140	2.15	0.24	0.753	0.682
1140–1180	2.19	0.8	0.620	0.305
1180–1225	1.98	0	0.829	0.949
1225–1260	1.91	0.25	0.5751	0.189
1260–1280	1.88	0.3	0.643	0.366

Summary of Empirical Results

Overall, the case for processes such as preferential attachment (expected for power-law fits) is clear for PII and probable for PIII kiva-size distributions, particularly in the CCP. With a few possible exceptions the site-size distributions also conform to power-law expectations.

Of course, these outcomes only hint at an explanation for the development of this structure. Can a process of preferential attachment, or something like it, that withstands the test of plausibility for the societies represented here be built into a model that generates power-law structures for size distributions? For example, do the largest settlements (or groups of settlements) grow ever larger by drawing in (or compelling the participation of) more people for ritual, exchange, and other social functions? We now describe a model providing a candidate explanation for the empirical results reviewed so far.

The Model

The Village simulation is built on a foundation of trees. Ring-width analysis generates temporal series of annually resolved estimates of temperature and precipitation from AD 600–1300 that in turn generate spatialized estimates of potential maize productivity and the productivity of the various plants that provide food for deer, rabbits, and hares, and wood for cooking and heating. The agents in this model represent Pueblo households who farm maize, hunt deer and leporids, raise turkeys, fetch water and fuel, trade resources, and react to local variability in environmental productivity (also affected by local densities of other households) by relocating their settlements to more productive land, or by intensifying (adding more farm plots, raising more turkey in lieu of hunting). On top of this base simulation, described extensively in Kohler and Varien (2012), we add a number of changes allowing the agents to live in territorial groups of varying political organization and form polities.[5]

The model we propose makes three important but well-founded assumptions. First, as warranted earlier, we assume the centrality of maize in the Pueblo diet. The best lands to produce maize were worth competing over due to the dominance of maize in the diet and the high spatial variability in potential production. Second, we assume a strong trend of population growth during the periods considered here, which is clearly demonstrated for the Southwest as a whole (Kohler and Reese, 2014) and for the VEPIIN area (Figure 5.1; Schwindt et al., 2016). Third, we build into the model the possibility of mortal conflict between groups, recognizing that these societies were subject to enough sporadic violence to rank them "among the most violent societies studied by anthropologists or archaeologists" (Kohler et al., 2014:458).

The model therefore features growing groups that may come into conflict over limited expanses of superior arable land. By virtue of their size, some of these groups are able to incorporate others, by force or threat, forming multi-settlement "polities" we call complex groups that can grow or shrink according to the climate-mediated production of the lands they encompass and the competition they encounter. These processes typically result in a chain of subordinate groups (or often a more tree-like structure) linked to a dominant group by flows of tribute in maize, mutual protection in defense, and coordinated action in offense. We demonstrate that this model results in territory sizes for these polities that are power-law distributed—unsurprising given that they are generated by a big-get-bigger dynamic—and we infer that flows of tribute and coordinated action could help generate the sorts of power-law-distributed settlement sizes (and therefore kiva sizes) we documented previously for the archaeological record.

Space limits necessitate deferring most model details to the Supplemental Materials. (See sections therein on the public goods game; parameter selection, group formation and territoriality; conflict, merging, and tribute; revolt in complex groups; and fission in simple groups; also Kohler et al. (n.d.) in review.)[6] To the base "Village" model, the model reported here adds a territorial, kin-based group structure in which households (agents) live in simple groups which annually play a within-group public goods game, deciding to elect a leader (the more costly alternative when groups are small) or perform mutual monitoring against defection (the more costly alternative when groups are large). Simple groups can therefore be either non-hierarchical or hierarchical. If a simple group reaches a population size parameterized in the simulation (either 50 or 100 households), it fissions (all parameters varied in the runs reported here are in Table 5.3).[7] When group territories begin to encroach on each other, groups may merge or fight, in either case linking them into complex groups with a hierarchical organization. Subordinate groups in complex groups pay tribute to the ultimate dominant group, passing through any intermediate groups in the chain (Steponaitis, 1981). Finally, simple groups (along with their subordinates, if any) may choose to revolt from their dominant group to form a simple group (by themselves) or a complex group (with their existing subordinates). Thus, the model unites the two relational mechanisms identified by Dubreuil (2010:140) as "intimately linked to the evolution of hierarchies"—emergence of corporate groups (our simple groups) and social division of sanction (the leaders who may appear in simple groups) (Table 5.3).

Our current model is generically similar to some earlier models (e.g., Cederman, 2002; Cegielski and Daniel Rogers, 2016; Griffin and Stanish, 2007; Turchin and Gavrilets, 2009) that feature competition, warfare, tribute, or polity emergence, disappearance, secession, and unification, and we gratefully acknowledge their inspiration. In general we endogenize more aspects of our model (e.g., production, population growth, and many household-level ecosystem interactions) than do others of which we are aware. To the extent that initial steps toward variability among households or groups of households in

TABLE 5.3 Parameters varied in the runs of the simulation reported here. This created 36 unique runs, each replicated 15 times; replicates are reported in Supplemental Table 4. Max simple group size is the number of households beyond which the group will fission. S is the percentage of fighters the smaller group will accept as casualties; e.g., a fight between a group with 100 warriors and a group with 200, and an s value of 0.02, will result in up to 2 fighters dieing. β is the tax on the net return to the public goods game, while μ is the tax on beta

Max simple group size (households)	S (acceptable proportion of fatalities among all combatants in the smaller group during warfare)	Β (proportion of net benefit to public goods game paid as tribute to direct dominant group)	μ (portion of β passed to next dominant group by an intermediate group)
50	0.02	0.1	0.1
100	0.05	0.5	0.5
—	—	0.9	0.9

wealth and power (as studied by Wilkinson et al., 2007 for example) and successful maintenance of existing polities depend on control of the best patches for maize production, these differences are important. In our case, we suggest that the modest correlation of community center size with local maize productivity suggests that the processes of polity growth are initiated, and then best maintained, by sites enjoying access to superior maize production.

Simulation Results

Each of the 36 unique parameter combinations (Supplemental Table 4) was run 15 times, creating 540 total runs. Figure 5.4 reports the population trajectories of agents in each of these runs and for each of the parameter combinations. Runs with low fatalities to warfare (s), low taxation (β), and low pass-through tribute (μ) (that is, high amounts of the tax from subordinate groups retained within each group as tribute moves up the chain) generate the highest populations, which are most similar to those in the empirical record (Figure 5.4, gray bars). We think that the main sources for the differences between the simulated populations and the empirical population estimates are the lack of immigration and emigration in the model, and the fact that we do not model low-frequency climate change, which influenced productivity in our region to an unknown extent; these issues are discussed at length in Kohler and Varien (2012). The runs with the highest populations are: Run 1, Run 2, and Run 3. The higher s-value and higher taxation values generate the lowest populations (e.g., run 18 with s = 0.05, β and μ = 0.9). Different thresholds for maximum simple group size do not

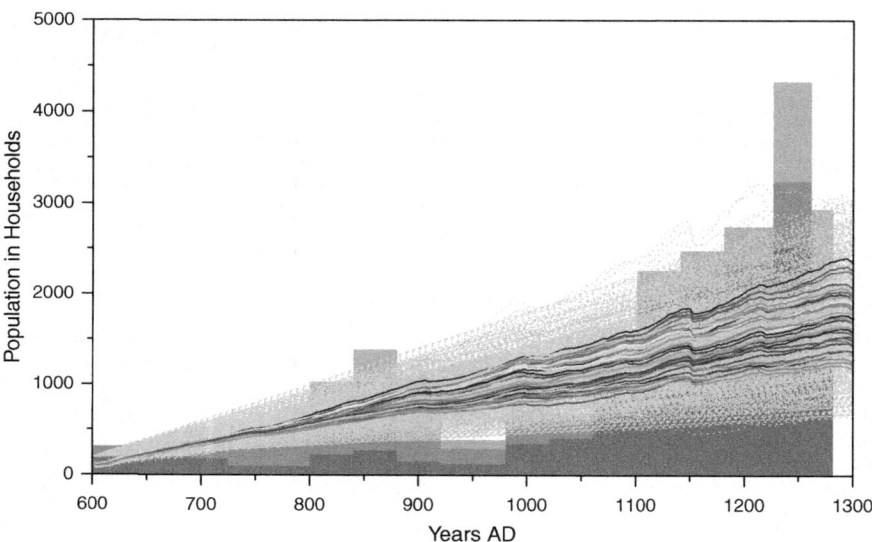

FIGURE 5.4 Central tendencies for simulated human population through time for each of 36 parameter combinations (in color), with each of the 540 unique runs plotted in grey over blocky histograms representing the empirical population estimates for the simulation area (from Varien et al., 2007). Schwindt et al. (2016) created newer population estimates, but for a larger region, so the older population estimates are retained here.

markedly affect total population size; both the smallest and largest total populations were produced when group-size threshold for fission was set to 50 (Figures 5.4 and 5.5).

To further illustrate the global dynamics, we graph results in Figure 5.5 for two contrasting parameter sets: Run 1 and replicates (maximum simple group size=50; s=.02, β=.1, μ=.1), and Run 35 and replicates (group size=100; s=.05, β=.9, μ=.5). Initially, Run 35 generates larger average group territories (Figure 5.5a), perhaps because its higher taxation rates fuel expansion, but eventually its higher fatality rates from warfare (and perhaps, too, the toll of higher taxation; Figure 5.5b) suppress both population (Figure 5.5c) and average group territory size (Figure 5.5a). In both parameter sets, warfare is relatively rare in the first two centuries (Figure 5.5b), since groups have room to grow without confronting others. Under Run 1 parameters, warfare (and its fatalities) more or less stabilize in the ninth century, whereas under Run 35 parameters, warfare and fatalities increase through the 1000s, after which they vary around fairly high values. Periods of poor production (e.g., around 900, 1000, and in the mid-1100s) tend to decrease deaths from warfare in both parameter sets, presumably because groups are not growing and therefore come into competition less frequently. Somewhat counterintuitively, periods of poor production that

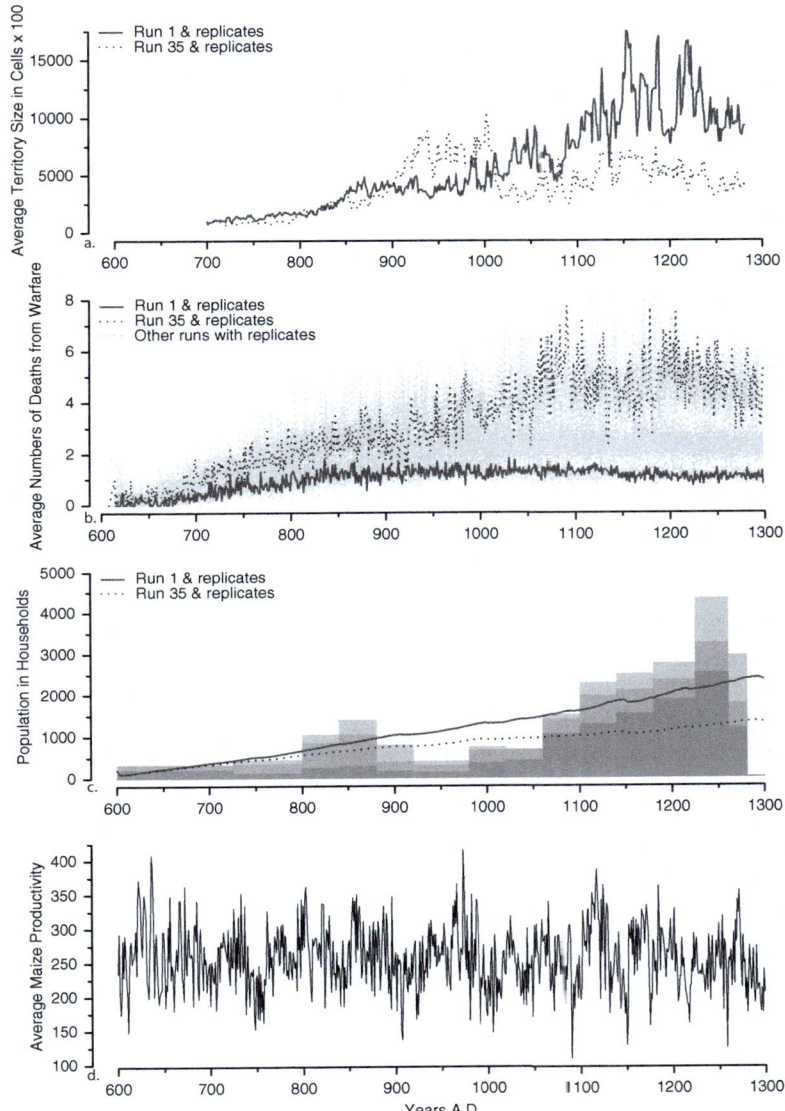

FIGURE 5.5 Panel 5.5a: Average territory sizes through time for the largest groups of which each simple group is a member, for Run 1 and replicates, and Run 35 and replicates. 5.5b: annual deaths from warfare. Grey lines indicate means for all runs with replicates; Run 1 and replicates and Run 35 and replicates are shown in black. 5.5c: average number of households through time for Run 1 and replicates, and Run 35 and replicates, shown over blocky histograms representing the empirical population estimate for the simulation area. 5.5d: average annual potential maize productivity for the simulation area.

are relatively short (Figure 4.5d) also tend to increase territory sizes (or set the stage for its increase immediately upon recovery). This appears to be the joint result of revolts being less common or less likely to be successful, and mergers being more common. In short, changes in productivity can destabilize polities for several different reasons, especially since productivity changes may not be completely simultaneous or of the same magnitude in nearby locations.

To illustrate how revolt affects the composition of groups we display the (aspatial) composition of the complex groups present in four periods in Run 1 (Supplemental Figure 5). Between AD 1020 and AD 1060, for example, the remnants of a revolt can be seen in the polity that is led by group 79. At the tail of this complex group, group 224 is subordinate to group 74. In AD 1020 group 74 is subordinate to group 248, yet group 74 revolts multiple times, each time then becoming subordinate to different dominants.

Since the dynamics of complex groups depend on total agent population, the next set of analyses concentrates on Run 1 and its replicates, which best fit the empirical populations. We calculated the territory size for each group at its highest organizational level in the last year in each of the 14 periods used to calculate empirical populations. That would be the simple group size for groups not subsumed in a complex group, otherwise we summed the territory sizes of each of the simple groups within each complex group. With the tools used for the kiva and settlement sizes we can then determine whether group territories through time correspond more closely to power-law or log-normal distributions. This is especially valuable because we understand the nature of the processes driving complex group size in the simulation, which includes an important role for dynamics of the "biggest-get-bigger" sort (Supplemental Figures 4.6 and 4.7).

Simulated territory sizes are log-normally distributed until the 980–1020 period (Table 5.4). At that point they begin to correspond to a power-law distribution, with some variability at the test-statistic level until strongly returning to a log-normal distribution in the final 1260–1280 period. This is precisely what we would expect if the power-law distributions are generated by the advantages in competition that larger groups come to have in the context of relative scarcity of agricultural land as populations grow (Table 5.4).

Discussion

We proposed that log-normal distributions may result from many different processes whose effects are roughly proportional to the size of entities in the previous time step. For log-normal distributions there is no signal that size itself is disproportionately advantaging further growth. Distributions corresponding to power laws, on the other hand, typically result from processes in which the largest entities in the previous time step are the most likely to grow even larger, as we might expect when power disparities or other advantages to size exist.

TABLE 5.4 Summary of conformity of simulation territory-size distributions to power-law expectations, evaluated in the last year of each of the empirically derived periods. "Power-law probabilities" between 0.1 and 1 indicate inability to reject the hypothesis that the data could have been generated by a power law. "Compare distributions" values of 0.6 to 1 indicate a power-law; values from 0 to 0.4 indicate a log-normal distribution; intermediate values are ambiguous. Positive values for the "Test statistic" indicate power laws; negative values indicate log-normal distributions

Year	Alpha	Power law stat	Compare distributions	Test statistic
725	1.291	0	0.042	−1.728
800	1.207	0.01	0.121	−1.169
840	1.202	0	0.164	−0.978
880	1.188	0	0.010	−2.343
920	1.178	0	0.010	−2.315
980	1.176	0	0.089	−1.346
1020	1.202	0.83	0.614	0.290
1060	1.181	0.19	0.570	0.177
1100	1.183	0.93	0.556	0.141
1140	1.182	0.23	0.427	−0.185
1180	1.193	0.81	0.613	0.288
1225	1.203	0.44	0.420	−0.203
1260	1.181	0.3	0.428	−0.182
1280	1.191	0	0.037	−1.781

In Table 5.5 we summarize the outcomes of the analyses from Tables 5.1–5.3 by classifying these as corresponding to a power law, corresponding weakly to a power law, corresponding to a log-normal distribution, or, finally, of ambiguous status. To be characterized as corresponding to a power law, a distribution must exhibit a power-law statistic of greater than 0.2, a compare distribution statistic of greater than 0.6, and a test statistic of greater than 0.5. If a distribution is characterized as weakly corresponding to a power law, its power-law statistic is above 0.1, its compare distribution statistic is between 0.4 and 0.6, and the test statistic is between 0 and −0.1. For a distribution to be characterized as log-normal, it must have a power-law statistic below 0.2, a compare distribution statistic of 0.4 or less, and a test statistic less than −0.5. Distributions classified as ambiguous may have a weak power-law statistic with the other statistics indicating a power-law, or a strong power-law statistic while the other statistics strongly indicate log-normality (Table 5.5).

In our view, the general convergence of empirical distributions of kiva and settlement sizes on power laws during PII times strongly suggests a consolidation of power into one or more multi-village hierarchies. The fact that the territory-size distributions generated by the simulation are similar further suggests

TABLE 5.5 Summary of analysis results for empirical and simulated distributions

Years AD	NSJ Kiva sizes (empirical)	MSJ Kiva sizes (empirical)	CCP Kiva sizes (empirical)	VEPIIN settlement sizes (empirical)	VEPI territory sizes (simulated)
600–725				Power-law	Log-normal
725–800				Power-law	Log-normal
800–840				Power-law	Log-normal
840–880				Power-law	Log-normal
880–920				Power-law	Log-normal
920–980	Weak power-law	Weak power-law	Power-law	Power-law	Log-normal
980–1020	Weak power-law	Weak power-law		Power-law	Power-law
1020–1060				Ambiguous	Power-law
1060–1100				Ambiguous	Power-law
1100–1140				Power-law	Weak power-law
1140–1180	Weak power-law	Weak power-law	Power-law	Power-law	Power-law
1180–1225	Weak power-law	Weak power-law		Ambiguous	Weak power-law
1225–1260				Weak power-law	Weak power-law
1260–1280				Power-law	Log-normal

that the processes we model—in which larger settlements and larger groups are advantaged by receiving flows of tribute, and by their ability to prevail in conflicts and subsume smaller groups—were also active in the prehispanic social settings of interest. The power-law signal in all three data streams is substantially weaker during the PIII period, which we take to suggest less highly structured organizations, with more power devolving to local centers. These themes are explored more in the following section.

Pueblo II Consolidation of Power

The primacy of Casa Rinconada in our studies, as well as the results of distributional analyses pointing unambiguously to power-law structure for the Chaco core and periphery, support the (non-controversial) notion of the CCP, and Chaco Canyon in particular, as a central place for ritual for the greater Southwest in the PII period. If our scaling logic is approximately correct, Casa Rinconada could have accommodated one or two representatives of each great kiva community in the far-flung population of outliers.

When we look to settlement sizes in the VEPIIN study area (resolved at a finer temporal scale than the Pecos periods to which the kivas are assigned) we see evidence of both power-laws, and ambiguous probabilities. One of the ambiguous periods, from 1060–1100, is precisely at the point when the Chaco great house pattern is first superimposed on the central Mesa Verde (Lipe, 2006). Our settlement data suggest that Chacoan influences, whatever their nature, had not completed their structuring work in the central Mesa Verde (VEPIIN) region until the 1100–1140 period, and continued to prevail through 1180 even if new great houses were not being built.

After producing log-normal territory distributions from 600 through 980, simulated territory-size distributions turn solidly toward power laws from 980 through 1100, after which they alternately exhibit power laws or weak power laws until 1260. Figure 5.5, top panel, illustrates a slow increase in the average territory size of groups—for Run 1 and replicates at least—through the 1000s and 1100s, until almost 1200. Since simple group size in these runs is capped at 50, this growth is through the process of chaining ever more simple groups into ever fewer large complex groups. This process is ultimately driven by generally high productivity during these times fueling population growth, expansion of complex groups through addition to their territories via warfare and merging, and successful resistance of revolt.

Although the processes in the simulation are complex, they are understandable, and the key to the appearance of power-law distributions in their territory sizes is that (all other things equal) large groups have an advantage over small because they can conquer or subsume them. Growth happens for those that are already large, within limits set by the productivity of dry-farming maize (explicit and endogenous in the simulation) and transport costs for people and materials (partially represented in the simulation). Within complex groups, simple groups pay tribute to their dominant groups, with tribute passing through to the highest dominant group in the hierarchy.

Analogies between the processes in the simulation and those in the archaeological record should be sought at a fairly high level of generality. In the real world, a growing polity might not have to come to blows with each of its neighbors, or threaten to do so, to expand its influence and power. Flows of tribute in maize in the simulation might, in the reference societies, materialize as contributions to centralized feasts. Mounting evidence shows that Chacoan great houses hosted feasting events that brought visitors carrying food and ceramics from elsewhere (Cameron, 2009; Harris, 2014; Windes, 1987). Often "potluck" in nature, such feasts could be seen as a type of tribute to the ritual power of central places (Mahoney and Kantner, 2000:10) do explicitly argue for tribute flow within the Chacoan system). Such "doings" (Fowles, 2013) reinforced the hierarchies materialized in the fabric of great houses and great kivas, much as "memory of [their] social construction probably provide[d] one of the most important elements of personal identity to groups" (Earle, 2001: 27).

It has long been understood, too, that the construction of Chaco's great houses would have required flows of labor from outside the canyon; that a highly significant proportion of the ceramic vessels and lithic raw materials used at Chaco came from the Chuska area (Cameron, 1997; Toll, 1991); that those great houses were built mostly from non-local timbers (Reynolds et al., 2005); and that in fact much maize probably *did* flow into Chaco Canyon from its periphery (e.g., Benson, 2010). Those uncomfortable with the idea of tribute can mentally substitute such flows whenever we use the more general term! Of course, what appears as a strictly political process in the simulation would likely be of inextricably mixed social, ceremonial, and political valence in this society (Earle, 2001: 27; Fowles, 2013; Heitman, 2015). From initial advantages to virtual simple groups controlling lands allowing them to grow more rapidly than their neighbors, who they came to dominate, to the long chains of dependencies grown in the simulation, in Pueblo society ritual and ceremony provided both a rationale for the wielding of power and an important means for wielding that power.

Pueblo III Reorganization and Depopulation

The characterization of group sizes in kivas does not change markedly between the PII and PIII periods except for the disappearance of the mid-sized court kiva in the CCP (they were never common in the other two areas), though the largest kivas decrease in size and number and the sample size of all kivas decreases everywhere, but particularly in the CCP (Supplemental Table 1). During PII times in the Chaco core/periphery, the largest kiva, Casa Rinconada, might accommodate some 130 people, while during PIII the largest kiva, the Chacra great kiva, likely accommodated 70-some participants. Aside from Chacra, CCP PIII kivas are quite small, with modes around 12 and 25 people. Both the decrease in kiva number and size support the dissolution of Chaco as the preeminent center.

In the NSJ, while great kivas continue to be used throughout PIII, the increase in smaller kivas (Figure 5.2b) may suggest a reorganization of ritual. This, coupled with the increase of plazas and multi-walled structures as central places, may indicate a switch from global (Chacoan) ritual to more local ritual serving single communities or relatively small groups of communities. Our settlement data suggests, though, that this restructuring took place mostly after 1180. Perhaps the hierarchy that persists after that date is less pan-regional or regional, and more local in nature: multiple competing groups rather than one large and connected complex. The proliferation of towers among the VEPIIN settlements after 1140 and of multi-walled structures after 1225 may suggest development of leaders extracting tribute at fairly local levels to build these walls and towers (of course, their construction could have been the tribute). In support of this idea, the complex groups in the simulation react to the generally low productivity in the 13th century with decreases in size (Figure 5.5a).

During the final two decades of occupation the settlement-size distribution again becomes a power law after 80 years of somewhat ambiguous structure.

Perhaps this should be regarded as revealing a structural backbone that remained after the departure of those not in settlements, organized in terms of the hierarchy that the last-to-leave settlements represented.

Our results show that interpretations of Ancestral Pueblo people as being egalitarian or hierarchical depends on when we look, and also on where we look. If we define our scale of inquiry to encompass all kivas, and not just (say) household kivas, coincident with the rise of Chaco we see increasing numbers of large kivas capable of enticing many individuals into integrative rituals. The largest great kiva, Casa Rinconada at Chaco Canyon, of a type completely different from the household kivas, stood at the apex of a polity with Chaco at its core. Similarly, the largest settlements in the PII period attracted people from smaller settlements through the processes required by staple finance (Earle, 2001) organized by ritual practice, but—we suggest—ultimately backed by threat of force.

The simulation takes the puzzling archaeological record for Chaco and the system it organized and exposes candidate mechanisms for producing this structure. Individual households interact with their local landscapes and with other local households, forming groups that cooperate more or less successfully through public goods games and protect their territories as best they can; those that are fortunate enough to land on the most productive soils reproduce the best. Particular lineages perpetuate themselves and as they grow may gain additional power by encompassing other such groups in large polities. The settlement-size scaling locates settlements within their regional and temporal context; kiva scaling examines how households and communities may have interacted in a ritual hierarchy; and the version of the Village simulation exercised here demonstrates how the emergence of local leadership facilitating cooperation for defense of arable land and producing other public goods, and structured tribute flow from subordinate to paramount groups, can stimulate and perpetuate hierarchical relationships resembling those reconstructed for the Chaco system.

One main reason that the archaeological record of Chaco is puzzling—clearly recognized by Earle (2001)—is that Chaco looks like a staple-financed organization, but the usual conditions for staple finance include a highly concentrated productive environment surrounded by unproductive areas, such as an irrigated river valley in a desert, causing circumscription. In such systems the costs of forcing households to contribute to a polity are very low, given their extremely limited outside options. The more extensive dry-farming that dominated maize production in the "dry-farming millennium" from AD 300–1300 (Kohler, 1993) is not so obviously conducive to controlling households and their communities.

But the places where dry farming could be successful on the Colorado Plateau in the years represented by the Chaco system were in fact rather limited (Bocinsky et al., 2016: Fig. 6D–F). More importantly, those areas were full—or at least that is a plausible inference based on the Southwest-wide sensitivity of life expectancies and birth rates to climatic fluctuations beginning around AD

1000 (Kohler and Reese, 2014). (Earlier, a less-packed maize-growing niche allowed households to escape climate-driven downturns in maize production through mobility, largely shielding their demographic rates from this variability.) Populations, through growth, circumscribed *themselves*, and it remained only for a polity to point this out, guaranteeing in the process that member groups need fear nothing from their neighbors in return for supporting the polity. This, however, is a fragile basis for coercion, as it depends on both the credibility of a ritual system claiming to underwrite production and the center's ability to support threatened member groups through manipulation of a complex set of debts, allegiances, force, and threats of force. It is perhaps more marvelous that it was able to endure for four to five generations, from about AD 1030–1140 in its fullest expression, than that it didn't last longer.

Conclusions

For some time southwestern archaeologists have been aware that hierarchies of site size, great house size, and kiva size are visible for significant spans of time in significant portions of the Pueblo world. We likewise understand that these must imply some hierarchical organization of practices connected with these structures. More recently, we have learned that variability in community center size (in the central Mesa Verde region at least) is only weakly connected with the potential maize productivity of their catchments, inviting other, complementary explanations for this variability.

What we add here is, first of all, some tools drawn from the analysis of complex adaptive systems that allow size distributions to be characterized in ways that suggest their generating processes. We acknowledge that these tools do not, for our data, always render clear and concise verdicts, but they have provided useful hints as to the directions in which we should look for the generating processes.

Second, we have briefly described and exercised a model that implements a set of processes widely considered to be universal (e.g., Johnson and Earle, 2000)—population growth, competition, and polity growth through conflict or threat of conflict generating flows of tribute of various sorts to dominant groups—that demonstrate one pathway by which size can generate further growth, within limits ultimately imposed by production, transportation, and communication technologies.

Although we coded it to help us understand how polities might grow, the simulation also provides several potential insights into the perennial problem of why poor production might imperil polities. At the basal level, simple groups shrinking in size might flip from hierarchical to non-hierarchical (see Kohler et al. (2017) in review). This, in turn, might reduce (and perhaps destroy) their returns to the public goods game, decreasing or eliminating the flow of tribute upwards in the social hierarchy. Intermediate groups who had been profiting from tribute might shrink too and perhaps flip in structure. As these processes worked their way up the chain, we can predict that successful revolts would become more common than new acquisitions to complex groups, and even absent successful revolt, complex groups could essentially crumble from below. Moreover, smaller remaining polities would be more vulnerable to attack, given fewer subordinate groups. The potential generality of such processes is illustrated by their similarity to the scenario envisaged for the late Bronze Age Argolid collapse by Maran (2009:255–256).

Our results reinforce the likelihood that one or more organizations (called polities here for convenience) existed in PII times and connected village-level communities into regional and (likely) pan-regional networks linked via flows of goods and labor. These results unsurprisingly point to Chaco Canyon as the place of pre-eminence and indirectly reinforce the notion that the decline of its hegemony was connected to conditions for maize farming that were likely markedly poorer in the San Juan Basin in the mid-1100s than in the northern San Juan, where regional systems endured into the FIII period, by which time they would have been influenced by Chaco's remembered example but not controlled by its leaders.

Our analyses also suggest a central role for great kivas (particularly during the PII period) as mechanisms to help reinforce hierarchy. As not every Puebloan could be accommodated for great kiva events, only those so empowered by their groups would attend. Such restricted access—with concomitant benefits for accumulating restricted knowledge—would have helped maintain the local and global hierarchies much as, among contemporary Pueblos, hierarchy is evident in differences between the "ceremonially rich" and the "ceremonially poor" (Ware, 2014: 41). It appears that representatives of all existing great houses in Chaco Canyon and in "outlier" communities with great kivas could have been (and we suggest were) accommodated in the largest of them all, at Casa Rinconada.

Acknowledgements

This chapter utilizes extensions to the "Village" ABM, originally developed with support from the National Science Foundation (BCS-0119981, DEB-0816400), which also generated and organized the empirical data on site sizes we use here. We thank the Templeton Foundation for funding part of this research. Our numerous colleagues in the Village Ecodynamics Project, as always, have provided much assistance and inspiration. Aaron Clauset, Matt Grove, Marcus Hamilton, Paul Reed, Ruth Van Dyke, and Tom Windes also provided useful advice. Crabtree acknowledges support by NSF Graduate Research Fellowship DGE-080667, an NSF GROW fellowship and a Chateaubriand Fellowship. This chapter is dedicated to the memory of Robert P. Powers, not just a fine friend but also, among many other achievements, the researcher providing the first useful estimates for Chaco Great House sizes across a broad portion of the Pueblo area.

Notes

1 700–890; all dates are A.D./C.E.; Pecos Classification dates from Bocinsky et al., 2016.
2 Ortman (2016: Figure 5.6) demonstrates that in the central Mesa Verde area, increasing site area scales against site population in a sublinear fashion, so that larger sites are more dense—a finding that suggests to us that defense was perhaps on average more important in site population growth than provision of areas for large-scale ritual involving populations of other ceremonial centers. The converse is true in the Tewa Basin of the northern Rio Grande in the 15th and 16th centuries: plaza area increases more rapidly than site population as site populations increase. In accordance with this interpretation, levels of interpersonal violence were also notably lower at that time in the northern Rio Grande than in the PII–PIII central Mesa Verde (Kohler et al., 2014).
3 Our identification of modes is visual, not rigorous. Zhou et al. (2005) illustrate a quantitative approach employing spectral analysis.
4 See http://www.chacoarchive.org/cra/outlier-database.
5 The version of the Village code reported here is archived and under active development on GitHub: https://github.com/crowcanyon/vep_sim_beyondhooperville.
6 Available as a Working Paper at https://www.santafe.edu/research/results/working-papers/sociopolitical-evolution-in-midrange-societies-the.
7 Although these limits may seem small, recent research suggests that average community size on Mesa Verde in any period never exceeded 26 momentary households, with the largest community, forming in the 1260–1280 period, estimated at 76 households (Reese, 2014).

Works Cited

Adler, Michael A. and Richard H. Wilshusen. 1990. Large-scale Integrative Facilities in Tribal Societies: Cross-cultural and Southwestern U.S. Examples. *World Archaeology* 22:133–146.

Aitchison, J. and J. A. C. Brown. 1957. *The Lognormal Distribution with Special Reference to its Uses in Economics*. University of Cambridge Department of Applied Economics Monograph 5.

Albert, R., H. Jeong, and A.-L. Barabási. 1999. Internet: Diameter of the World-Wide Web. *Nature* 401:130–131. doi:10.1038/43601

Alberti, Gianmarco. 2014. Modeling Group Size and Scalar Stress by Logistic Regression from an Archaeological Perspective. *PLoS ONE* 9(3): e91510. doi:10.1371/Journal.pone.0091510

Auerbach, F. 1913. Das Gesetz der Bevolkerungskonzentration. *Petermans Geographische Mitteilungen* LIV: 73–75.

Benson, Larry V. 2010. Who Provided Maize to Chaco Canyon After the Mid-12th-century Drought? *Journal of Archaeological Science* 37:621–629.

Bernardini, Wesley. 1996. Transitions in Social Organization: A Predictive Model from Southwestern Archaeology. *Journal of Anthropological Archaeology* 15:372–402.

Bettencourt, Luís M. A. 2013. The Origins of Scaling in Cities. *Science* 340:1438–1441.

Bettencourt, Luis M. A., Jose Lobo, Dirk Helbing, Christian Kühnert, Geoffrey B. West. 2007. Growth, Innovation, Scaling, and the Pace of Life in Cities. *PNAS* 104:7301–7306.

Bocinsky, R. Kyle, Johnathan Rush, Keith W. Kintigh, and Timothy A. Kohler. 2016. Exploration and Exploitation in the Macrohistory of the Pre-Hispanic Pueblo Southwest. *Science Advances* 2: e1501532.

Bowles, Sam. 2009. Did Warfare Among Ancestral Hunter-Gatherers Affect the Evolution of Human Social Behaviors? *Science* 324:1293–1298.
Brown, Clifford T., April A. Watson, Ashley Gravlin-Berman, and Larry S. Liebovitch. 2012. Poor Mayapan. In *The Ancient Maya of Mexico: Reinterpreting the Past of the Northern Maya Lowlands*, edited by Geoffrey E. Braswell, pp. 306–324. Equinox Publishing Ltd, Bristol CT.
Cameron, Cathy. 1997. The Chipped Stone of Chaco Canyon, New Mexico. In *Ceramics, Lithics, and Ornaments of Chaco Canyon*, edited by F. Mathien, pp. 531–658. Publications in Archaeology 18G. Chaco Canyon Studies, National Park Service, Santa Fe.
Cameron, Cathy. 2009. *Chaco and After in the Northern San Juan*. University of Arizona Press, Tucson.
Cederman, Lars-Erik. 2002. Endogenizing Geopolitical Boundaries with Agent-based Modeling. *PNAS* 99:7296–7303.
Cegielski, Wendy H., and J. Daniel Rogers. 2016. Rethinking the Role of Agent-Based Modeling in Archaeology. *Journal of Anthropological Archaeology* 41:283–298
Clauset, Aaron, Cosma Rohilla Shalizi, and M. E. J. Newman. 2009. Power-Law Distributions in Empirical Data. *SIAM Review* 51(4):661–703.
Coffey, Grant. 2014. The Harlan Great Kiva Site: Civic Architecture and Community Persistence in the Goodman Point area of Southwestern Colorado. *Kiva* 79:380–404.
Coffey, Grant. 2016. Creating Symmetry: The Cultural Landscape in the Sand Canyon Locality, Southwestern Colorado. *Kiva* 82:1–21.
Coltrain, Joan Brenner, Joel C. Janetski and Shawn W. Carlyle. 2006. The Stable and Radio-Isotope Chemistry of Eastern Basketmaker and Pueblo Groups in the Four Corners Region of the American Southwest: Implications for Anasazi Diets, Origins, and Abandonments in Southwestern Colorado. In *Histories of Maize: Multidisciplinary Approaches to the Prehistory, Linguistics, Biogeography, Domestication, and Evolution of Maize*, edited by John E. Staller, Robert H. Tykot and Bruce F. Benz, pp. 276–289. Elsevier.
Cordell, Linda S., and Fred Plog. 1979. Escaping the Confines of Normative Thought: A Reevaluation of Puebloan Prehistory. *American Antiquity* 44:405–429.
Coward, Fiona, and R. I. M. Dunbar. 2014. Communities on the Edge of Civilization. In *Lucy to Language: The Benchmark Papers*, edited by R. I. M. Dunbar, Clive Gamble, and J. A. J. Gowlett, pp. 380–405. Oxford University Press, Oxford.
Dubreuil, Benoît. 2010. *Human Evolution and the Origins of Hierarchies: The State of Nature*. Cambridge University Press, Cambridge.
Duffy, Paul R. 2015. Site Size Hierarchy in Middle-range Societies. *Journal of Anthropological Archaeology* 37:85–99.
Earle, Timothy. 2001. Economic Support of Chaco Canyon Society. *American Antiquity* 66:26–35.
Feinman, Gary M., Kent G. Lightfoot, and Steadman Upham. 2000. Political Hierarchies and Organizational Strategies in the Puebloan Southwest. *American Antiquity* 65:449–470.
Fowles, Severin M. 2013. *An Archaeology of Doings: Secularism and the Study of Pueblo Religion*. SAR Press, Santa Fe.
Gillespie, Colin S. 2015. Fitting Heavy Tailed Distributions: The powerRlaw Package. *Journal of Statistical Software* 64:1–16.
Glowacki, Donna M. 2015. *Living and Leaving: A Social History of Regional Depopulation in Thirteenth-Century Mesa Verde*. The University of Arizona Press, Tucson
Glowacki, Donna M., and Scott G. Ortman. 2012. Characterizing Community-Center (Village) Formation in the VEP Study Area, A.D. 600–1280. In *Emergence and Collapse of Early Villages: Models of Central Mesa Verde Archaeology*, edited by Timothy A. Kohler and Mark D. Varien, pp. 219–246. University of California Press, Berkeley.

Goffman, Erving. 1959. *The Presentation of Self in Everyday Life*. Doubleday Anchor. Garden City, NJ.

Griffin, Arthur F., and Charles Stanish. 2007. An Agent-based Model of Prehistoric Settlement Patterns and Political Consolidation in the Lake Titicaca Basin of Peru and Bolivia. *Structure and Dynamics: eJournal of Anthropological and Related Sciences* 2:2. http://escholarship.org/uc/item/2zd1t887

Grove, Matt. 2011. An Archaeological Signature of Multi-level Social Systems: The Case of the Irish Bronze Age. *Journal of Anthropological Archaeology* 30:44–61. doi:10.1016/j.jaa.2010.12.002

Gruner, Erina. 2015. Replicating Things, Replicating Identity: The Movement of Chacoan Ritual Paraphernalia Beyond the Chaco World. In *Practicing Materiality*, edited by Ruth M. Van Dyke, pp. 56–78. University of Arizona Press, Tucson.

Haas, W. Randall Jr., Cynthia J. Klink, Greg J. Maggard, and Mark S. Aldenderfer. 2015. Settlement-Size Scaling among Prehistoric Hunter-Gatherer Settlement Systems in the New World. *PLoS One* 10(11): e0140127. doi:10.1371/journal.pone.0140127

Hamilton, Marcus J., B.T. Milne, R.S. Walker, Oskar Burger, and J.H. Brown. 2007. The Complex Structure of Hunter-gatherer Social Networks. *Proceedings of the Royal Society B: Biological Sciences* 274:2195–2202.

Harris, Rachel M. 2014. *Comparative Analysis of Ceramics from Three Great Houses and One Small House Site in Southeastern Utah*. Unpublished master's thesis, Department of Antropology, Brigham Young University, Provo, UT.

Heitman, Carrie C. 2015. The House of Our Ancestors: New Research on the Prehistory of Chaco Canyon, New Mexico, A.D. 800–1200. In *Chaco Revisited: New Research on the Prehistory of Chaco Canyon, New Mexico*, edited by Carrie C. Heitman and Stephen Plog, pp. 215–248. University of Arizona Press, Tucson.

Horton, Robert E. 1945. Erosional Development of Streams and their Drainage Basins: Hydro-physical Approach to Quantitative Morphology. *Geological Society of America Bulletin* 56:275–370.

Inomata, Takeshi, and Lawrence S. Coben. 2006. *Archaeology of Performance: Theaters of Power, Community, and Politics*. Alta Mira Press, New York.

Johnson, Allen W., and Timothy K. Earle. 2000. *The Evolution of Human Societies: From Foraging Group to Agrarian State*. Stanford University Press, Stanford.

Johnson, Gregory A. 1982. Organizational Structure and Scalar Stress. In *Theory and Explanation in Archaeology*, edited by C. Renfrew, M.J. Rowlands, and B.A. Segraves, pp. 389–421. Academic Press, New York.

Johnson, Gregory A. 1989. Dynamics of Southwestern Prehistory: Far Outside—Looking In. In *Dynamics of Southwest Prehistory*, edited by Linda S. Cordell and George J. Gumerman, pp. 371–389. Smithsonian Institution Press, Washington, DC.

Judge, W. James. 1989. Chaco Canyon—San Juan Basin. In *Dynamics of Southwest Prehistory*, edited by Linda S. Cordell and George J. Gumerman, pp. 209–261. Smithsonian Institution Press, Washington, D.C.

Kantner, J. 2003. Rethinking Chaco as a System. *Kiva* 69:207–227.

Kantner, J. and R. Hobgood. 2003. Digital Technologies and Prehistoric Landscapes in the American Southwest. In *The Reconstruction of Archaeological Landscapes through Digital Technologies*, edited by M. Forte and P. R. Williams, pp. 117–124. Archaeopress, Oxford, England.

Kohler, Timothy A. 1993. News from the Northern American Southwest: Prehistory on the Edge of Chaos. *Journal of Archaeological Research* 1:267–321.

Kohler, Timothy A. 2012. Modeling Agricultural Productivity and Farming Effort. In *Emergence and Collapse of Early Villages: Models of Central Mesa Verde Archaeology*, edited by T. A. Kohler and M. D. Varien, pp. 85–111. University of California Press, Berkeley.

Kohler, Timothy A., Denton Cockburn, Paul Hooper, R. Kyle Bocinsky, and Ziad Kobti. 2012. The Coevolution of Group Size and Leadership: An Agent-based Public Goods Model for Prehispanic Pueblo Societies. *Advances in Complex Systems* 15:29.

Kohler, Timothy A., Stefani A. Crabtree, R. Kyle Bocinsky and Paul Hooper. 2017. In review. Developing General Methods for Explaining Sociopolitical Evolution in Prehispanic Pueblo Societies. In *The Principles of Complexity*, edited by Jeremy Sabloff et al. Princeton University Press. https://www.santafe.edu/research/results/working-papers/sociopolitical-evolution-in-midrange-societies-the

Kohler, Timothy A., and Rebecca Higgins. 2016. Quantifying Household Inequality in Early Pueblo Villages. *Current Anthropology* 57(5) doi: 10.1086/687982

Kohler, Timothy A., Scott G. Ortman, Katie E. Grundtisch, Carly M. Fitzpatrick and Sarah M. Cole. 2014. The Better Angels of Their Nature: Declining Violence through Time Among Prehispanic Farmers of the Pueblo Southwest. *American Antiquity* 79:444–464.

Kohler, Timothy A., and Kelsey M. Reese. 2014. Long and Spatially Variable Neolithic Demographic Transition in the North American Southwest. *PNAS* 111:10101–10106.

Kohler, Timothy A., and Mark D. Varien. 2010. A Scale Model of Seven Hundred Years of Farming Settlements in Southwestern Colorado. In *Becoming Villagers: Comparing Early Village Societies*, edited by M. Bandy and J. Fox, pp. 37–61. Amerind Foundation and the University of Arizona Press, Tucson.

Kohler, Timothy A., and Mark D. Varien (Eds.). 2012. *Emergence and Collapse of Early Villages: Models of Central Mesa Verde Archaeology*. University of California Press, Berkeley and Los Angeles, CA.

Kosse, Krisztina. 1994. The Evolution of Large, Complex Groups: A Hypothesis. *Journal of Anthropological Archaeology* 13: 35–50.

Kosse, Krisztina. 2000. Some Regularities in Human Group Formation and the Evolution of Societal Complexity. *Complexity* 6(1): 60–64.

Lehman, Julia, Phyllis Lee, and R. I. M. Dunbar. 2014. Unravelling the Function of Community-level Organization. In *Lucy to Language: The Benchmark Papers*, edited by R. I. M. Dunbar, Clive Gamble, and J. A. J. Gowlett, pp. 245–276. Oxford University Press, Oxford.

Lekson, Stephen H. 1990. Cross-Cultural Perspectives on the Community. In *On Vernacular Architecture: Paradigms and Environmental Response*, edited by Mete Turan, pp. 122–145. Avebury, Aldershot.

Lekson, Stephen H. (Ed.). 2006a. *The Archaeology of Chaco Canyon, an Eleventh-Century Pueblo Regional Center*. SAR Press, Santa Fe.

Lekson, Stephen H. 2006b. Chaco Matters: An Introduction. In *The Archaeology of Chaco Canyon, an Eleventh-Century Pueblo Regional Center*, edited by S. H. Lekson, pp. 3–44. SAR Press, Santa Fe.

Lekson, Stephen H. 2015. *The Chaco Meridian: One Thousand Years of Political and Religious Power in the Ancient Southwest*. 2nd edition. Rowman & Littlefield, Lanham, Maryland.

Lekson, Stephen H., William B. Gillespie, Thomas C. Windes. 1984. *Great Pueblo Architecture of Chaco Canyon, New Mexico*. Publications in Archaeology, Chaco Canyon Studies, 18B. Albuquerque, NM.

Lightfoot, Kent G. and Gary M. Feinman. 1982. Social Differentiation and Leadership Development in Early Pithouse Villages in the Mogollon Region of the American Southwest. *American Antiquity* 47:64–86.

Lipe, William D. 2002. Social Power in the Central Mesa Verde Region, A.D. 1150–1290. In *Seeking the Center Place: Archaeology and Ancient Communities in the Central Mesa Verde Region*, edited by Mark D. Varien and Richard H. Wilshusen, pp. 203–232. University of Utah Press, Salt Lake City.

Lipe, William D. 2006. Notes from the North. In *The Archaeology of Chaco Canyon: An Eleventh-century Pueblo Regional Center*, edited by Stephen K. Lekson, pp. 261–313. SAR Press, Santa Fe.

Lyman, Lee R. 2009. *Prehistory of the Oregon Coast: The Effects of Excavation Strategies and Assemblage Size on Archaeological Inquiry*. Left Coast Press, Walnut Creek.

Mahoney, Nancy M., and John Kantner. 2000. Chacoan Archaeology and Great House Communities. *Great House Communities Across the Chacoan Landscape*, edited by John Kantner and Nancy M. Mahoney, pp. 1–18. University of Arizona Press, Tucson.

Maran, J. 2009. The Crisis Years? Reflections on Signs of Instability in the Last Decades of the Mycenaean Palaces. *Scienze dell'antichità: Storia archeologia antropologia* 15:241–262.

Matson, R. G. 2016. The Nutritional Context of the Pueblo III Depopulation of the Northern San Juan: Too Much Maize? *Journal of Archaeological Science: Reports* 5:622–631.

McGregor, John C. 1943. Burial of an Early American Magician. *Proceedings of the American Philosophical Society* 82(2):270–298.

Mills, Barbara J. 2007. Performing the Feast: Visual Display and Suprahousehold Commensalism in the Puebloan Southwest. *American Antiquity* 72:210–239.

Mitzenmacher, Michael. 2004. A Brief History of Generative Models for Power Law and Log-normal Distributions. *Internet Mathematics* 2:226–251.

Morris, Earl H. 1924. Burials in the Aztec Ruin and the Aztec Ruin Annex. *Anthropological Papers of the American Museum of Natural History, Volume XXVI, Parts II and IV*. American Museum of Natural History, New York.

Ortman, Scott G. 2016. Discourse and Human Securities in Tewa Origins. In *Archaeology of the Human Experience*, edited by Michelle Hegmon, pp. 74–94. Archeological Papers of the American Anthropological Association, Number 27.

Pepper, George H. 1909. The Exploration of a Burial-Room in Pueblo Bonito, New Mexico. In *Putnam Anniversary Volume: Anthropological Essays Presented to Frederic Ward Putnam in Honor of His Seventieth Birthday, April 16, 1909, by His Friends and Associates*, pp. 196–252. G. E. Stechert & Co., New York.

Plog, Stephen. 1995. Equality and Hierarchy: Holistic Approaches to Understanding Social Dynamics in the Pueblo Southwest. In *Foundations of Social Inequality*, edited by T. Douglas Price and Gary M. Feinman, pp. 189–206. Plenum, New York.

Plog, Stephen and Carrie Heitman. 2010. Hierarchy and Social Inequality in the American Southwest, A.D. 800–1200. *PNAS* 107:19619–19626.

Powers, Robert P., William B. Gillespie, and Stephen H. Lekson. 1983. *The Outlier Survey: A Regional View of Settlement in the San Juan Basin*. Reports of the Chaco Center 3. NPS, USDI, Albuquerque.

Reese, Kelsey M. 2014. Over the Line: A Least-cost Analysis of "Community" in Mesa Verde National Park. Unpublished Master's thesis, Department of Anthropology, Washington State University, Pullman.

Reid, J. J., and S. M. Whittlesey. 1990. The Complicated and the Complex: Observations on the Archaeological Record of Large Pueblos. In *Perspectives on Southwestern Prehistory*, edited by P. E. Minnis and C. L. Redman, pp. 184–195. Westview Press, Boulder.

Reynolds, A.C., J. L. Betancourt, J. Quade, et al. 2005 ^{87}S/^{86}Sr Sourcing of Ponderosa Pine Used in Anasazi Great House Construction at Chaco Canyon, New Mexico. *Journal of Archaeological Science* 32:1061–1075.

Ryan, Susan C. 2013. Architectural Communities of Practice: Ancestral Pueblo Kiva Production During the Chaco and Post-Chaco Periods in the Northern Southwest. Unpublished Ph.D. dissertation, Department of Anthropology, University of Arizona, Tucson.

Ryan, Susan C. 2016. Integration and Disintegration: The Role of Kiva Production in Community Formation in the Prehispanic U.S. Southwest. In *Coming Together: Comparative Approaches to Population Aggregation and Early Urbanization*, edited by A. Gyucha. Institute for European and Mediterranean Archaeology, Buffalo (expected 2017).

Schwindt, Dylan M., R. Kyle Bocinsky, Scott G. Ortman, Donna M. Glowacki, Mark D. Varien, and Timothy A. Kohler. 2016. The Social Consequences of Climate Change in the Central Mesa Verde Region. *American Antiquity* 81:74–96.

Sebastian, Lynne. 1992. *The Chaco Anasazi: Sociopolitical evolution in the prehistoric Southwest*. Cambridge University Press, Cambridge.

Steponaitis, Vincas P. 1981. Settlement Hierarchies and Political Complexity in Nonmarket Societies: The Formative Period of the Valley of Mexico. *American Anthropologist* 83:320–363.

Toll, H. W. 1991. Material Distributions and Exchange in the Chaco System. In *Chaco and Hohokam: Prehistoric Regional Systems in the American Southwest*, edited by P. L. Crown and W. J. Judge, pp. 77–108. School of American Research Press, Santa Fe.

Turchin, Peter, and Sergey Gavrilets. 2009. The Evolution of Complex Hierarchical Societies. *Social Evolution & History* 8:167–198.

Van Dyke, R. M. 2007a. Great Kivas in Time, Space, and Society. In *The Architecture of Chaco Canyon, New Mexico*, edited by Stephen H. Lekson, pp. 93–126. University of Utah Press, Salt Lake City.

Van Dyke, R. M. 2007b. *The Chaco Experience: Landscape and Ideology at the Center Place*. SAR Press, Santa Fe.

Van Dyke, R. M., R. K. Bocinsky, T. Robinson, and T. C. Windes. 2016. Great Houses, Shrines, and High Places: Intervisibility in the Chacoan World. *American Antiquity* 81:205–230.

Varien, Mark D., Scott G. Ortman, Timothy A. Kohler, Donna M. Glowacki, and C. David Johnson. 2007. Historical Ecology in the Mesa Verde Region: Results from the Village Project. *American Antiquity* 72:273–299.

Vivian, Gordon, and Paul Reiter. 1965. *The Great Kivas of Chaco Canyon and Their Relationships*. Monograph 22, School of American Research. University of New Mexico Press, Albuquerque.

Ware, John. 2014. *A Pueblo Social History: Kinship, Sodality, and Community in the Northern Southwest*. SAR Press, Santa Fe.

Wilkinson, T. J., J. H. Christiansen, J. Ur, M. Widell, and M. Altweel. 2007. Urbanization within a Dynamic Environment: Modeling Bronze Age Communities in Upper Mesopotamia. *American Anthropologist* 109:52–68. doi: 10.1525/aa.2007.109.1.52

Windes, Thomas C. 1987. *Investigations at the Pueblo Alto Complex, Chaco Canyon, New Mexico, 1975–1979. Vol II*, Part 2. Publications in Archeology 18F, Chaco Canyon Studies. National Park Service, Santa Fe.

Windes, Thomas C. 2015. The Chacoan Court Kiva. *Kiva* 79:337–379.

Windes, Thomas C., and Eileen Bacha. 2008. Differential Wood Use at Salmon Ruin. In *Chaco's Northern Prodigies: Salmon, Aztec, and the Ascendancy of the Middle San Juan Region after A.D. 1100*, edited by Paul F. Reed, pp. 113–139. The University of Utah Press, Salt Lake City.

Zhou, W.-X., D. Sornette, R. A. Hill, and R. I. M. Dunbar. 2005. Discrete Hierarchical Organisation of Social Group Sizes. *Proceedings of the Royal Society, London* 272B:439–444.

6
NETWORK ANALYSIS AND FOOD WEBS CASE STUDY

As we explored in Chapter 4, network analysis is one of the foundational pillars drawn from complex adaptive systems science that has found particularly fertile ground in archaeological inquiry. In my own research, I deploy the tools of network science to examine both social and ecological networks—especially trophic networks, or food webs—to shed light on how people in the past were entangled within broader systems of interaction. These approaches allow us to move across scales, from the individual to the community to the ecosystem, revealing the structural dynamics that linked humans to their environments, and each other, across space and through time.

Among the more recent and revelatory applications of trophic network analysis is the explicit inclusion of humans within ecological food webs—not merely as consumers acting upon nature, but as embedded agents participating within it. This marks a fundamental shift in both archaeological and ecological thought. Whereas earlier paradigms often treated human subsistence strategies as linear or unidirectional—humans hunt, gather, domesticate, and thus reshape the world—contemporary network approaches reveal a more reciprocal, dynamic system. Human actions reverberate through food webs, influencing the abundance and behavior of species, but these ecological shifts, in turn, constrain or expand human choices.

For example, Maschner et al. (2009) demonstrated that selective culling of sea lions for kayak skins in Alaska likely kept predator populations low enough to reduce pressure on fisheries, thereby stabilizing the system (see also: Dunne et al., 2016). In contrast, Murphy and Romanuk (2014) analyzed how human disturbances—particularly those that are sudden or intense—can drastically reduce species richness and ecological resilience. These two studies, taken together, illustrate the dual role humans can play in ecosystems: either

DOI: 10.4324/9781003585251-7

cultivating biodiversity and equilibrium, or serving as a stressor that tips systems into decline. The difference lies not only in human intent, but also in the structure of the ecological network, the strength of feedback loops, and the adaptive capacity of both species and societies.

In my own work, I have examined how humans have at times served as ecological stabilizers—binding together otherwise disconnected trophic interactions, reinforcing biodiversity, and enhancing system robustness. In such cases, the removal of humans from the network precipitated dramatic ecological restructuring (Crabtree et al., 2019). Predator-prey dynamics shift, competition among herbivores intensifies, and the fine-tuned balances that had persisted begin to unravel. In other instances, human overreach—through overhunting, habitat fragmentation, or agricultural intensification—has destabilized food webs.

Indeed, truly "pristine" ecosystems without human influence are exceedingly rare, both in the past and present. This makes it imperative to understand how human communities have historically interacted with, modified, and been reciprocally shaped by their ecosystems. Only by reconstructing these relationships can we begin to understand the broader dynamics of adaptation and transformation that human societies have faced, particularly in times of environmental stress. The application of network models enables us to do just that—offering a quantitative, systems-level lens through which to examine the entanglements of people and place.

In this chapter, I present the largest terrestrial food web compiled to date (Crabtree et al., 2017). This web focuses on the Ancestral Pueblo Southwest—a dataset that draws on both archaeological and modern ecological data to reconstruct trophic interactions over six centuries of occupation. We analyze food webs from three key archaeological periods and sites: Pueblo I (AD 750–900), Pueblo II (AD 900–1150), and Pueblo III (AD 1150–1300). By tracking changes in network structure across these temporal snapshots, we gain insight into how Ancestral Pueblo people fit within their ecosystems, how they responded to environmental variability, and how their subsistence strategies affected—and were affected by—broader ecological transformations.

A central question animating this work is whether Ancestral Pueblo predation choices contributed to the destabilization of local food webs. If so, what were the consequences for broader settlement patterns, population movement, and eventual regional depopulation? Overexploitation of key prey species, particularly large-bodied game, may have driven communities to pivot toward secondary or fallback foods with lower caloric and nutritional returns. These substitutions likely required more labor, offered diminishing returns, and may have been insufficient to sustain growing populations. For those living in environmentally marginal areas, the cost-benefit balance of staying in place may have tipped, leading to the large-scale migrations observed in the late 13th century.

This hypothesis aligns with broader patterns documented in both historical and ethnographic contexts. Across the globe, societies experiencing resource depletion—whether due to overhunting, deforestation, or agricultural exhaustion—often exhibit similar dynamics: dietary simplification, increased mobility, and eventual social reorganization. In the case of the Ancestral Pueblo Southwest, many explanatory models for migration emphasize megadroughts and other exogenous climatic factors. While climate undoubtedly played a role, this study suggests that human-ecosystem feedbacks—the cumulative effects of subsistence intensification, species depletion, and shifting ecological networks—also deserve close attention. Rather than passive victims of drought, these communities may have found themselves at the center of cascading ecological thresholds, wherein decisions made at the household or community level scaled up to regional transformations.

To explore these dynamics rigorously, we employ a suite of analytical techniques. First, we reconstruct the food web topology for each period, assessing overall network connectivity, trophic diversity, and the presence of key structural features such as keystone nodes and trophic loops. These metrics allow us to characterize the robustness or fragility of each web—whether energy flows are distributed evenly or concentrated in vulnerable bottlenecks. Second, we perform targeted species removal experiments, simulating human predation by removing specific taxa and measuring the resulting cascade effects. This approach helps us test the resilience of the food webs to anthropogenic pressure and helps to identify which species were linchpins in maintaining stability. Third, we integrate archaeological data to assess how documented changes in diet and demography correlate with modeled network disruptions.

The results are telling. During Pueblo I, food webs are relatively diverse and balanced, with a wide range of prey species and strong redundancy across trophic levels. Pueblo II, however, shows signs of increasing pressure—particularly on large game—and a narrowing of dietary options. By Pueblo III, the network becomes increasingly fragmented, with greater dependence on less nutritious species and a noticeable loss of trophic redundancy. These shifts mirror the archaeological record: a move toward marginal land use, evidence of intensified foraging, and eventually, widespread depopulation of the Four Corners region.

The implications of this study extend beyond Ancestral Pueblo archaeology. Understanding how past societies navigated ecological constraints is crucial for informing contemporary discussions about sustainability and resilience. Many modern food systems face similar challenges—overexploitation of key resources, shifting species distributions due to climate change, and the increasing reliance on lower-quality food sources in stressed environments. By reconstructing how Ancestral Pueblo communities adapted (or failed to adapt) to these pressures, we can extract lessons applicable to present-day resource management and conservation.

In sum, this chapter seeks to move beyond simplistic narratives of environmental determinism and explore the complex interdependencies between humans and their ecosystems. The Ancestral Pueblo Southwest provides a compelling case study for examining these dynamics, offering both empirical richness and theoretical insight into the ways human societies shape—and are shaped by—their ecological surroundings. As network-based approaches continue to refine our understanding of past human-environment interactions, they also underscore a fundamental truth: no society operates in isolation from its ecosystem, and the consequences of ecological change ripple outward, influencing human decisions, adaptations, and ultimately, survival.

Works Cited

Crabtree, Stefani A., Douglas W. Bird, and Rebecca Bliege Bird. 2019. Subsistence Transitions and the Simplification of Ecological Networks in the Western Desert of Australia. *Human Ecology* 47(2):165–177. https://doi.org/10.1007/s10745-019-0053-z

Crabtree, Stefani A., Lydia J.S. Vaughn, and Nathan T. Crabtree. 2017. Reconstructing Ancestral Pueblo Food Webs in the Southwestern United States. *Journal of Archaeological Science* 81:116–127. https://doi.org/10.1016/j.jas.2017.03.005

Dunne, Jennifer A., Herbert Maschner, Matthew W. Betts, Nancy Huntly, Roly Russell, Richard J. Williams, and Spencer A. Wood. 2016. The Roles and Impacts of Human Hunter-Gatherers in North Pacific Marine Food Webs. *Scientific Reports* 6:21179.

Maschner, Herbert D.G., Matthew W. Betts, Joseph Cornell, Jennifer A. Dunne, Bruce P. Finney, Nancy Huntly, James W. Jordan, et al. 2009. An Introduction to the Biocomplexity of Sanak Island, Western Gulf of Alaska. *Pacific Science* 63(4):673–709.

Murphy, Grace E.P., and Tamara N. Romanuk. 2014. A Meta-Analysis of Declines in Local Species Richness from Human Disturbances. *Ecology and Evolution* 4(1):91–103. https://doi.org/10.1002/ece3.909

CASE STUDY: RECONSTRUCTING ANCESTRAL PUEBLO FOOD WEBS IN THE SOUTHWESTERN UNITED STATES*

Introduction

After seven centuries of successful farming and habitation (Kohler and Varien, 2012; Schwindt et al., 2016), the Ancestral Pueblo people completely abandoned the Four Corners area circa AD 1300. For over a century, archaeologists have been examining the question of why this abandonment occurred. A consensus has not been reached as to the causes of this depopulation, with explanations resting on environmental causes such as drought (e.g., Badenhorst and Driver, 2009; Douglass, 1929; Flint-Lacey, 2003; Schoenwetter and Dittert, 1968), social causes such as violence (LeBlanc, 1999), or more recently a combination of the two (e.g., Glowacki, 2015; Nelson and Schachner, 2002; Ortman, 2012).

Recently, researchers (e.g., Bocinsky et al., 2016; Schwindt et al., 2016) have revisited this question with new tools and approaches that look to overarching climate patterns as potential drivers of depopulation. Yet these papers do not take into account how overuse of the environment would have itself destabilized animal and plant populations creating new microclimates. This chapter revisits the debate on the depopulation of the central Mesa Verde utilizing modern tools to examine the extent to which anthropogenic change destabilized the northern Southwest, making migration essential. This study re-examines this long-standing question using a tool rarely (and only recently) used in archaeological studies: food web analysis (e.g., Dunne et al., 2016). We ask how the interactions between environmental and human systems influenced ecosystems in the Four Corners region, and whether such feedback between environmental

---

* Reprinted from Stefani A. Crabtree, Lydia J.S. Vaughn, and Nathan T. Crabtree. (2017). Reconstructing Ancestral Pueblo Food Webs in the Southwestern United States. *Journal of Archaeological Science* 81: 116–127. https://doi.org/10.1016/j.jas.2017.03.005.

and social pressures may have precipitated abandonment. In contrast to more traditional archaeological methods (e.g., Badenhorst and Driver, 2009) we use a food web framework to examine archaeological assemblages from three periods, Pueblo I (AD 750–900—Grass Mesa Pueblo), Pueblo II (AD 900–1150—Albert Porter Pueblo), and Pueblo III (AD 1150–1300—Sand Canyon Pueblo). This diachronic approach allows us to identify changes in species presence and prevalence through time, an important indicator of ecosystem shifts (Parmesan, 1996; Parmesan et al., 1999). The use of archaeological food webs enables us to focus on species that directly affect humans within the context of the overarching food web, thereby directly examining feedback between humans and the environment and clarifying interpretations of the Ancestral Pueblo ecosystem.

While traditional studies enable an understanding of feeding links, the power of food web (i.e., trophic) studies lies not just in documenting presence of species but also in examining linkages among predators and prey. By studying the network topology of trophic webs, it is possible to identify important structural properties that promote stability or increase vulnerability of the web (Tecchio et al., 2013). Moreover, food web approaches are the only means to analyze the effects of species removals and introductions on the other species and links in the web (Fritts et al., 1998). This study leverages this analytical approach, building on long-standing studies of Four Corners area archaeology, such as those finding that deer depletion forced Ancestral Pueblo people to rely on other protein sources (Badenhorst and Driver, 2009; Bocinsky et al., 2012; Cowan et al., 2012; Schollmeyer and Driver, 2012). This work additionally adds to a growing body of human food web studies, which will enable comparison of environments worldwide (Crabtree et al., 2019; Dunne et al., 2016).

To date, this study is the largest terrestrial food web compiled. We take the approach of compiling a large database of feeding links for all known species in the Four Corners area, creating full-scale trophic webs to examine how humans were connected to the greater Four Corners ecosystem through time. This chapter shows that human use and modification of the landscape dramatically changed the environment of the Four Corners region during occupation, destabilizing the ecosystem, influencing the development of new strategies, and precipitating depopulation through three main findings:

- Food web analysis provides new evidence for feedback between anthropogenic environmental impacts and their subsequent effects on humans.
- Aridification and human-mediated deforestation are visible in the archaeological record through the disappearance of two woodland-dependent species and the appearance of two grassland-dependent species over time.
- When human density is low, omnivory allows humans to be resilient to environmental fluctuations, whereas when human density is high, the availability of key prey decreases, and humans must rely on other means of survival, such as migration.

Studying Trophic Interactions to Inform Understanding of Environmental and Social Change

Food web studies aim to understand species interactions in a defined environment by mapping the network of predator-prey relationships (trophic networks). Computational approaches to studying these trophic relationships enable the use of large datasets to investigate individual inter-species interactions and how changing interactions can cause cascading system-wide changes. Understanding how species losses affect food webs (Dunne et al., 2002a; Srinivasan et al., 2007), identifying commonalities among food web structures (e.g., Dunne et al., 2002b; Stouffer et al., 2005; Williams et al., 2002), and determining how individual species interactions cascade across trophic levels (Micheli et al., 2005) has advanced our understanding of complex ecosystem structures and dynamics.

Within a food web, each species is assigned a trophic level, representing how organisms of that species obtain energy and carbon. At the basal trophic level, primary producers generate biomass from inorganic materials (e.g., plants photosynthesize). With increasing trophic level, primary consumers eat primary producers, secondary consumers eat primary producers and primary consumers, and so forth up to apex predators, which consume prey residing at high trophic levels (see Bonhommeau et al., 2013). By tallying the complete set of species historically eaten and used by humans and then connecting those species to other species they consumed (and are consumed by), we can evaluate human resilience to environmental fluctuations. Using trophic webs constructed from distinct time periods, we can identify species introductions and local extinctions through time and calculate their effects on food web properties, thereby better understanding how humans were interconnected to the greater environment and how this connection evolved and fluctuated through time.

The American Southwest

The northern US Southwest is unique for archaeological inquiry. Preserved wood from Pueblo structures permits dendrochronologists to pinpoint when sites were built and abandoned, while the semi-arid climate helps preserve faunal remains (Nash, 1999). This high degree of preservation coupled with relative precision of demographic reconstruction means that archaeological food webs can be examined at multiple sites from multiple time periods and placed in their correct regional demographic context. The ability to synthesize information across timescales provides a powerful way to relate incremental changes to cascading environmental consequences. By studying how anthropogenic changes such as deforestation, soil erosion, or harvest pressure coincide with the distribution of flora, fauna, and human populations in the region, and how these changes likely led to social strategies, we can better understand the depopulation of the central Mesa Verde region.

The area used in this study is in the Central Mesa Verde Region and the Village Ecodynamics Project's (VEP) northern study area (Figure 6.1). The VEP is a multi-disciplinary project aiming to understand the prehispanic Pueblo occupation of the Four Corners area through empirical research and modeling. The 4600 sq km northern VEP study area supports seven biotic communities—sagebrush, grasslands, pinyon-juniper woodland, gambel oak scrubland, pine/Douglas fir forest, spruce/fir forest, and alpine tundra (Adams and Petersen, 1999:15)—and encompasses the "Great Sage Plain" (Newberry, 1876), parts of Canyons of the Ancients National Monument, and the Mesa Verde landform (Figure 6.1). This area is a diverse ecological zone encompassing some of the most densely populated areas of the Ancestral Pueblo occupation (Hill et al., 2010; Schwindt et al., 2016). This study focuses on three sites, Grass Mesa Pueblo, Albert Porter Pueblo, and Sand Canyon Pueblo, all of which had roughly equal access to these seven biotic communities.

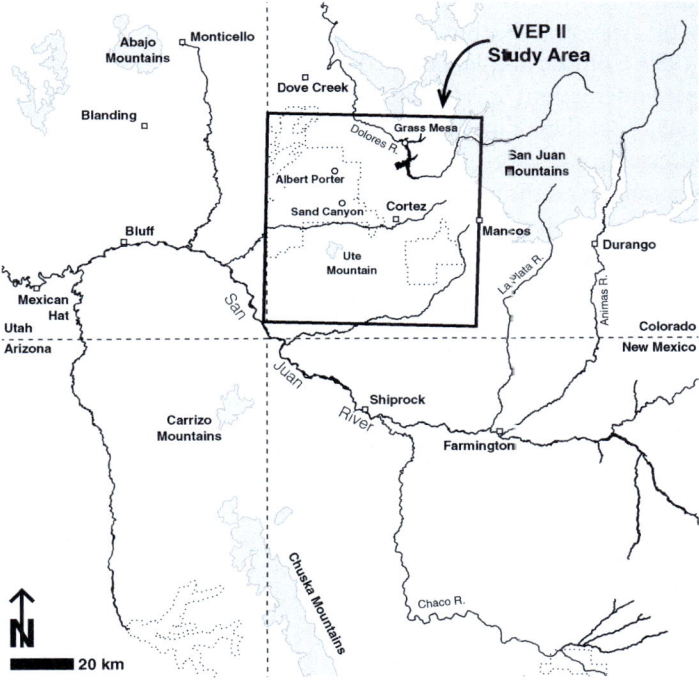

FIGURE 6.1 Central Mesa Verde area; box shows study area used for this research. Sites used for analyses in this chapter (Grass Mesa Pueblo, Albert Porter Pueblo, and Sand Canyon Pueblo) represented by circles. Figure courtesy of R. Kyle Bocinsky.

We focus our study on maize farmers living during the Pueblo I (AD 750–900), Pueblo II (AD 900–1150), and Pueblo III times (AD 1150–1300, Table 6.1). During this time the inhabitants of the area were maize farmers who supplemented their calories by hunting deer, rabbits, and later domesticating turkey. Briefly, Pueblo I times are marked first by population growth indicative of a Neolithic Demographic Transition (Kohler and Reese, 2014) followed by population decline at the end of the Pueblo I period. High rates of local population growth recommenced during the mid-Pueblo II period (Schwindt et al., 2016), ultimately reaching about 27,000 people in the mid-1200s (the finale of Pueblo III), a level more than twice that reached during the Pueblo I peak. Throughout the history of occupation of this area, people moved from dispersed hamlets to relatively dense villages (Crabtree, 2015). The density of habitation combined with the high level of population would have had dramatic effects on the environment, including clearing vegetation for habitations and fields, burning vegetation to increase hunting opportunities, and hunting large quantities of animals to feed the growing population (Figure 6.1).

In this study we pay particular attention to environmental changes due to farming and effects of environmental change on farmers, since 70–80 percent of the diets of Ancestral Pueblo people was composed of maize (Decker and Tieszen, 1989; Coltrain and Janetski, 2013). In spite of a range of known human–environment interactions, it is tempting for archaeologists studying early farming populations to set these farmers apart from many environmental pressures; our work addresses these oversights. The invention of agriculture arguably made humans less reliant on the unpredictable nature of foraging, but it brought a host of other challenges. Many of the known effects that Ancestral Pueblo people had on the environment, such as deforestation and erosion, are directly related to clearing native vegetation for fields for farming maize (Kohler, 2004) (Table 6.1).

Clearing of forests for agricultural fields changes the functioning of ecosystems (Diaz and Cabido, 1997; Wardle, 2011). Changes in plant cover can

TABLE 6.1 Periods and sites examined here

Years AD	Cultural period	Description
Prehistory to 500	Paleoindian/Archaic/Basketmaker II	No sites in this study
600–750	Basketmaker III	No sites in this study
750–900	Pueblo I	Grass Mesa Pueblo
900–1150	Pueblo II	Albert Porter Pueblo
1150–1300	Pueblo III	Sand Canyon Pueblo
1300–1500	Pueblo IV	No sites in this study
AD 1500 to present	Colonial period	Modern data used to understand species composition

change carbon and nitrogen cycling (Wardle, 2011), influence water availability and local and regional climate (Jackson et al., 2009; Bala et al., 2007; Gehlhausen et al., 2000), and affect organisms at all trophic levels (Knops et al., 1999; Schmitz et al., 2000). In the Four Corners region, forest clearing in favor of intensive farming of maize, beans, and squash likely affected the local environment in this manner.

Sediment cores from Prater Canyon, an intensely inhabited canyon in the northeast of Mesa Verde National Park, show intensive burning episodes during occupation, suggesting that Native Americans used fire to modify landscapes (Herring et al., 2014); maize, the primary crop of the Ancestral Pueblo people, is a notoriously nitrogen-greedy plant that would have thrived on the short-term increase in nutrients mobilized by these fires (Benson, 2011; Wan et al., 2001). Fire also may have been used as a tool for hunting, creating ecosystems that were more favorable for Ancestral Pueblo people to pursue game. Elsewhere, scientists have shown that repeated landscape burning and planting of nitrogen-greedy crops reduces long-term soil fertility (Monleon et al., 1997), which may have occurred over time in the ecosystem reported here.

Another known effect of maize farming on the greater Four Corners environment is erosion. It is noted that the Ancestral Pueblo people living in Mesa Verde applied check dams by the 1200s to improve the short-term productivity of their fields (Kohler, 2004; Rohn, 1963). While these efforts would have decreased erosion in the short-term, the rapidly growing population may have outstripped the ability of these measures to alleviate long-term effects (Herring et al., 2014; Kohler, 2004: 225).

Plant species were not the only species to be affected by human arrival. While Ancestral Pueblo people depended on rabbit and hare for protein after deer depression, they also domesticated turkey, feeding them from their maize storage (Rawlings and Driver, 2010). Keeping turkeys thus caused Ancestral Pueblo people to clear more land, creating a more open landscape. The combination of field clearing (which would remove trees as well as other native flora and drive out pest species, preferred prey, and large predators) with the introduction of domesticated turkey (which would intensify field clearing for more maize gardens), and the introduction of the domesticated dog (which likely chased out many other species) likely created zones of habitation devoid of native flora and fauna, potentially causing crowding of native species on the periphery (Urban, 2015).

The story of Ancestral Pueblo people unfolds on a changing landscape with occasional severe droughts that are independent of human actions. Human actions made some of these conditions worse (e.g., erosion) and enhanced the presence of some species on the landscape (e.g., rabbits). In the following, we first discuss important species presences/absences observed when compiling the food web database. Second, we consider properties of a reconstructed composite food web for the entire Four Corners area. Finally, we present network metrics derived from specific archaeological assemblages: Grass Mesa Pueblo, a Pueblo I village; Albert Porter Pueblo, a Pueblo II village; and Sand Canyon Pueblo, a Pueblo III village. Methods are detailed at the end of the chapter. The trophic webs presented herein derive from large, well-preserved samples excavated using a consistent set of practices that should approximate a complete set of human prey species.

Materials and Methods

Data for this article were collected in a 4,600 sq km area in southwestern Colorado that overlaps some of the densest archaeological habitations in the American Southwest and corresponds to the Village Ecodynamics Project II's northern study area (Figure 6.1). We identified every plant and vertebrate animal within this study area and catalogued them in our database; invertebrate data is coarse-grained to the order level. Within this area, modern vegetation cover was downloaded from the US Soil Survey or from US Forest Service reports. Initial vertebrate data was compiled from Mesa Verde National Park's database on animals that live in the park. Further data per animal class is defined in the following.

Data were compiled from trusted online field guides to ensure that future users could easily access background information on species. Avian data was compiled from the Cornell Lab of Ornithology, amphibian and reptile data from the Field Guide to Reptiles of Arizona and mammal data from the University of Michigan Museum of Zoology. If a species was not represented in the preferred online field guide, either (a) species data was found at another reliable source, such as the Audubon Society, or (b) a similar species was identified and its data was used. For example, Hammond's spadefoot toad prey data was not found on any reliable site, so data for the plains spadefoot toad was substituted. The avian data was crosschecked by an expert to ensure that all species were accounted for and that vague diet descriptions were properly coded.

Each species is numbered from 1 to 334 to give it an individual identifier. Species were then individually researched according to reliable sources, as described in this section. Verbal data on species consumption patterns was compiled in the database as presence/absence. For example, the long eared myotis is described as preying "mainly on moths, but their diet also includes beetles, flies, and spiders." In compiling the matrixes for our analysis we noticed several species from archaeological assemblages that were not present in modern data, or that were present in modern data but not the archaeological data; both of these were included to create a complete database of organisms. To create the overall food web, we include all species that were characterized in the matrix and all of their feeding links. This gives us the inferred species that humans would have interacted with throughout the Four Corners area.

When we pared down our analyses to the individual archaeological assemblages, first we created a matrix of all human prey (e.g., humans→ deer), corresponding to their temporal assignment. Then the prey species of the primary prey of humans were added to the matrix (humans→ deer → herbaceous grasses). Predators of the primary prey species of humans were also added to the matrix (wolves→ deer). Thus, these webs represent those species that would be directly affected by human intervention. This means many nodes will be represented, but not all links might be represented. Webs with high connectance (the realized proportion of possible links among all species; Cockburn et al., 2013) show much higher complexity, while those with low path-length (the number of edges it takes to connect all nodes) are likely to be connected in a small world network (all nodes are connected to all others; Crabtree, 2015; Dunne et al., 2002b). Understanding the distribution of links in the web can have important ramifications for understanding extinction events (since redundancy of species makes webs more stable—Yeakel et al., 2014), the vulnerability or resilience of the overall food web, and for understanding how invasive species will link in with the web (Dunne et al., 2002a).

The assemblages in the archaeological food webs are smaller than in the composite food web, potentially influencing the decreased clustering coefficients seen in the following analyses. The high percentages of excavation in each of these sites suggest, however, that it is not sampling bias but rather a real signature with the smaller assemblages. The database for this project is available at https://wsu.academia.edu/StefaniCrabtree, which indicates data sources and the 334 species identified in this project.

Choice of Sites

One well-excavated site per period (Pueblo I, Pueblo II, and Pueblo III) was chosen for analysis. Grass Mesa Pueblo was chosen because it is one of the largest and most completely excavated Pueblo I villages in the Central Mesa Verde region and was excavated as part of the Dolores Archaeological Project (DAP). The methods developed for the DAP influenced those used by Crow Canyon Archaeological Center who excavated and analyzed Albert Porter Pueblo and Sand Canyon Pueblo. This minimizes any differences among these three assemblages due to sampling or analytical biases. Albert Porter Pueblo was chosen due to it having a large Pueblo II component and being excavated by Crow Canyon Archaeological Center. Albert Porter was occupied into Pueblo III, but only the Pueblo II occupation was used for these studies. Sand Canyon Pueblo was chosen due to being the largest site occupied during Pueblo III times and being well excavated by Crow Canyon Archaeological Center.

Excavation Techniques

Grass Mesa Village was excavated with shovel, trowel, and backhoe. Deposits were screened through ¼" mesh (Kohler, 1983: 28). Excavations at both Albert Porter Pueblo and Sand Canyon Pueblo were by trowel and shovel, and most deposits were screened through ¼" mesh. (Special features were screened through ⅛" mesh; Ryan, 2003; Crow Canyon Archaeological Center, 2004.)

Zooarchaeological Methods

Zooarchaeological analysis was not performed by the authors of this study but was compiled from existing archaeological reports. Zooarchaeological methods are outlined in Adams (2015); Badenhorst and Driver (2015); Crow Canyon Archaeological Center (2004); Muir (2007); Neusius and Gould (1988); and Matthews, (1988).

There are challenges in identifying fauna. In the zooarchaeological studies here, only those species that could be positively identified were catalogued as such; otherwise they were assigned to lump categories such as "large bird" or "large mammal" (Adams, 2015; Badenhorst and Driver, 2015; Crow Canyon Archaeological Center, 2004; Muir, 2007; Neusius and Gould, 1988; Matthews, 1988). Only those fauna that were positively identified were catalogued in the food webs database. Fauna analysis for the Pueblo I site of Grass Mesa Pueblo was performed by Sarah Neusius (Neusius and Gould, 1988), fauna analysis for the Pueblo II site of Albert Porter Pueblo was performed by Shaw Badenhorst and Jon Driver (Badenhorst and Driver, 2015), and fauna analysis for the Pueblo III site of Sand Canyon Pueblo was performed by Robert Muir following protocol developed by Jon Driver (Muir, 2007).

Invertebrates

Invertebrate data, unfortunately, could not be verified at the species level. While charismatic megafauna have been well studied, most insects in the Southwest have not been studied to the same resolution. After consulting with an expert, invertebrate data was coarse grained to the Order level. It is hoped that future studies can resolve invertebrates to a more fine-grained level.

Specialists Versus Generalists

The most important distinction in coding the data was determining if an animal was a specialist or a generalist. This was preserved in coding by not overrepresenting those species that make up a very small proportion of the diet of the animal. For example, the mourning dove is said to gain 99 percent of its daily food intake from seeds. Consequently, those plants that produce seeds are represented as their prey, while plants that do not produce seeds (but could, conceivably, be a part of the diet when seeds are unavailable) are not represented.

Carrion Feeders

Carrion feeders can presumably feed on any dead animal. Animals that had a small portion of their diet as carrion were not presumed to eat every represented animal, but only the named prey was represented (for similar reasons to the preceding specialist versus generalist concerns). Animals that receive most of their diet from carrion (e.g., turkey vulture) are presumed to eat every animal represented.

Cannibalism

If a key characteristic of an animal was eating its own species it was coded as cannibal. Mammals were not coded as cannibals by default. While suckling does represent a type of cannibalism (young cannot survive without feeding on their mother's milk) we removed this link in this analysis.

Dogs

We include dogs in our food web analyses despite the lack of evidence that humans preyed on them. For one, we know that dogs existed during the occupation of the Central Mesa Verde region, so they must be included in the composite food web for it to be complete. Additionally, domestic dog DNA has been used as proxy for humans when human DNA is unavailable to examine migratory events (Witt et al., 2015). Thus dogs are included in this study. While dogs did enter the Southwest with the earliest Paleoindian migrants, the very high human populations of the Pueblo II and III periods were likely accompanied by a similarly high number of dogs, as is seen in the assemblages we analyze here, and may have expanded the ecological footprint of habitations due to the propensity of dogs to hunt wild resources. Modern packs of feral dogs in the Southwest have been known to hunt deer and pronghorn (ASPCA, 2015), and Pueblo dogs in the Southwest likely ate wild birds and rodents in considerable numbers.

Results

Species Change as Evidence for Aridification

The presence and absence of certain fauna can be viewed as indicators of local environmental changes. Here we will discuss four such species whose presence in the species assemblages change through time: elk, snowshoe hare, sandhill crane, and scaled quail. None of these species had many bones recovered, as illustrated in Supplementary Table 2. However, we argue that the presence of these bones in tandem with recent climate studies (Bocinsky and Kohler, 2014) indicates an environmental signature.

Elk bones are present in the Pueblo I assemblage, but not later assemblages. Likewise, snowshoe hare were present in the Pueblo I assemblage but were not present in later assemblages and are not listed as a common species in the guides we consulted. As we discuss later (Discussion), elk and snowshoe hare

are both dependent on relatively moist forests for survival. Sandhill crane and scaled quail, however, depend on sparse, dry grasslands for survival. Sandhill crane are present in Pueblo I (NISP 1) and Pueblo III assemblages yet are not listed as native to the area in the guides we consulted. The modern bird sighting website *eBird*, managed by the Audubon Society, was used to determine modern sandhill crane sightings in the study area. (Birders use *eBird* to report rare sightings nationwide.) Only 11 individual sightings of sandhill cranes have been reported for the region since 1909 (*eBird*), primarily along the modern Dolores reservoir. While sandhill cranes are ubiquitous roughly 200 miles to the east in Alamosa, Colorado, their presence is rare in the present study area. Similarly, scaled quail bones are present in the Pueblo III assemblage but not earlier assemblages, and they are not listed as a common species in our study area. Modern scaled quail range does not overlap with southwestern Colorado (Cornell Lab of Ornithology). While scaled quail are common in the Farmington area, roughly 50 miles south of Sand Canyon Pueblo, they have been documented in only two locations within the study area (*eBird*). These are: Mesa Verde National Park (one sighting) and Four Corners National Monument area (one sighting).

The disappearance of two species that rely on woody corridors and high moisture and the concomitant appearance of two species that do not currently reside in the region and rely on dry grasslands provide evidence of a shift toward a relatively drier ecosystem. Explanations to the shift toward large quantities of elk in the region today and no scaled quail or sandhill crane are likely based on modern anthropogenic effects on grasslands being different than those created by Ancestral Pueblo people.

The Composite Food Web

We used the compiled trophic database to assemble a composite food web (Figure 6.2). This food web contains 334 nodes representing 298 distinct species (plants and vertebrates) and 36 invertebrate orders. Joining these 334 nodes are 11,344 links representing flows of biomass between consumers (predators) and the species they consume, creating a highly interconnected food web, with many species having overlapping prey. For example, both black-chinned hummingbirds and broad-tailed hummingbirds are represented in the food web, but their primary prey species are the same (Figure 6.2). While other studies (e.g., Yodzis and Winemiller, 1999) collapse species into multi-species functional groups, individual species were represented here to illustrate the complete ecosystem of southwestern Colorado. To characterize this composite food web we calculate metrics focusing on the human niche in the food web (Table 6.2).

Predation vulnerability and generality: Predation vulnerability and generality, calculated respectively as the quantity of predators per prey species (Lotze et al., 2011) and the quantity of prey per predator species, characterize the

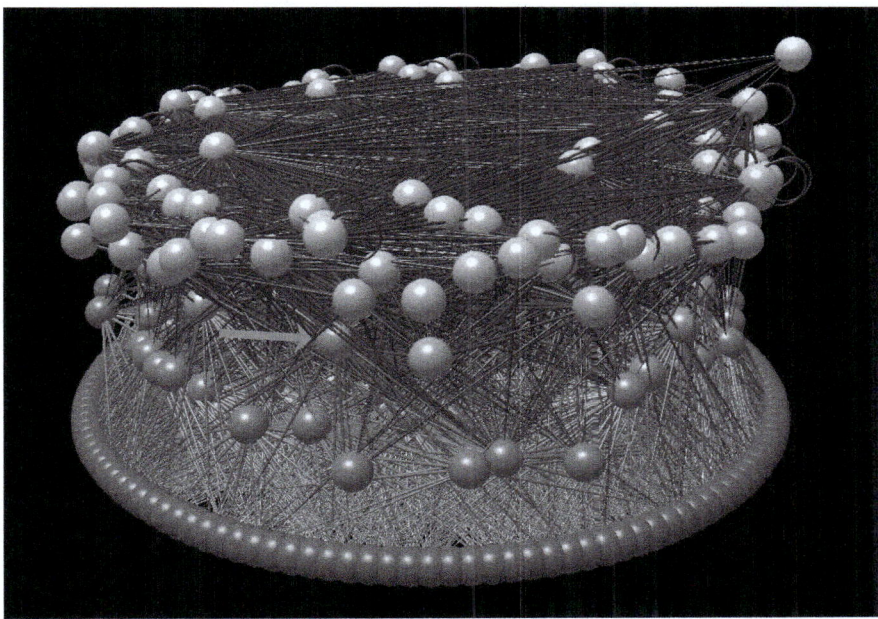

FIGURE 6.2 Graph of overall food web. Trophic level on y-axis. Dark nodes indicate primary producers, lighter primary consumers, lightest true carnivores. Humans pointed at by arrow. The common poorwill, an insectivore, is represented by the node in the upper right-hand corner.

TABLE 6.2 Scores for human trophic level, generality, vulnerability, connectivity, and clustering coefficient by food web

Trophic web	Trophic level	Generality	Vulnerability	Connectivity	Clustering coefficient
Composite	2.521	3.710	0.265	1.987	0.103
Grass Mesa	2.468	2.233	0.264	1.249	0.117
Albert Porter	2.658	1.452	0.267	0.859	0.106
Sand Canyon	2.642	2.496	0.264	1.380	0.126

vulnerability of a species to increases in predation and decreases in prey. Humans in the composite web have a low vulnerability score (0.264), showing that they have few predator species, limited to large predators such as wolves and cougars (Table 6.2). The generality of humans in the composite web is high at 3.71. For comparison, the black-billed magpie and common raven, both carrion eaters, are the most general species, with humans as the 27th most general species (Figure 6.2).

The vulnerability scores of the primary prey of humans are reported in Table 6.3 and displayed in Figure 6.3. Unlike humans, the primary prey species of humans exhibit high predation vulnerability. With a score of 2.27, maize is the most vulnerable plant to predation (the only nodes more vulnerable than maize are invertebrates, which may be a reflection of aggregating across many species). Many studies of vertebrate species specifically mention maize as a preferred food source (sandhill cranes for example, Supplementary Table 1). Many of these animals likely plagued the storage and gardens of Ancestral Pueblo people (Figure 6.3).

Trophic Level: Here, we use Williams and Martinez's (2004) estimates of trophic level (short-weighted trophic level). Typically, a trophic level of 1 is assigned to plants. A trophic level of 2 is generally herbivores, 3 omnivores, and 4 and above carnivores. Food webs display vertical organization (Figure 6.2), with node color corresponding to trophic level; red nodes represent primary producers (plants), orange nodes represent herbivores, yellow-orange nodes represent omnivores, and true yellow nodes represent carnivores. Vertices attenuate down the trophic level—they are thicker at the predator end and thinner at the prey end. Loops indicate cannibalism. Humans have a trophic level of 2.52, placing them at the 122nd highest trophic position out of 334 nodes. Carrion-eating animals and true carnivores are located at the highest trophic level. As evident in this figure, humans rank closer to herbivores than to carnivores—a fact that would be even more evident if the food web accounted for the abundance of maize in the diet (Table 6.3).

TABLE 6.3 Vulnerability and generality scores of primary prey for humans. White-tailed jackrabbit and snowshoe hare were not originally coded in the dataset but were positively identified in an archaeological assemblage. Consequently, their vulnerability score only reflects being eaten by a few top species (humans, bobcat, cougars) and thus should not be taken as a true vulnerability score for these leporids

Species	*Vulnerability (# of predators)*	*Generality (# of prey)*
Maize	2.27	n/a
Beans	1.21	n/a
Squash	1.21	n/a
Mule deer	0.47	3.39
Desert cottontail	1.15	0.41
Black-tailed jackrabbit	1.21	1.53
White-tailed jackrabbit	0.12*	1.68
Snowshoe hare	0.12*	1.68
Nuttall's cottontail	1.15	1.68

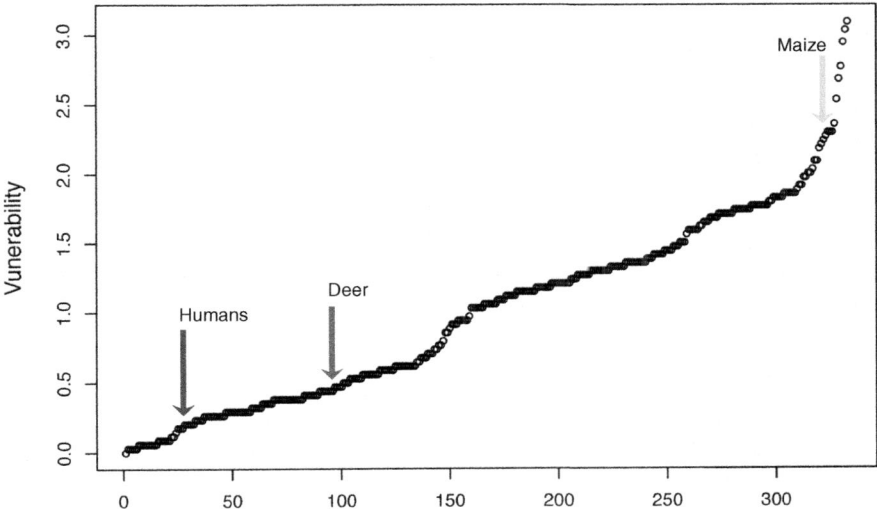

FIGURE 6.3 Vulnerability measures of species to predation; maize is the most vulnerable plant in our study area.

There are two main benefits for displaying data as in Figure 6.2. First, the density of links and quantity of nodes shows the high level of interconnection within the study area's ecosystem, taking discussions of environmental complexity from the abstract to the concrete. Second, as many food web studies also use the Networks 3D software (e.g., Dunne et al., 2016; Williams, 2010), displaying information this way allows for comparison among studies.

To focus on species most closely connected to humans, Figure 6.4 flattens the composite web and shows humans, human prey, and the prey of humans' primary prey (deer, turkeys, leporids). Here, line thickness shows the strength of interaction between humans and the other nodes, demonstrating the relative feeding strength for these species in human diet.

Clustering Coefficient: The clustering coefficient of a node measures how nodes within a given neighborhood are connected (Figure 6.5). The clustering coefficient can range from 0 to 1, with a value of 1 indicating that the node is completely connected to a clique (all nodes in a neighborhood are connected, i.e., each species preys on every other species in that neighborhood). A clustering coefficient close to 0 means that the focal node connects to other species, but those other species do not connect to one another. In Figure 6.6, species are sorted along the x-axis by clustering coefficients with the least-connected nodes near zero on both axes.

In the composite food web of southwestern Colorado, the highest clustering coefficients correspond to bird and bat species—these species are in the most connected cliques (Supplementary Table 2). Humans, on the other hand, have

130 Thinking Through Archaeological Complexity

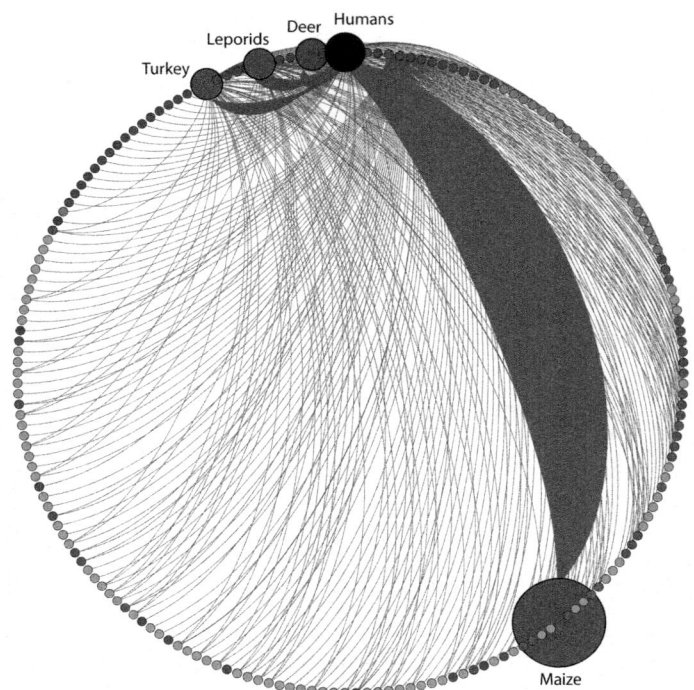

FIGURE 6.4 Primary prey of humans, leporids (cottontail and jackrabbit), deer and turkey taken from composite web. Darker nodes are nodes that are connected to humans through predation. Size of node and thickness of edges approximates importance of species to consumer, with narrow edges being not important, and wide edges being very important. Maize makes up between 70 and 85 percent of diet. Deer, leporids, and turkey each became important in the human diet through Pueblo occupation. Primary prey of humans, leporids (cottontail and jackrabbit), deer, and turkey taken from composite web.

a clustering coefficient value of 0.103, meaning that many of the species they prey upon do not prey on each other (Figure 6.6).

Connectivity: Connectivity measures how many other nodes a node is connected to. Here, the species with the highest connectivity are carrion eaters, such as the common raven (4.48) and the black-billed magpie (4.48), which will opportunistically eat almost all species, and which are eaten by many species as well (Figure 6.7). Humans are the 38th most connected species (1.99), though

Case Study: Reconstructing Ancestral Pueblo Food Webs   **131**

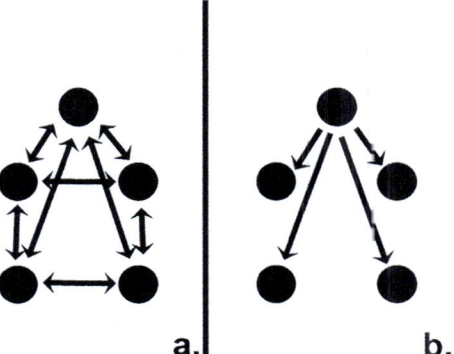

FIGURE 6.5   Ideal Clustering Coefficients. In (a) all species prey on each other, showing a complete connectance (or 1). In (b) only one predator preys on all other species, which do not prey on each other, showing a clustering coefficient close to 0.

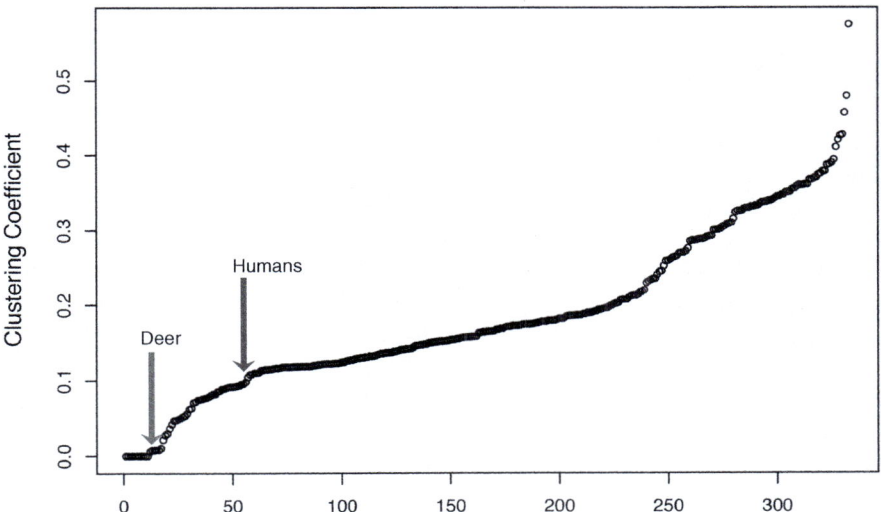

FIGURE 6.6   Clustering coefficient for the overall food web. Humans are mapped at point 51 on the x-axis, showing that humans are connected but are well below the median species in this food web.

these links are mostly through consumption, not predation. Mule deer, with a connectivity value of 1.93, are the 40th most connected species in this analysis; they both consume and are preyed upon by many species (Figure 6.4).

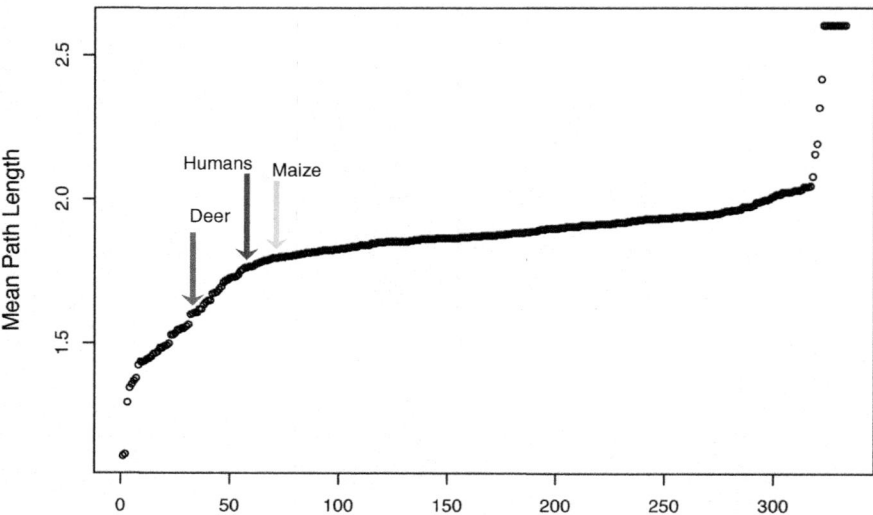

FIGURE 6.7 Connectivity measures. Here, humans are the 37th most connected species with a score of 1.987.

The Archaeological Food Webs

We reconstructed trophic webs from three archaeological sites: Grass Mesa Pueblo (Figure 6.8) (Pueblo I; Neusius and Gould, 1988; Matthews, 1988), Albert Porter Pueblo (Figure 6.9) (Pueblo II; Adams, 2015; Badenhorst and Driver, 2015), and Sand Canyon Pueblo (Figure 6.10) (Pueblo III; Crow Canyon Archaeological Center, 2004). Grass Mesa Pueblo was one of the largest villages excavated as part of the Dolores Archaeological Project (DAP). The methods developed for the DAP influenced those used by Crow Canyon Archaeological Center to excavate the Pueblo II and III sites discussed here. This minimizes any differences among these three assemblages due to sampling or analytical biases (see Methods) (Figure 6.8).

The human-specific food web from the archaeological excavations at Grass Mesa Pueblo includes 314 nodes with 2,764 feeding links and an average number of links per species of 8.81, resulting in a much simpler trophic web than the composite web (Figure 6.8). In contrast, the human-specific food web for Albert Porter Pueblo is smaller, with only 249 species represented with 1,246 links among species, showing an average number of links per species of 5.01 (Figure 6.9). The Sand Canyon Pueblo's human-specific food web is the most connected human-specific web, with 321 nodes and 4,045 links among them, resulting in 12.63 links on average per node (Figure 6.10). Sand Canyon Pueblo was the largest site occupied of its time.

Trophic Level: The trophic level of humans is highest in the Albert Porter food web (2.658) and lowest in the Grass Mesa food web (2.468) (Table 6.2).

FIGURE 6.8 Human specific food web for Grass Mesa Pueblo, Pueblo I period. Arrow identifies humans.

While this study does not take into account the percent of the diet these organisms constitute, Ancestral Pueblo people did have a predominantly vegetarian diet (Matson and Chisholm, 1991) (Figure 6.9).

Clustering Coefficient: The clustering coefficients for the archaeological assemblages are all marginally higher than for the composite food web showing that humans and their prey are in slightly more connected cliques, with the highest clustering coefficient in the Sand Canyon Pueblo assemblage (Table 6.2).

Connectivity: As noted, connectivity shows how connected a species is to every other species. During Grass Mesa Pueblo occupation humans score 1.25 and are the 74th most connected species of 334 species. During Albert Porter Pueblo occupation, humans score 0.86 and are the 135th of 334 most connected species. During Sand Canyon Pueblo occupation humans score 1.38 and are the 60th most connected species. While humans are not the most connected species, they are still connected to many of the species in the environment (Figure 6.10).

Nodal Knockout Food Webs

The preceding food web metrics do not take into account the strength of interactions between individual predator and prey nodes. However, we can examine

134 Thinking Through Archaeological Complexity

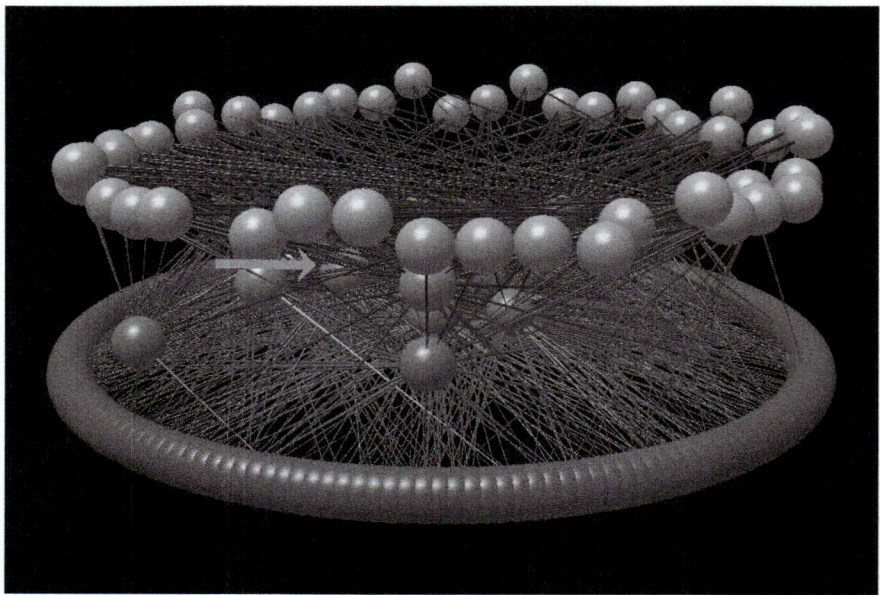

FIGURE 6.9 Human specific food web, Albert Porter Pueblo, Pueblo II period. Arrow identifies humans.

FIGURE 6.10 Human specific food web, Sand Canyon Pueblo, Pueblo III period. Arrow identifies humans.

the relative importance of nodes by performing a "nodal knockout" analysis and keeping only those species that are the most important to humans as prey in the constricted food webs. Species identified as most important by the nodal knockout analysis were corn, beans, squash, deer (before being hunted out), rabbit/hare, and turkey (after being introduced as a food source). Note that we did not remove those species that prey on humans but simply replaced the matrix of human prey with these constricted assemblages.

Our first nodal-knockout analysis generated a constricted food web from Grass Mesa Pueblo including foods that were most common during Pueblo I occupation: maize, beans, squash, rabbits, hare, and deer. While turkey are occasionally present in early assemblages, their use seems to be more for ritual than for food (Bocinsky and Kohler, 2015). Humans' generality decreases in this web to 0.26, lower than in the complete Grass Mesa food web (Table 6.4). Second, the Albert Porter constricted food web from the Pueblo II period represents the period after deer were locally hunted out but before the introduction of domesticated turkey. In this constricted food web, humans' generality score decreases to 0.23 (Table 6.4). Finally, in the Sand Canyon constricted food web from the Pueblo III period we introduce turkey as a food source and see the generality score raise to 0.26 again (Table 6.4). These nodal knockout results are important for identifying changes over time in humans' most important prey (Table 6.4).

Discussion

To tie the food web findings to the broader archaeological context we discuss implications of the presence/absence data and network results in light of existing archaeological data. In particular, we examine evidence for human-mediated environmental change and discuss how social choices can promote environmental degradation. These environmental changes and social adaptations create social-environmental feedback that led to the depopulation of the Four Corners area.

This study shows that both elk and showshoe hare were present during Pueblo I times and completely absent in later assemblages. The National Resource Conservation Service lists lowland woodland cover as essential for

TABLE 6.4 Generality scores for both empirical data and the reduced food web, where only the most important species to Pueblo diet were included. These include corn, beans, squash, deer (before being hunted out), rabbit/hare, and turkey (after being introduced as a food source)

	Empirical	*Reduced (hypothetical)*
Pueblo I (Grass Mesa)	2.23	0.26
Pueblo II (Albert Porter)	1.45	0.23
Pueblo III (Sand Canyon)	2.50	0.26

winter survival and migration of both Rocky Mountain and Roosevelt elk (NRCS, 1999). Elk also require high precipitation and are thus found in higher elevations (Driver, 2011). Similarly to elk, snowshoe hare require dense coniferous forests, bushy undergrowth, and high moisture (National Geographic, 2015). If woody corridors become too patchy or woodland cover is clearcut, elk cannot successfully migrate to survive the winter and snowshoe hare would not be able to find proper forage or cover for reproduction (NRCS, 1999). Given comparable needs for woodland cover, the regional loss of both elk and snowshoe hare may have resulted from forest clearance during Pueblo I times (Badenhorst and Driver, 2009). If these species were hunted or forced out of the high elevations of Mesa Verde, they may have become locally extinct, with forest disappearance preventing elk from migrating back into the area. While it is possible that these bones could have been transported into the area through long hunting forays or trade, their co-occurrence potentially suggests otherwise.

The disappearance of woodland-dependent species coupled with the arrival of species dependent on dry environments suggests severe environmental aridification and deforestation during Pueblo occupation. A recent study in *Science* (Morell, 2015) shows that the feeding patterns of elk have detrimental effects on grass abundance; as long as there are high numbers of elk, grasslands suffer. The coincident disappearance of elk—which reduce grass abundance and depend on forested areas—and appearance of bird species—which depend on sparse grasslands and cannot live in dense woodland—suggests a large habitat shift in the Four Corners area, likely brought upon by centuries of clearcutting by maize farmers. With a natural environmental shift from moist in Pueblo I times to dry in Pueblo III times (Benson et al., 2007; Bocinsky and Kohler, 2014) and the concurrent clearcutting of forests for maize fields (Wyckoff, 1977), scaled quail and sandhill crane thrived while elk and snowshoe hare suffered.

In the Rocky Mountains, 19th-century pioneer journals rarely mention elk, suggesting that once their numbers became depressed it took centuries for them to rebound (Kay, 1994, 1995). Explanations for the depressed numbers of elk recorded in explorers' journals include a combination of "aboriginal overkill" (Kay, 1994) and habitat loss through fire. Further south in Bandelier National Monument archaeological assemblages yield few elk remains (Allen, 2004:56), though today elk are abundant. In the Four Corners, elk habitat disappeared during Pueblo occupation, and the recolonization of this species took centuries after the region was abandoned, coinciding with the disappearance of sandhill crane and scaled quail.

The presence of sandhill crane during the Pueblo period (but not during modern times) also suggests an environmental shift between AD 1300 and the present. Sandhill cranes require large expanses of grassland abutting standing water or marshland. Scaled quail also prefer sparse grasses and desert shrublands and will not live in the thicker, woodier habitats of other quail and bobwhite species (Cornell Lab of Ornithology, 2025). The rarity of sandhill crane and scaled quail sightings during the modern period suggests that their habitat, open grasslands, became scarce. A recent mapping project displaying landcover (USGS Navajo Project, 2016) suggests that much of the land separating the study region from Farmington, NM, the site of dense scaled quail populations, is currently forested, though this deserves more study.

In the face of changing environmental conditions and prey availability, human resilience is related to the ability of humans to be "versatilists" (Potts, 1998), changing their prey choices to reflect current environmental and cultural conditions. Ancestral Pueblo people unintentionally decreased their versatility through practices related to their farming. Studies suggest that forests were clearcut during Ancestral Pueblo times in the Four Corners area. In the feature of Mummy Lake in Mesa Verde National Park, Wyckoff (1977) found that only 15 percent of pollen from AD 1000–1225 was arboreal, a percentage that is so low as to suggest deforestation (Kohler, 2004; Wyckoff, 1977). That same pollen core from Mummy Lake suggests rapid forest replacement following the depopulation of Central Mesa Verde, strongly pointing to humans as the agents of deforestation.

These pollen cores bolster findings that Pueblo farmers clearcut areas (through a combination of cutting, girdling, and burning) to make way for their farms (Kohler, 2004; Wyckoff, 1977). Deforestation during Ancestral Pueblo times could have also led to soil erosion, depending on which type of vegetation (if any) replaced the trees (Kohler, 2004:225), reducing the long-term ability of substrates to support vegetation. Further, pollen core studies also confirm that grassland dependent species could have benefited from deforestation during Pueblo occupation, while after Pueblo abandonment habitats shifted with the encroachment of pinyon-juniper forests. Our findings show that this woody encroachment coincided with the disappearance of sandhill cranes and scaled quail from common bird species of the modern era; the window in which they existed in this region was only during Ancestral Pueblo occupation.

Generality and vulnerability scores from this study's network analysis are evidence for changes in the versatility of Ancestral Pueblo people. Low predation vulnerability scores are beneficial to the focal species, meaning few animals prey on that species. The opposite is true for generality—a low generality score means that species preys on few animals. Low predation vulnerability and high generality scores characterize a robust species, while a less robust species would exhibit low generality and high predation vulnerability scores.

Humans have low predation vulnerability scores in all of the food webs, as they are preyed on by only large predators (e.g., wolves and cougars). In the composite and archaeological food webs humans have high generality scores, suggesting that they are generalists who may easily switch among prey, a finding well known in the anthropological literature (Staddon, 1983). Note, however, that while the composite and archaeological webs document the presence and absence of species and feeding links, they do not take into account the relative importance of species to the diet (the strength of links). The nodal knockout analyses examine those species that were the most abundant in human diets. In the constricted food webs resulting from nodal knockouts, the generality scores of humans alternate between 0.26 and 0.23—both quite small—indicating that humans would have had few options for error in this environment. Anthropologists have noted the health effects of a starch-heavy diet (Mertz, 1970:352) and the social effects of prey depression (Badenhorst and Driver, 2009), which may both have been consequences when humans couldn't rely on a full suite of prey. In the nodal knockout analysis, humans have the 20th *lowest* generality score of all consumer species (non-plants).

The fact that humans have high generality scores if they can make use of the whole assemblage but low generality scores if they can only rely on the most important prey advances a line of reasoning that environmental pressures and human prey choice were intimately interconnected. We suggest that some families may have had access to preferred prey more easily than others, and so the generality score for the composite web may represent only those families that could readily prey switch, while the generality scores in the nodal knockout webs may in fact represent those families who faced constraints (e.g., population density) that limited their ability to prey switch.

Along with the generality score, the clustering coefficient is also related to human resilience. A high clustering coefficient indicates that the primary prey of humans also fed on each other, so the consumption of one organism may have cascading effects, either increasing or reducing the abundance of other prey species. Here we see that humans have a relatively low clustering coefficient across the composite and archaeological food webs. By consuming mostly species that are independent, cascading effects due to prey switching are limited. This strategy, intentional or unintentional, helps humans to minimize burdens they may otherwise place on themselves. The archaeological assemblages have a slight increase in mutual predation, most clearly in Sand Canyon Pueblo.

Another source of decreased robustness for humans can be seen in their trophic level. Energy is lost at every trophic level. The closer an organism is to the producer level, the more efficient that organism is in receiving energy from the basal trophic level (Yodzis and Inness, 1992). In the preceding results we show that humans have a relatively low trophic level. By consuming low on the pyramid of biomass, humans are able to increase reproductive efficiencies (Kling, 2015) while also accessing more biomass and calories. In contrast, consuming higher on the pyramid of biomass reduces reproductive efficiencies due to constraints of prey availability; the biomass that can be supported decreases by about 90 percent with each step up the trophic pyramid. The changing trophic level of Ancestral Pueblo people may indicate when times were good—during Pueblo II times they ate more meat—and when times were bad—during Pueblo III times they could not predictably eat the dense energy of meat.

The Albert Porter Pueblo assemblage represents fewer species than the other assemblages. If the size of the Albert Porter assemblage is a typical Pueblo II assemblage it indicates that Pueblo peoples relied on fewer prey during the Pueblo II period than in other time periods. Further south along the Salt and Gila rivers of Arizona, Dean (2007) showed that prior to the Hohokam collapse, increased diet breadth correlated with high demographic stress, while decreased diet breadth, seen in constricted assemblages, correlated with low demographic stress. The constricted assemblage in Albert Porter Pueblo suggests that Ancestral Pueblo people had low demographic stress and were able to rely on their preferred prey more easily than during other periods. Sand Canyon Pueblo, on the other hand, has the highest generality score. While this means that people living during Pueblo III times could prey-switch, the species richness may also suggest demographic stress and the inability for humans to rely on their preferred food sources. Toward the end of the occupation of Sand Canyon Pueblo, archaeologists find that humans were unable to rely on domesticated crops due to drought and thus switched to a wild foods diet (Kuckelman, 2010). An increase in diversity, such as at Sand Canyon Pueblo, means that at the assemblage level people relied on undesirable species. However, we stress *at the assemblage level* because there were likely many strategies for each family in each archaeological site—some families may have met their needs through preferred prey, while others could not. Higher populations have greater effects on the overall environment, making it difficult to switch from cultivated foods. In light of the nodal knockout analysis, which shows low generality when humans rely on their preferred foods, we can see how detrimental a reduction of species would be for the Ancestral Pueblos. If soil fertility decreased following deforestation, these small increases in mutual predation and trophic level may have had important effects on the susceptibility of Ancestral Pueblos to environmental shifts.

Conclusions

The environmental footprint of the 27,000 inhabitants of the study area (Schwindt et al., 2016) would have included forest clearing to find beams for houses and woody fuels for fires, and to clear land for maize gardens. In addition to this, the ability to relocate, or even rotate fields, would be curtailed by density—where once there were large enough tracts of arable land to enable fallowing of nutrient-poor soils, people would instead be forced to innovate new ways to maintain their fields. The inability to move because of human density coupled with the environmental effects *of* human density (erosion, nitrogen poor soils, traveling far for woody fuels, scarce or absent prey species) would have gradually decreased the quality of life of Ancestral Pueblo people. And while it is true that during some times humans could switch prey to other native species ("starvation foods" as Kohler et al. (2008) call them), this choice was only available for all people when human density was low.

While it is easy to discuss deforestation, species shifts, and prey depression in the abstract, ecological changes would have been felt differently by different people in the Ancestral Pueblo world. Decisions were likely made at the individual, family, village, and clan levels. While *in the aggregate* humans may have been resilient to environmental shifts, aggregate conditions would not have applied to individual families who experienced starvation. The individual effects of ecological changes would have been dramatic and devastating for many Pueblo farmers. The high populations resulting from the Neolithic demographic transition forced humans into a rigidity trap, enabling overall survival only through high agricultural production. Once turkeys were introduced, maize farming became even more critical, and the ability to use other weedy species decreased (Bocinsky and Kohler, 2015). If the soil became too poor to support maize fields due to centuries of human use, the Ancestral Pueblo people needed to prey switch to survive. In such circumstances, if previously available forage had become scarce (elk, snowshoe hare, the forests that supported them), the people would have been faced with a difficult decision: starve, develop social responses to starvation (e.g., violence), or migrate.

People along the margins of the Central Mesa Verde region likely felt climatic changes first (Schwindt et al., 2016). These farmers were unable to sustain rain-fed agriculture in the face of a shrinking maize-growing niche (Bocinsky and Kohler, 2014). Those farmers on the margins may have been the first to attempt to utilize the suite of foodstuffs available to them via prey switching. This would only be available in the short term, however. As human settlement density increased and forests were cleared, and as humans decreased fallowing periods for their fields (increasing erosion), the effects of environmental changes would be felt more strongly. This would lead to *further* social adaptations—trades with neighbors, raiding those you don't know—which may in turn increase other types of social pressures (paying back donated gifts, building defenses against invaders). If the environment did not bounce back quickly—which here we suggest it did not—the environmental and social pressures may have become unbearable, especially for those families that colonized marginal lands. Due to the density and extent of human habitation and years of environmental degradation decreasing native flora and fauna, farmers on the margins were likely the first to decide to migrate away from the Central Mesa Verde.

Future Food Webs Studies

The research we present here is part of an increasing body of studies using food webs to evaluate human/ecosystem interactions. The detailed analysis of archaeological cultures and the ecosystems in which they lived provide a means to examine human reactions to changing environments worldwide.

Dunne et al. (2016) have placed humans in trophic webs from western Alaska. Creating dynamic models of food webs, they show that Aleuts were "super generalists," feeding on many species in the region. The researchers on this project (Dunne et al., 2016; Maschner et al., 2009) suggest that humans are important managers of ecosystems who promote ecological integrity. This research also further shows the necessity of including humans to gain a full understanding of ecosystem structure and dynamics.

Recent research in French Polynesia examines the sustainability of humans in island ecosystems of the South Pacific (Martinez et al., 2013–2017). This research seeks to understand the trajectory of human/environment interaction, using those methods developed by Dunne et al. (2016). While this project is ongoing, it is promising a third well-developed case study to compare human–environment interactions in the same manner as applied both in the research presented here and that presented by Dunne et al. (2016).

The research we presented in this chapter provides a terrestrial case study that can be directly compared with the island systems studied by Dunne et al. (2016) and Martinez et al. (2013–2017). Our results show how important a nuanced understanding of a culture and its environment is to truly understand the challenges that culture faced. Even agricultural groups are intimately connected with their environments, and to understand environments we need to understand how humans structure them. Further, small acts may have unintended consequences that benefit some species (such as scaled quail benefiting from decreased forests) while simultaneously hurting other species (such as elk or snowshoe hare). These domino effects can only be understood through large-scale analyses, using the "big data" of food web matrices, and only through studying the unique contingencies that these cultures faced may we begin to understand patterns of human/environment interaction, social adaptation, and the effects of species addition and removal. The increasing body of knowledge we have on food webs shows the importance of humans in structuring ecosystems: how we dramatically alter ecosystems and how we can manage ecosystems to prevent potential species loss. By comparing these well-developed cases we can better understand our place in the global ecosystem.

Acknowledgements

This research was made possible by grant DEB-0816400 and was conducted while supported by NSF Graduate Research Fellowship DGE-080667, the NSF GROW fellowship, and the Chateaubriand Fellowship. An earlier version of this research won the American Association for the Advancement of Science 2012 poster competition, social sciences division. Several researchers have contributed to the success of this research. This research was first presented at the Santa Fe Institute Complex System Summer School in 2011; feedback from Jennifer Dunne, David Krakauer, and Cormac McCarthy advanced this research. Thanks to the Sao Paolo School of Ecological Networks and Thomas

Lewinsohn for feedback on the next steps. Great thanks for feedback on earlier manuscripts by Kathryn Harris, Laura Ellyson, Andrew Duff, Tim Kohler, Kyle Bocinsky, and Mindy Wilkinson. S. Crabtree developed the study, performed analyses, compiled matrixes, performed background research, and helped design study methodology; any problems with the chapter are strictly hers. N. Crabtree helped compile matrixes and perform research on species in the Four Corners area. Vaughn helped design study methodology and assisted in writing.

Works Cited

Adams, K. R., and V. E. Bowyer. 2002. Sustainable Landscape: Thirteenth-Century Food and Fuel Use in the Sand Canyon Locality. In *Seeking the Center Place: Archaeology and Ancient Communities in the Mesa Verde Region*, edited by M. D. Varien and R. H. Wilshusen, pp. 101–120. University of Utah Press, Salt Lake City, UT.

Adams, Karen. 2015. Plant Use. In *The Archaeology of Albert Porter Pueblo: A Great House Community Center in Southwestern Colorado*, edited by Susan C. Ryan. Crow Canyon Archaeological Center, Cortez, CO.

Adams, Karen, and Ken L. Petersen. 1999. Environment. In *Colorado Prehistory: A Context for the Southern Colorado River Basin*, edited by William D. Lipe, Mark D. Varien, and Rich H. Wishusen, pp. 14–50. Colorado Council for Professional Archaeologists and Crow Canyon Archaeological Center, Colorado, CO.

Allen, Craig 2004. Ecological patterns and environmental change. In *Archaeology of Bandelier National Monument: Village Formation on the Pajarito Plateau, New Mexico*, edited by Timothy A. Kohler, pp. 19–67. University of New Mexico Press, Albuquerque, NM.

ASPCA, American association for the prevention of cruelty to animals. 2015. Predatory behavior in dogs, technical report. https://www.aspca.org/pet-care/general-pet-care/behavioral-help-your-pet6

Badenhorst, Shaw and Jon C. Driver. 2015. Faunal Remains. In *The Archaeology of Albert Porter Pueblo: A Great House Community Center in Southwestern Colorado*, edited by Susan C. Ryan. Crow Canyon Archaeological Center, Colorado, CO.

Badenhorst, Shaw and Jonathan C. Driver. 2009. Faunal Changes in Farming Communities from Basketmaker II to Pueblo III (A.D. 1–1300) in the San Juan Basin of the American Southwest. *Journal of Archaeological Science* 36(9):1832–1841. https://doi.org/10.1016/j.jas.2009.04.006

Bala, G. K. Caldeira, M. Wickett, T. J. Phillips, D. B. Lobell, C. Delire, A. Mirin 2007 Combined climate and carbon-cycle effects of large-scale deforestation. *Proceedings of the National Academy of Sciences* 104:6550–6555.

Benson, L. V. 2011. Factors Controlling Pre-Columbian and Early Historic Maize Productivity in the American Southwest, Part 1: The Southern Colorado Plateau and Rio Grande Regions: *Journal of Archaeological Method and Theory*, 18:1–60.

Benson, L. V., K. Petersen, J. Stein. 2007. Anasazi (Pre-Columbian Native-American) Migrations During The Middle-12th and Late-13th Centuries – Were they Drought Induced? *Climate Change* 83(1), pp. 187–213.

Bocinsky, R. Kyle, Jason A. Cowan, Timothy A Kohler, and C. David Johnson. 2012. How Hunting Changes the VEP World, and How the VEP World Changes Hunting. In *Emergence and Collapse of Early Villages*, edited by Timothy A. Kohler and Mark D. Varien, pp. 145–152. University of California Press, Berkeley.

Bocinsky, R. Kyle, and Timothy A. Kohler. 2014. A 2,000-Year Reconstruction of the Rain-Fed Maize Agricultural Niche in the US Southwest. *Nature Communications* 5:5618.

Bocinsky, R. Kyle, and Timothy A. Kohler. 2015. Complexity, Rigidity, and Resilience in the Ancient Puebloan Southwest. In *Viewing the Future in the Past: Historical Ecology Applications to Environmental Issues*, edited by H. T. Foster II, L. Paciulli, and D. Goldstein. University of South Carolina Press, Columbia, SC.

Bocinsky, R. Kyle, Johnathan Rush, Keith W. Kintigh, and Timothy A. Kohler. 2016. Exploration and Exploitation in the Macrohistory of the Pre-Hispanic Pueblo Southwest. *Science Advances* 2(4).

Bonhommeau, Sylvain, Laurent Dubroca, Olivier Le Pape, Julien Barde, David M. Kaplan, Emmanuel Chassot, and Anne-Elise Nieblas. 2013. Eating up the World's Food Web and the Human Trophic Level. *Proceedings of the National Academy of Sciences* 110(51):20617–20620. https://doi.org/10.1073/pnas.1305827110

Cockburn, Denton, Stefani A. Crabtree, Ziad Kobti, Timothy A. Kohler, R. Kyle Bocinsky 2013. Simulating Social and Economic Specialization in Small-Scale Agricultural Societies. *JASSS* 16(4) 4.

Collar, Anna, Fiona Coward, Tom Brughmans, and Barbara J. Mills. 2015. Networks in Archaeology: Phenomena, Abstraction, Representation. *Journal of Archaeological Method and Theory* 22:1–32. https://doi.org/10.1007/s10816-014-9235-6

Coltrain, Joan Brenner, and Joel C. Janetski. 2013. The Stable and Radio-Isotope Chemistry of Southeastern Utah Basketmaker II Burials: Dietary Analysis Using the Linear Mixing Model SISUS, Age and Sex Patterning, Geolocation and Temporal Patterning. *Journal of Archaeological Science* 40(12):4711–4730. https://doi.org/10.1016/j.jas.2013.07.012

Cowan, Jason A., Timothy A. Kohler, C. David Johnson, Kevin Cooper, and R. Kyle Bocinsky. 2012. Supply, Demand, Return Rates, and Resource Depression: Hunting in the Village Ecodynamics World. In *Emergence and Collapse of Early Villages*, edited by Timothy A. Kohler and Mark D. Varien, pp. 129–144. University of California Press, Berkely.

Crabtree, Stefani A. 2015. Inferring Ancestral Pueblo Social Networks from Simulation in the Central Mesa Verde. *Journal of Archaeological Method and Theory* 22(1):144–181. https://doi.org/10.1007/s10816-014-9233-8

Crabtree, Stefani A., R. Kyle Bocinsky, Paul L. Hooper, Susan C. Ryan, and Timothy A. Kohler. 2017. How to Make a Polity (In the Central Mesa Verde Region). *American Antiquity* 82(1):71–95. https://doi.org/10.1017/aaq.2016.18

Crabtree, Stefani A., Douglas W. Bird, and Rebecca Bliege Bird. 2019 Subsistence Transitions and the Simplification of Ecological Networks in the Western Desert of Australia. *Human Ecology* 47: 165–177. https://doi.org/10.1007/s10745-019-0053-z

Crow Canyon Archaeological Center 2004 The Sand Canyon Pueblo Database. Available: http://www.crowcanyon.org/sandcanyondatabase

Dean, Rebecca M. 2007. Hunting Intensification and the Hohokam "Collapse". *Journal of Anthropological Archaeology* 26(1):109–132. https://doi.org/10.1016/j.jaa.2006.03.010

Decker, Kenneth W., and Larry L. Tieszen. 1989. Isotopic Reconstruction of Mesa Verde Diet from Basketmaker III to Pueblo III. *Kiva* 55(1):33–46.

Diaz, S., M. Cabido 1997. Plant functional types and ecosystem function in relation to global change. *Journal of Vegetation Science*, 8, 463–474.

Douglass, AE 1929. Secret of the Southwest Solved by Talkative Tree Rings. *National Geographic Magazine*, https://ltrr.arizona.edu/sites/ltrr.arizona.edu/files/bibliodocs/Douglass%2C%20AE_Secret%20of%20the%20Southwest%20Solved%20by%20Talkative%20Tree%20Rings_1929.pdf

Driver, J. C. 2011. Human impacts on animal populations in the American Southwest. In *Movement, Connectivity and Landscape Change in the Ancient Southwest*, edited by M.C. Nelson, C. Strawhacker, University Press of Colorado, Boulder, pp. 179–198.

Dunne, Jennifer A., Herbert Maschner, Matthew W. Betts, Nancy Huntly, Roly Russell, Richard J. Williams, and Spencer A. Wood. 2016. The Roles and Impacts of Human Hunter-Gatherers in North Pacific Marine Food Webs. *Scientific Reports* 6:21179.

Dunne, Jennifer A., Richard J. Williams, and Neo D. Martinez. 2002a. Network Structure and Biodiversity Loss in Food Webs: Robustness Increases with Connectance. *Ecology Letters* 5(4):558–567. https://doi.org/10.1046/j.1461-0248.2002.00354.x

Dunne, Jennifer A., Richard J. Williams, and Neo D. Martinez. 2002b. Food-Web Structure and Network Theory: The Role of Connectance and Size. *Proceedings of the National Academy of Sciences* 99(20):12917–12922. https://doi.org/10.1073/pnas.192407699

Flint-Lacey, P.R. 2003. The Ancestral Puebloans and their piñon–juniper woodlands. In *Ancient Piñon–Juniper Woodlands*, edited by M.L. Floyd, pp. 309–320. University Press of Colorado, Boulder, CO.

Fritts, Thomas H., Thomas Frittsusgsgov, and Gordon H. Rodda. 1998. The Role of Introduced Species in the Degradation of Island Ecosystems: A Case History of Guam 1. *Annual Review of Ecology and Systematics* 29(29):113–140.

Gehlhausen, Sophia M., Mark W. Schwartz, Carol K. Augspurger 2000 Vegetation and microclimatic edge effects in two mixed-mesophytic forest fragments. *Plant Ecology* 147:21–35.

Glowacki, Donna M. 2015 Living and Leaving: A Social History of Regional Depopulation in Thirteenth-Century Mesa Verde. University of Arizona Press, Tucson.

Havens, Karl E. 1993. Predator-Prey Relationships in Natural Community Food Webs. *Oikos* 68(1):117–124.

Herring, E.M., R. S. Anderson, G. L. San Miguel 2014. Fire, vegetation and Ancestral Puebloans: A sediment record from Prater Canyon in Mesa Verde National Park, Colorado, U.S.A., *The Holocene*, pp. 1–11.

Hill, J. Brett, Jeffrey J. Clark, William H. Doelle, and Patrick D. Lyons. 2010. Depopulation of the Northern Southwest: A Macro-Regional Perspective. In *Leaving Mesa Verde: Peril and Change in the Thirteenth Century Southwest*, edited by T. A. Kohler, M. D. Varien, and A. M. Wright, pp. 34–52. University of Arizona Press, Tucson, AZ.

Jackson, R. B., E. G. Jobbágy, M. D. Nosetto 2009. Ecohydrology in a human-dominated landscape. *Ecohydrology* 2:383–389.

Kay, C. E. 1994. Aboriginal Overkill: The role of Native Americans in structuring western ecosystems. *Human Nature* 5:359–398.

Kay, C. E. 1995. Aboriginal overkill and native burning: implications for modern ecosystem management, *Western Journal of Applied Forestry* 10, pp. 121–126.

Kling, G.W. 2015. *The flow of energy: Higher trophic levels*, Global Change, University of Michigan Lecture.

Knops, J. M. H., D. Tilman, N. M. Haddad, S. Naeem, C. E. Mitchell, J. Haarstad, M. E. Ritchie, K. M. Howe, P. B. Reich, E. Siemann, J. Groth. 1999. Effects of plant species richness on invasion dynamics, disease outbreaks, insect abundances and diversity, *Ecology Letters* 2(5), pp. 286–294.

Kohler, T. A. 1983. Dolores archaeological program technical reports, Report Number DAP-084, Cultural Resources Mitigation Program: Dolores Project Bureau of Reclamation, Upper Colorado Region, Contract No. 8-07-40-S0562.

Kohler, Timothy A. 2004. Pre-Hispanic Human Impact on North American Southwestern Environments: Evolutionary Ecological Perspectives. In *The Archaeology of Global Change: The Impact of Humans on their Environment*, edited by C. L. Redman, S. R. James, P. R. Fish, and J. D. Rogers. Smithsonian Institution Books, Washington, DC.

Kohler, Timothy A., and Kelsey M. Reese. 2014. Long and Spatially Variable Neolithic Demographic Transition in the North American Southwest. *Proceedings of the National Academy of Sciences* 111(28):10101–10106. https://doi.org/10.1073/pnas.1404367111

Kohler, Timothy A., and Mark D. Varien (editors) 2012 *Emergence and Collapse of Early Villages: Models of Central Mesa Verde Archaeology*. University of California Press, Berkeley
Kohler, Timothy A., Mark D. Varien, Aaron Wright, and Kristin A. Kuckelman. 2008. Mesa Verde Migrations. *American Scientist* 96: 146–153.
Kuckelman, Kristin A. 2010. Catalysts of the Thirteenth-Century Depopulations of Sand Canyon Pueblo and the Central Mesa Verde Region. In *Leaving Mesa Verde: Peril and Change in the Thirteenth Century Southwest*, edited by Timothy A. Kohler, Mark D. Varien, and Aaron M. Wright, pp. 180–199. University of Arizona Press, Tucson, AZ.
Laland, Kevin N. and Michael J. O'Brien. 2010. Niche Construction Theory and Archaeology. *Journal of Archaeological Method and Theory* 17(4):303–322.
LeBlanc, Stephen A. 1999. *Prehistoric Warfare in the American Southwest*. University of Utah Press, Salt Lake City, UT.
Lotze, Heike K., Marta Coll, and Jennifer A. Dunne. 2011. Historical Changes in Marine Resources, Food-Web Structure and Ecosystem Functioning in the Adriatic Sea, Mediterranean. *Ecosystems* 14(2):198–222. https://doi.org/10.1007/s10021-010-9404-8
Martinez, N., J. Dunne, P. Kirch, N. Davies, J. Kahn. Award dates (2013-2017). Coupled Human and Natural Systems Grant, CNH: Socio-Ecosystem Dynamics of Human-Natural Networks on Model Islands, Award Abstract #1313830, National Science Foundation, http://www.nsf.gov/awardsearch/showAward?AWD_ID=1313830
Maschner, Herbert D. G., Matthew W. Betts, Joseph Cornell, A. Dunne, Bruce Finney, Nancy Huntly, James W. Jordan, et al. 2009. An Introduction to the Biocomplexity of Sanak Island, Western Gulf of Alaska. *Pacific Science* 63(4):673–709.
Matson, R. G. 2016. The Nutritional Context of the Pueblo III Depopulation of the Northern San Juan: Too Much Maize? *Journal of Archaeological Science: Reports* 5:622–631. https://doi.org/10.1016/j.jasrep.2015.08.032
Matson, R. G., and Brian Chisholm. 1991. Basketmaker II Subsistence: Carbon Isotopes and Other Dietary Indicators from Cedar Mesa, Utah. *American Antiquity* 56(3):444–459. https://doi.org/10.2307/280894
Matthews, Meredith M. 1988. The Macrobotanical Data Base: Applications in Testing Two Models of Socioeconomic Change. In *Dolores Archaeological Program: Anasazi Communities at Dolores, Grass Mesa Village*, edited by William D. Lipe, James N. Morris, and Timothy A. Kohler, pp. 1137–1158. Bureau of Reclamation, US Department of the Interior, Denver, CO.
Mertz, E. T. 1970. Nutritive Value of Corn and Its Products. In *Corn: Culture, Processing, Products, Major Feed and Food Crops in Agriculture and Food Series*, edited by G. E. Inglett, pp. 350–359. AVI Publishing Company Incorporated, Roslyn, NY.
Micheli, Fiorenza, Lisandro Benedetti-Cecchi, Silvia Gambaccini, Iacopo Bertocci, Costanza Borsini, Giacomo Chato Osio, and Federico Romano. 2005. Cascading Human Impacts, Marine Protected Areas, and the Structure of Mediterranean Reef Assemblages. *Ecological Monographs* 75(1):81–102. https://doi.org/10.1890/03-4058
Monleon, V. J., K. Cromack, J. D. Landsberg 1997. Short-and long-term effects of prescribed underburning on nitrogen availability in ponderosa pine stands in central Oregon. *Canadian Journal of Forest Research*, 27:369–378.
Morell, V. 2015. Lessons from the wild lab, *Science* (20) pp. 1302–1307.
Muir, R. J. 2007. Faunal Remains In *The Archaeology of Sand Canyon Pueblo*. Cortez, CO: Crow Canyon Archaeological Center.
Muir, Robert J., and Jonathan C. Driver. 2002. Scale of Analysis and Zooarchaeological Interpretation: Pueblo III Faunal Variation in the Northern San Juan Region. *Journal of Anthropological Archaeology* 21(2):165–199. https://doi.org/10.1006/jaar.2001.0392

Nash, S. E. 1999. *Time, Trees, and Prehistory: Tree-Ring Dating and the Development of North American Archaeology, 1914-1950*. Salt Lake City, UT: The University of Utah Press.

Nelson, M. C., G. Schachner. 2002. Understanding abandonments in the North American Southwest. *Journal of Archaeological Research* 10(2):167–206.

Neusius, S. W., and M. Gould. 1988. Faunal Remains: Implications for Dolores Anasazi Adaptations. In *Dolores Archaeological Program: Anasazi Communities at Dolores: Grass Mesa Village*, edited by W. D. Lipe, J. N. Morris, and T. A. Kohler. U. S. Department of the Interior, Bureau of Reclamation, Denver, CO.

Newberry, J. S. 1876. Geological Report. In *Report of the Exploring Expedition from Santa Fé, New Mexico, to the Junction of the Grand and Green Rivers of the Great Colorado of the West, in 1859, under the Command of Capt. J. N. Macomb, Corps of Topographical Engineers*, edited by J. N. Macomb. U. S. Government Printing Office, Washington, DC.

NRCS: National Resources Conservation Service. 1999. American Elk (Cervus elaphus), Fish and Wildlife Habitation Leaflet, Number 11, November.

Ortman, S. G. 2012. *Winds from the North: Tewa Origins and Historical Anthropology*. Salt Lake City, UT: The University of Utah Press.

Parmesan, C. 1996. Climate and species range. *Nature* 382, pp. 765–766.

Parmesan, C., N. Ryrholm, C. Stefanescu, J. K. Hill, C. D. Thomas, H. Descimon, B. Huntley, L. Kaila, J. Kullberg, T. Tammaru, W. J. Tennent, J.A. Thomas, M. Warren. 1999. Poleward shifts in geographical ranges of butterfly species associated with regional warming. *Nature* 399, pp. 579–583.

Potts, Richard. 1998. Variability Selection in Hominid Evolution. *Evolutionary Anthropology: Issues, News, and Reviews* 7(3):81–96.

Rawlings, Tiffany A., and Jonathan C. Driver. 2010. Paleodiet of Domestic Turkey, Shields Pueblo (5MT3807), Colorado: Isotopic Analysis and Its Implications for Care of a Household Domesticate. *Journal of Archaeological Science* 37(10):2433–2441. https://doi.org/10.1016/j.jas.2010.05.004

Rohn, A.H. 1963. Prehistoric soil and water conservation on Chapin Mesa, southwestern Colorado, *American Antiquity*, 28(4), pp. 441–455.

Romanuk, Tamara N., Yun Zhou, Ulrich Brose, Eric L. Berlow, Richard J. Williams, and Neo D. Martinez. 2009. Predicting Invasion Success in Complex Ecological Networks. *Philosophical Transactions of the Royal Society B: Biological Sciences* 364(1524): 1743–1754.

Ryan, Susan C. 2003 Albert Porter Pueblo, (Site 5MT123), Montezuma County, Colorado, Annual Report Field Season 2003, Crow Canyon Archaeological Center.

Schmitz, O. J., P. A. Hambäck, A. P. Beckerman 2000. Trophic Cascades in Terrestrial Systems: A Review of the Effects of Carnivore Removals on Plants, *The American Naturalist* 155(2), pp. 141–153.

Schoenwetter, A. E., J. Dittert 1968. Ecological interpretation of Anasazi settlement patterns. In *Anthropological Archaeology in the Americas*, edited by B. J. Meggers, pp. 41–66.

Schollmeyer, K. G., and Jonathan C. Driver. 2012. The Past, Present, and Future of Small Terrestrial Mammals in Human Diets. In *Conservation Biology and Applied Zooarchaeology*, edited by S. Wolverton and R. L. Lyman, pp. 179–207. The University of Arizona Press, Tucson, AZ.

Schwindt, Dylan M., R. Kyle Bocinsky, Scott G. Ortman, Donna M. Glowacki, Mark D. Varien, and Timothy A. Kohler. 2016. The Social Consequences of Climate Change in the Central Mesa Verde Region. *American Antiquity* 81(1):74–96.

Smith, Bruce D. 2011. General Patterns of Niche Construction and the Management of 'Wild' Plant and Animal Resources by Small-Scale Pre-Industrial Societies. *Philosophical Transactions of the Royal Society B: Biological Sciences* 366(1566): 836–848.

Smith-Ramesh, Lauren M., Alexandria C. Moore, and Oswald J. Schmitz. 2017. Global Synthesis Suggests that Food Web Connectance Correlates to Invasion Resistance. *Global Change Biology* 23(2):465–473. https://doi.org/10.1111/gcb.13460

Srinivasan, U. Thara, Jennifer A. Dunne, John Harte, and Neo D. Martinez. 2007. Response Of Complex Food Webs to Realistic Extinction Sequences. *Ecology* 88(3):671–682. https://doi.org/10.1890/06-0971

Staddon, J. E. R. 1983. Foraging and Behavioral Ecology. In *Adaptive Behavior and Learning*, pp. 182–200. 1st ed. Cambridge University Press, Cambridge.

Stouffer, D. B., J. Camacho, R. Guimera, C. A. Ng, and L. A. Nunes Amaral. 2005. Quantitative Patterns in the Structure of Model and Empirical Food Webs. *Ecology* 86(5):1301–1311.

Tecchio, Samuele, Marta Coll, Villy Christensen, Joan B. Company, Eva Ramírez-Llodra, and Francisco Sardà. 2013. Food Web Structure and Vulnerability of a Deep-Sea Ecosystem in the NW Mediterranean Sea. *Deep Sea Research Part I: Oceanographic Research Papers* 75:1–15. https://doi.org/10.1016/j.dsr.2013.01.003

The Sand Canyon Pueblo Database. 2004.

Urban, Mark C. 2015. Accelerating Extinction Risk from Climate Change. *Science* 348(6234): 571–573.

USGS 2025. Navajo Land Use Planning Project. http://geomaps.wr.usgs.gov/navajo/4corners/index.html

Wallach, Arian D., Anthony H. Dekker, Miguel Lurgi, Jose M. Montoya, Damien A. Fordham, and Euan G. Ritchie. 2017. Trophic Cascades in 3D: Network Analysis Reveals How Apex Predators Structure Ecosystems. *Methods in Ecology and Evolution* 8(1):135–142. https://doi.org/10.1111/2041-210X.12663

Wan, S., D. Hui, Y. Luo 2001. Fire effects on nitrogen pools and dynamics in terrestrial ecosystems: a meta-analysis. *Ecological Applications*, 11, 1349–1365.

Wardle, D. A. 2011. Terrestrial ecosystem responses to species gains and losses, *Science* pp. 1273.

Williams, R. J. 2010. Network3D Software. Microsoft Research, Cambridge.

Williams, Richard J., Eric L. Berlow, Jennifer A. Dunne, Albert-László Barabási, and Neo D. Martinez. 2002. Two Degrees of Separation in Complex Food Webs. *Proceedings of the National Academy of Sciences* 99(20):12913–12916. https://doi.org/10.1073/pnas.192448799

Williams, Richard J., and Neo D. Martinez. 2004. Limits to Trophic Levels and Omnivory in Complex Food Webs: Theory and Data. *The American Naturalist* 163(3):458–468. https://doi.org/10.1086/381964

Witt K. E. K. Judd, A. Kitchen, C. Grier, T. A. Kohler, S. G. Ortman, B. M. Kemp, R. S. 2015. DNA analysis of ancient dogs of the Americas: Identifying possible founding haplotypes and reconstructing population histories, *Journal of Human Evolution 79*, pp. 105–118.

Wyckoff, Don G. 1977. Secondary Forest Succession Following Abandonment of Mesa Verde. *Kiva* 42(3/4):215–231.

Yeakel, Justin D., Mathias M. Pires, Lars Rudolf, Nathaniel J. Dominy, and Paul L. Koch. 2014. Collapse of an Ecological Network in Ancient Egypt. *Proceedings of the National Academy of Sciences* 111(40):14472–14477. https://doi.org/10.1073/pnas.1408471111

Yodzis, P, Innes, S. 1992. Body size and consumer-resource dynamics. *American Naturalist* 139:1151–1175.

Yodzis, P., K. O. Winemiller 1999. In search of operational trophospecies in a tropical aquatic food web, *Oikos* 87 pp. 327–340.

Yoon, Ilmi, Rich Williams, Eli Levine, Sanghyuk Yoon, Jennifer Dunne, and Neo Martinez. 2004. Webs on the Web (WOW): 3D Visualization of Ecological Networks on the WWW for Collaborative Research and Education. *Proceedings of SPIE - The International Society for Optical Engineering* 5295:124–132.

7
CONCLUSIONS

Traditionally, archaeologists have relied on inferential, historical approaches to unravel the complexities of past societies. In contrast, this book introduces a more dynamic perspective—one grounded in complex adaptive systems science. This framework provides a model-based, deductive approach, harnessing the tools of network analysis, agent-based modeling, and settlement scaling theory to interrogate the archaeological record. Rather than viewing the past as a collection of discrete events or isolated moments frozen in time, this approach highlights the processes, interactions, and emergent behaviors that underlie the observed patterns in archaeological material. By leveraging computational methods, we are no longer confined to static interpretations; we can test hypotheses about social and ecological dynamics, simulating scenarios that would otherwise remain elusive to field-based data alone. Through this lens, we see the past not as a set of fixed facts, but as a web of interconnected actions and consequences—where individual choices ripple through time, shaping the very structure of societies and ecosystems. This model-based approach opens new avenues for understanding human organization, resilience, and transformation over the *longue durée*.

At the outset of this book, I suggested that while archaeologists inherently seek to understand human relationships, the study of material culture does not always lend itself to tracing the social webs of past societies. However, by applying the tools of complex adaptive systems—agent-based modeling, network analysis, and settlement scaling—we have been able to uncover those latent connections that so often remain invisible in traditional archaeological analyses. These methodologies allow us to move beyond static artifacts and reconstruct the dynamic, relational networks that governed past human behavior. By modeling the interactions of individuals, communities, and species, we

DOI: 10.4324/9781003585251-9

gain a deeper insight into how choices at the household or individual level could cascade into broader societal changes, reshaping landscapes, economies, and ecosystems.

At the heart of this work lies a central tenet of complexity science: individual decisions matter. The small, often overlooked choices of people—whether deciding where to plant crops, which species to hunt, or how to divide resources—have the potential to set in motion rapid and profound societal changes. Through the computational techniques of agent-based modeling and network analysis, we can quantify and trace the consequences of these decisions, providing a clearer understanding of how past societies adapted to—and struggled with—internal and external pressures.

In Chapter 5, I created an agent-based model to examine the ways that Ancestral Pueblo farmers interacted in the dry uplands of Mesa Verde from AD 600 to AD 1280. In this model, part of the Village Ecodynamics Project's universe of agent-based models, agents are households made up of individuals that form groups and play a public goods game within their group. Groups of agents come into conflict over arable land, and hierarchical groups of groups form, which we term "complex groups." I demonstrated that the distribution of simulated complex-group sizes followed a power-law distribution during Pueblo II times, with the distribution weakening toward a log-normal distribution during Pueblo III times. By comparing the distribution of group sizes in the simulation output against distributions of kiva-membership sizes and the sizes of momentized household populations within sites I suggested that the trend toward power-law distributions during Pueblo II demonstrated the consolidation of power of groups at the top of the hierarchy. This consolidation of power, I suggested, weakened during Pueblo III times, away from one paramount group and toward localized power, at the site (community) or group-of-sites (communities) level. The model enabled the analysis of group-level properties—in the article presented therein, group hierarchy. While the archaeological analyses shed new light on the social structure of groups in the Ancestral Pueblo Southwest, it was only through the comparison with the agent-based model that the plausibility of the development of a multi-tiered hierarchy could be determined. This study reinforced the utility of agent-based modeling in examining complex processes that could not be clearly understood from the archaeological record alone. It also reinforced the use of settlement scaling theory, here used in different ways than other studies presented in Chapter 2, but nevertheless demonstrating the way that understanding how the scaling of settlements can tell us about the processes of their formation.

In Chapter 6 the discussion moved from the individual household to the aggregate of the species. However, the analyses presented therein demonstrate how decisions by Ancestral Pueblo people of which species to hunt and of where to plant their fields would have had dramatic ramifications for species richness on the landscape. While the immediate effects might only be felt locally, the analyses presented in Chapter 6 show that enough of these local decisions can dramatically alter environments, making them inhospitable for certain species (such as snowshoe hare and elk) and eventually eradicating them altogether. These changes, I suggest, led to increased vulnerability of Ancestral Pueblo people and made those living on the margins more susceptible to environmental fluctuations. The specific deployment of network science—here a way to understand the connections of Ancestral Pueblo people to their ecosystem—demonstrates the ways that humans embed themselves in ecosystems, and how small choices can have implications for the network as a whole.

Through the application of complex systems theory, I demonstrated the power of modeling to reveal the forces driving societal change. By comparing simulated outputs to archaeological data, we gain a deeper understanding of the factors that shaped ancient societies. More importantly, these models provide a platform for exploring how past societies responded to ecological and social pressures—insights that are crucial for addressing similar challenges in our present world.

Lessons from These Studies

There are two types of lessons from these studies: those that forge new methodological approaches for archaeology, and those that suggest an understanding of humanity in both prehistory and today.

Methodological Advances

The two studies I present here show the utility of complex adaptive systems approaches for studying the archaeological record. I approached the century-long debate as to the hierarchical nature of Ancestral Pueblo people via an agent-based modeling approach. I showed that through a simple process of territorial expansion, large village-spanning polities could form in the prehispanic American Southwest. This did not require top-down processes, but rather a bottom-up process from households competing over arable land.

This model demonstrates that simulations built with a keen understanding of the system being modeled can provide insights that traditional archaeological analyses cannot. This is not to say that my model was the first to propose the mechanisms; Lekson (2015), for example, and some others have been proponents of a pan-regional hierarchy centered around Chaco Canyon. Rather, the model I presented allowed for the examination of these ideas suggested from other researchers, and it is only due to the decades (almost centuries) of archaeological research that I was even able to build an agent-based model built upon sound historical data.

Agent-based modeling provides a way to see the actions and interactions of individuals (or families/households) that are difficult to reconstruct with traditional archaeological methods. While agent-based modeling is still evolving as a discipline, models have increasingly been able to include diverse strategies and viewpoints, including one unique agent-based model (built by an archaeologist) attempting to model the sense of smell (Rocks-McQueen 2014).

The food webs case study presented in Chapter 5 also utilizes a tool from complex adaptive systems—network analysis—to understand cascading effects of prey choice and ecosystem shifts in the Southwest. This chapter demonstrates how simple actions can have dramatic unintended consequences. Large tracts of arable land were cleared in the Southwest to make way for maize, changing the ecosystem in ways that may still be felt today. While food web studies have been used for decades, long before the advanced computational tools we see today, the approach used here enables a true modeling of interactions of every species, helping to understand not just the complexity of the ecosystem of the central Mesa Verde (it was certainly complex!) but also the nuanced ways the ecosystem shifted through time.

Understanding the Trajectory of Humanity

Beyond their methodological contributions, the studies in this book also offer important lessons about the trajectory of humanity. By examining how past societies interacted with their environments, we gain valuable insights into the challenges we face today. In Chapter 6, for instance, we see how small, localized decisions regarding subsistence practices—when multiplied across generations—can lead to significant ecological disruptions. The disappearance of key species, such as elk and snowshoe hare, not only alters the landscape but also fundamentally shifts the structure of the food web. When the food web structure changes dramatically it will alter the way that humans interact within their own ecosystems, forcing humans to adapt in novel ways.

As human populations grow, we increasingly find ourselves confronting the limits of our ecosystems, with species loss and ecosystem degradation threatening our future. The resilience of the Ancestral Pueblo people—exemplified by their migration in response to environmental stress—suggests that adaptability and flexibility are crucial in the face of ecological change. However, such resilience becomes more difficult as population density increases, and the luxury of migration may no longer be available to modern societies. Understanding how human actions impact ecosystems, and vice versa, is essential for ensuring long-term sustainability.

The study of ancient societies also provides a valuable lens for examining the development of political systems. In Chapter 5, we saw how increased population density can catalyze the formation of larger, more complex polities. This process, driven by competition for resources, may mirror the formation of early states and empires throughout history. As modern societies grow more interconnected and resource pressures intensify, understanding how early societies navigated these challenges can offer valuable lessons for managing political and social conflict today.

These studies offer a foundation for future research into the dynamics of human-environment interaction. As we face unprecedented global challenges, understanding how past societies adapted to environmental and social pressures is more crucial than ever. We are poised at a crossroads as a civilization, plagued by many of the same issues that our ancestors faced. An understanding of our past can help us make informed decisions about our future.

Works Cited

Lekson, Stephen H. 2015. *The Chaco Meridian: One Thousand Years of Political and Religious Power in the Ancient Southwest*. 2nd ed. Rowman & Littlefield, Lanham, Maryland.

Rocks-McQueen, Doug. 2014. *Agent Based Modelling and the Person*. Paris, France.

GLOSSARY*

A glossary of terms that appear in this book or are in general useful for studying complex adaptive systems.

agent-based model   a computer model that simulates the actions and interactions of individuals across time and through space and examines how those interactions can lead to larger system-wide behaviors.
algorithm   a sequence of instructions given to a computer.
artificial data   model output that can be compared to real archaeological data.
average degree   the average number of edges per node in a network.
average shortest path length   the mean number of steps between all pairs of nodes in a network.
betweenness centrality of a network   the average betweenness centrality of all nodes of a network.
betweenness centrality of a node   the number of shortest paths between all pairs of nodes that cross through the node.
Boolean   a variable with only two possible values. Also called a binary variable.
bounded rationality   the idea, first proposed by Herbert Simon in 1956 that humans will often settle on a "good-enough" solution rather than exert time and resources to find the optimal one.
calibration   using an external data source to reduce parameter ranges to a narrower and more plausible set.

---

* Adapted from Iza Romanowska, Colin D. Wren, and Stefani A. Crabtree. (2021). *Agent-based Modeling for Archaeology: Simulating the Complexity of Societies*. SFI Press, Santa Fe, NM.

chaotic system   a type of dynamic system that is highly sensitive to the initial conditions. Chaotic systems, for example weather, are unpredictable beyond the horizon of predictability determined by our ability to measure the initial conditions.

coefficient of variation   the variance divided by the mean of a variable.

conformist bias   probability of adopting a cultural trait proportional to its popularity in the population. The inverse is known as anti-conformist bias.

cultural diffusion   concerns the spread of an idea, such as an innovation, a decorative pattern, or a belief.

cultural trait   different content transmitted between individuals: a skill, reference, piece of information, strategy, or particular behavior.

directed edge   one-way connection, such as a consumer (predator) eating a resource (prey; trophic networks).

edge   the relationships between the entities in a network (the lines).

emergence   a property of model dynamics where an unexpected effect arises from the aggregated interactions of the individual entities, i.e., when the whole becomes more than the sum of its parts.

equifinality   a principle stating that a given state may be reached through many different routes.

Erdős-Rényi network   a network, also known as a graph in network science, created by repeatedly connecting two random nodes with an edge until the specified number of edges is reached.

exchange   nonmonetary trade of goods, services, and ideas.

experiment design   the final phase of the modeling process in which the modeler experiments on the modeled world by running the simulation in different configurations (scenarios).

fitness   a measure of an agent's "quality," usually relative to other agents, such as likelihood of reproduction or survivability in a biological system, or presence of preferred traits or behaviors that bring an economic or social benefit in a cultural system.

game theory   a mathematical framework studying models of interaction between competing agents, usually rational decision makers.

model   a simplified, often abstract, representation of a system.

model-based bias   probability of adopting a cultural trait based on the characteristics of individuals who carry this trait.

model selection   an idea borrowed from statistics whereby one looks to an assemblage of potential models and identifies the one that best fits the data.

models from first principles   simulate how the world would look under the most basic of assumptions.

Moore neighborhood   consists of the immediately adjacent eight cells (including diagonals).

multilevel models   models that explicitly code dynamics that occur at multiple scales (e.g., individual and household).

mutation   a random change of an element in the genome. Here used to denote a random change in the value of a cultural trait.

Nash equilibrium   a set of agent choices such that no agent can benefit by altering its choice, assuming that the choices of the other agents remain unchanged.

network   a set of entities (nodes) connected through a set of relationships (edges or links). Edges between the nodes could represent any type of relationship, from kinship and friendship to trade flows and material culture similarity.

network science   branch of science concerned with relational data and its collection, management, analysis, interpretation, and presentation.

node   the entities in a network (the dots).

ontology   the full representation of the model's world, including names and definitions of entities and their categories and properties, the relationships between entities, and the rules of behavior.

open science   a philosophy of research transparency in science that advocates for open-access publishing, open-data sharing, and transparent methods.

open source/open code   a pillar of the open-science movement that encourages the publication of all scientific code, including analysis scripts.

optimal foraging theory   a model of resource acquisition behavior that maximizes the net benefit (i.e., after costs have been accounted for).

overfitting   the model is overfitted when it fits the data too closely, thus reflecting noise rather than significant trends.

parameter   a constant used to describe the modeled world and a particular scenario, such as the initial number of agents, population growth rate, or carrying capacity of a patch.

parameter sweep   systematically testing a range of parameter values, i.e., scenarios to determine the range of outcomes.

parameterization   the process of choosing individual or ranges of parameter values.

parsimony   the idea that a model should have as few details as possible while still representing the modeled phenomenon. Often defined as the Occam's razor principle.

phase space   often multidimensional space of all possible states of the model.

point of equilibrium   a moment in the simulation run when the model stabilizes and nothing new can be learned from it.

random drift   random change in the frequency of traits; often occurs in small populations.

replication   a reimplementation of a model by another researcher to verify the original model's correctness.

resilience   the capacity of a system to recover from a perturbation.

self-organized criticality   a phenomenon in which a system undergoes a transition from one semi-equilibrium state to another without any external influence.

simulation   dynamic model of a system. A model with a time axis.
stochasticity   degree of randomness in a model's dynamics and outcomes; involving randomly generated numbers.
theory-driven models   models maximizing generalism, usually exploring relationships and causality and often used to explain phenomena.
tractability   a feature of models denoting how easy it is to understand the internal dynamics, interactions between processes, and causality chain that leads to the patterns in output.
trade   exchange that involves money as intermediary and is market-based.
tragedy of the commons   a phenomenon that extends well beyond collective agreements in small-scale agrarian populations.
undirected edge   two-way connection, such as a reciprocal relationship.
validation   establishing that the model is conceptually correct with respect to the system being modeled.
variable   attribute of an agent, patch, or the world that can change over the course of a simulation run, such as age, fitness, grass, or number of agents alive.
verification   establishing that the code, as written, works correctly.
von Neumann neighborhood   consists of the immediately adjacent four cells (i.e., no diagonals).

INDEX

adaptation 3, 30
agent-based modeling, definition of 15, 34
algorithm 45
analysis 14, 27, 43, 62, 89, 126
Artificial Anasazi 35–36

Bayesian approaches 40–42
betweenness centrality 59, 63
biology 8, 64
bottom-up models 34, 150
boundedness 26

calibration 40, 49, 69
cellular automata (CA) 41
ceramics 65, 78, 101
climate change 11, 95, 114
clustering 67, 123, 127, 129
code 43, 45, 48
complexity 2–4, 6, 16, 22, 37, 69, 73, 76, 149
cultural transmission 66

datasets 67, 69, 74, 80
diffusion 59–60, 64, 66
dimension 27, 38–39, 41
distribution: normal (Gaussian) 83–85, 89, 91, 99–100; power-law (preferential attachment) 83–85, 89, 91, 94, 99–100

ecology 6, 14, 37, 42
economic 27, 62, 64, 66–67, 82, 89

edge 55, 57, 60–62, 65, 123
emergence 4, 30
equilibrium 47, 113
evaluation 39, 41, 49, 68
exchange 5, 21, 37, 62–63, 66, 93
exponential random graph model 67–69

fractal 20
frequency 83, 87, 95

Gell-Mann, Murray 3, 46
generality 126–128, 135
geographic information system (GIS) 13, 36, 41–42
graph theory 55–56, 60, 68
grid 38
growth 21, 27–28, 35, 77, 80, 84

heterogeneity 14, 38–40, 42
histogram 82, 86, 92, 96

interaction 42, 57, 62–63, 81, 112, 129, 141, 152
intractable 6, 35, 59, 65

kiva 74–75, 80, 82–85, 88, 92, 100, 103

lithics 2, 7–8, 36, 57, 101

methods 59–60, 64, 73, 117

NetLogo 36, 39
network science 53–54, 56, 59–60, 112, 150
node 24, 55, 57, 63, 127
noise 8

ODD protocol 49
optimization 84

parameter 38, 44, 46–47, 88–89, 94, 96
parsimony 11–12, 40, 45, 47, 54
patch 36, 95
path 56, 123
pottery *see* ceramics
prediction 40–42, 48
preferential attachment *see* distribution, power-law

resilience 62–63, 69, 112, 114
resource 60, 114
robustness 61–62, 113–114, 138

simulation 14–15, 34–35, 39, 41–42, 44, 49, 59, 73–75, 79–80, 83, 93, 95, 101, 149

space syntax 60
stochastic 75

temporal dimension 38–39, 43
time step 35, 38–39, 84, 98
topology 15, 114, 117
trade *see* exchange
transition, Neolothic Demographic 120, 140

uncertainty 67–68

validation 75
variability 74, 82, 93, 104, 113
Village Ecodynamics Project 36, 74, 80, 119, 122, 149

weighted 128

x-axis 129

yield 61, 136

zooarchaeological 124

For Product Safety Concerns and Information please contact our EU representative GPSR@taylorandfrancis.com Taylor & Francis Verlag GmbH, Kaufingerstraße 24, 80331 München, Germany

Printed and bound by CPI Group (UK) Ltd, Croydon, CR0 4YY

11/11/2025

01995617-0001